Duck Stamps and Prints

Duck Stamps and Prints

The Complete Federal and State Editions

Best Wishes—
McCaddin
12-68

INTRODUCTION BY JOE McCADDIN

HUGH LAUTER LEVIN ASSOCIATES, INC., NEW YORK

DISTRIBUTED BY MACMILLAN PUBLISHING COMPANY, NEW YORK

ACKNOWLEDGEMENTS

I would like to extend special thanks to these individuals: Jeff Hurvitz, whose advice and participation in writing this book was invaluable; Burnett Harshman, publisher and president of Midwest Marketing, whose cooperation in providing photographs and information was immeasurable; Patty Béchard, for her support; Harkavy Publishing Service and Harry L. Wagner, for their preparation of the catalogue and artist-biography portions of the book; Martin Lubin and Betty Binns Graphics, for the outstanding design; Craig Schaeffer, who inspired the publisher; and finally, Charlotte, my wife and friend, whose patience and confidence aided me greatly.

J. McC.

Printed in Hong Kong by Mandarin Offset

ISBN 0–88363–688–3

INTRODUCTION

Duck stamp prints are limited-edition works of wildlife art that are available to collectors in two main categories—federal and state issues. The federal duck stamp print is for many people the most coveted wildlife art collectible in the United States. Collectors would be hard-pressed to find another collectible anywhere in the world that has achieved such a rapid increase in popularity and value.

The duck stamp itself—which many people collect apart from the art prints—is a hunting license stamp that first appeared in 1934, issued by the federal government. Since then, this annual series has never been interrupted, making it unique among federal stamp series.

A signed and numbered limited-edition print, based on the stamp's design, is available for each stamp issued since 1934. A complete collection of these print and stamp sets is now worth more than $100,000. There remain fewer than fifty-five complete collections of these sets today. But—a fact of great interest to collectors—a collection of federal duck stamps and prints from just 1970 to 1986 can now be sold for $40,100! All that from an initial investment of just $1140.

The federal collection is the granddaddy, the benchmark for duck stamp and print collecting. But the emergence of duck stamps and prints from the individual states, beginning in the early 1970s, and from private conservation organizations in the 1980s, has created a wider field of collecting with equal, if not greater, increases in value. In this book, we shall examine each important aspect of duck stamps and prints and the reasons they continue to gain widespread popularity.

The Federal Duck Stamp Program

One man's deep concern for the plight of migratory birds set into motion in 1934 a program that has given birth to hundreds of original wildlife art treasures and raised many millions of dollars for conservation.

Before he became chief of the Biological Survey in Washington, D.C., Jay Norwood "Ding" Darling was an accomplished cartoonist and ardent conservationist. The resulting merger of his vocation and avocation, respectively, afforded Darling the honor of creating the first duck stamp design when the U.S. Congress enacted the 1934 Migratory Bird Hunting Stamp Act. Darling's simple pencil drawing of Mallards dropping down to a body of water formed the basis of the first stamp, which became required under the new act for all individual hunting licenses. The proceeds of the stamp's sale benefitted many lovers of

the outdoors, including hunters, campers, fishermen, backpackers, leaf collectors, and bird watchers. Thus began a series of conservation efforts that continues to this day.

The first stamp went on sale in August 1934, and a total of 635,000 were sold at a price of $1 each. (The price of the 1987 stamp was $10.) A sales peak was reached in 1971, when nearly 2,442,000 stamps were sold. Collectors who have purchased each year's stamp at its issue price—for a total cost of $179—currently have a collection worth over $4000. After three years all unsold stamps are destroyed, by July 1, thus preserving the value of the limited edition.

The first print was created nearly four years after the first stamp was issued, following repeated requests from friends, politicians, neighbors, and admirers of Joseph D. Knap, the designer of the 1937 stamp. The previous designs by Darling, Frank Benson (1935), and Richard E. Bishop (1936) all had caused people to request larger versions of the stamp images—to no avail.

Knap decided to redo his stamp as an etching so it could be used for multiple impressions. The previous artists then decided to do the same so that their admirers, too, could put a copy of the federal stamp design on display. The collecting of stamps and signed prints had begun.

The Federal Stamp Design Competition

From 1934 to 1949, the honor of competing for the annual stamp design selection was by invitation only. In fact, only three people were asked to submit their designs for this award in 1949. But the U.S. Bureau of Biological Survey—the forerunner of today's U.S. Fish and Wildlife Service in the Department of the Interior—changed all that in 1950 when it opened the competition to all artists. This resulted in a rapid increase in the number of applicants; by 1981, there were 2099. When the U.S. Fish and Wildlife Service began requiring an entry fee of $50 in 1986, the number of submissions dropped.

Under the banner of the U.S. Fish and Wildlife Service, the Migratory Bird Hunting and Conservation Stamp Program now oversees all activities concerning the federal competition. (For its first five years, the program was the province of the Department of Agriculture.) In order to compete in the contest, an applicant must follow a stringent set of rules. For instance, the image size of the design must be 7 inches high by 10 inches wide. It must appear in a single white mat, with outside dimensions of 9 by 12 inches and a width of 1 inch.

What started out as a rather simple judging process has evolved over fifty-four years into a panel of five judges. (This panel is replaced each year.) Some judges may have backgrounds as waterfowl experts, biologists, conservationists, or wildlife artists. The service tries to maintain a balance on the panel, particularly so that the stamps' subjects can be competently scrutinized for accuracy.

Although it is the limited-edition print that has catapulted the print and stamp set into a highly prized collectible, the service has not lost sight of the original premise: to produce a stamp. The Bureau of Engraving and Printing must have a design that is compatible with its process for producing this stamp. Since a piece of metal is used by the engraver to "strike" the stamp, clarity of design is vital. If it lacks clarity, an otherwise excellent piece of artwork could be excluded from further consideration.

The final judging of the design entries is held in Washington, D.C. The judges have several hours to review the art work, which is mounted on large display boards in an auditorium. Once the judging begins, one designated person presents each of the entries to the panel.

In order for a work to advance to the second phase of judging, at least three judges must vote in favor of it. (In the 1987 competition, fifty works advanced to the second round.) The process then evolves into a point system, whereby each judge awards each of the surviving works a point total ranging from zero to nine. The lowest and highest scores for each painting are then thrown out. Works with the five highest scores continue to the third and final round. If ties occur

for the top five positions, the number of paintings that advance to the final round will actually be greater than five. In 1987 there were nineteen designs in the final round. The final round is scored in the same fashion as the second round, leading to the selection of a single painting.

After the competition is completed, a public display of the top twenty entries and the winner is traditionally held in the town of Easton, on Maryland's eastern shore. (For further information concerning the competition, write to the Federal Duck Stamp Competition, U.S. Fish and Wildlife Service, Department of the Interior, Washington, D.C. 20240.) The following week, before Thanksgiving, this exhibition of twenty, augmented by one hundred other entries, is displayed for three days in Redlines, California, and then hangs in the San Bernadino County Museum for a further two weeks.

Design Considerations and Trends

For the duck stamps—which, strictly speaking, may depict geese or swans also —the Program excludes certain species of the duck family from consideration each year. In the 1987 competition, for instance, applicants were not permitted to paint five of the forty-three listed species. The Fulvous Whistling Duck, Cinnamon Teal, Widgeon, Pintail, and Canvasback were excluded because they had been the subjects of the five previous stamps. The coordinator of the program, Norma Opgrand, elaborated on recent requirements, saying of the 1986 and 1987 designs: "We specifically asked for waterfowl in action last year and this year. The judges could select others, but we urged action and identification of habitat in the water. It is so much easier for an engraver to make a stamp out of something that's more realistic than surrealistic." Asked for how the designs have changed in recent years, she said, "We used to have more designs [with ducks] sitting in the water."

In the early years of the competition, winning stamp designs almost always featured birds in flight. Ding Darling's 1934 design of two Mallards gracefully descending was followed in 1935 by Frank Benson's depiction of three Canvasbacks taking flight. In the following year, Richard E. Bishop depicted the popular Canada Geese soaring. (Canada Geese also appear on the 1958 and 1976 stamps, by Leslie C. Kouba and Alderson Magee, respectively.)

Joseph D. Knap's 1937 creation shows a flock of five Greater Scaup flying over whitecaps, with a shoreline visible in the distance.

7

A major change occurred in the design of 1939, when Lynn B. Hunt positioned two Green-Winged Teal, possibly mates, along a shoreline, their privacy about to be surrendered as a flock of their species approaches.

A family of Ruddy Ducks was introduced in Edwin R. Kalmbach's 1941 work. A peaceful swim by the ten subjects gives it a unique flair in terms of both quantity and quality.

An innovation occurred in the 1944 painting by Walter A. Weber: The three White-Fronted Geese appear in the extreme foreground of the design, revealing intricate characteristics of their bellies and wings.

Reeds first appeared in a 1948 rendering of Buffleheads by Maynard Reece. The reeds are bending from a stiff wind that does not seem to deter the birds.

Graceful Trumpeter Swans were introduced in Weber's second design, in 1950. Their fluid motion is offset by mountaintops, which also make their first appearance on a duck stamp.

In his 1951 depiction of Gadwalls, Reece introduced an element of disturbance to the water. The two subjects seem to be excited by some unseen stimulus, thus creating swirls.

In the 1956 work by Edward J. Bierly, a tree in winter is reflected against undisturbed waters, and the two approaching American Mergansers appear to be flying into the reflection.

An animal other than a waterfowl appeared for the first and only time in the 1959 work by Reece. His painting of a Labrador Retriever carrying a Mallard drake proved to be quite popular.

There were no major innovations in stamp design during the 1960s, but that would prove to be the calm before the storm.

Edward Bierly had already painted two federal winners (in 1956 and 1963) when his 1970 design of Ross's Geese was selected. It was the first to use a full-color lithography printing process.

The color series, too, evolved over the years. In 1974, for instance, first-time winner David A. Maass painted two Wood Ducks "jumping" into flight against the backdrop of winter trees. This was the first time in the color series that a painting of ducks in flight had displayed a true feeling of depth.

In 1982, Maass's second winning design depicted three Canvasbacks in flight over a shoreline. A stormy background, from the rippling waves to the swaying reeds, marked the first time in the color series that water was given a look of activity. Whether peacefully rippling or churning, water has been given this quality in the '80s, as in the 1987 print by Arthur G. Anderson, depicting a cluster of trees, turbulent water, and three Redheads in flight.

The move into full color also signaled a surge in the value of these collectibles. For instance, the 1970 Bierly print that originally sold for $60 rapidly escalated in value: By 1987, a signed and numbered print with mint stamp was worth $2700.

As an artist with a strong design history, Maynard Reece created the greatest rate of appreciation when his work appeared in full color. Reece, who operated a Des Moines, Iowa, gallery, had won four federal contests by 1969. The print of his 1969 painting, which depicts White-Winged Scoters, was reproduced in a single color. The signed-print and mint-stamp set are currently valued at $1000.

In contrast, Reece's unprecedented fifth winning design, in 1971, of Cinnamon Teal has appreciated in value to over $6000. The hand-colored print's original purchase price: $75.

The 1975 print, by James L. Fisher, of a trio of Canvasbacks flying with a Canvasback decoy in the foreground was the last to depict anything other than live waterfowl in their environment as the dominant feature of the design. This was the result of a change in rules. From that year on, all prints were numbered.

An attempt was made to eliminate the correlation between the stamp and the hunting purpose for which it was intended; thus, decoys, small boats (such as the Barnegat Bay sneak box), or dogs (such as the black Labrador depicted on Reece's 1959 design), came to be excluded. Consequently, both the 1959 and the 1975 prints have risen substantially in value, with the Labrador design now valued at $3000 and the decoy design at $1800.

Stamp Production

As the pictorial elements of the duck stamp have changed over the years, so, too, has the actual printing process used in its production.

Each year, the winning stamp design is reviewed by the U.S. Postal Service. After receiving approval, the stamp is forwarded to the Bureau of Engraving and Printing. The Bureau's designer then creates a model of the stamp, combining the art work, inscription (words), and denomination. Then the Bureau decides the manner in which the stamp will be printed. Finally, the U.S. Fish and Wildlife Service must approve the model prior to production.

The method of printing most commonly used has been the intaglio process. *Intaglio* is derived from the Italian word *intagliare*, meaning *to engrave, cut*. The term encompasses the various methods of engraving: etching, aquatint, drypoint and soft-ground etching, and mezzotint. All of these processes utilize lines or areas cut below the surface of the printing plate.

The intaglio method was used on a single-color, flat-bed press from 1934 through 1958. From 1959 through 1986, a rotary (Giori) press was used. It has the ability to print up to three colors simultaneously from a single plate. Between 1970 and 1986, stamps were printed in a combination of engraving and offset lithography. For the 1987 design, the printing was done on a web-set press.

Through the 1953 issue, ungummed paper was "webbed" prior to intaglio printing and the application of gum. In later years, pregummed paper was used with dry printing. In 1987, pregummed paper with a white coating was used to improve the vibrancy of color and the sharpness of the stamp image.

From 1934 to 1945, the printing plates were created without gutters, or dividing areas. Thus, stamps adjacent to the cut lines between the four panes (quadrants) of each plate had imperforate (straight) edges.

Beginning in 1946, the plates were laid out with vertical and horizontal gutters dividing a sheet of 112 subjects into four panes of twenty-eight stamps each. This permitted the complete perforation of all stamps on all sides. The sheets were cut into panes along the center lines of the gutters.

When the printing press was changed from flat-bed to rotary in 1959, the sheet size was increased to 120 subjects, the number of stamps per pane to 30. The current stamp design is 1.26 inches high by 1.82 inches wide, while the overall stamp size, including perforations, is 1.41 by 1.96 inches. The stamps are "gauge 11," which means they have 11 perforations for every 2 centimeters. The 1987 production marked the first time that stamps were perforated on an off-line web perforator, which results in a perfect center hole at the intersection of the perforations of four stamps.

Stamp Collecting

There is no single collectible that is more popular worldwide than stamps. And the duck stamp, although not used for postage, is very popular among stamp collectors (and is available at post offices). It is the longest ongoing stamp series ever issued by the United States government, uninterrupted since its inception in 1934.

The beginning collector usually strives to obtain single mint stamps—in other words, stamps that are "post office fresh." The second most collected version is a used—that is, signed—duck stamp. The signature is usually that of the stamp's original owner, or licensee. It is required by federal law that if the stamp is purchased for the right to hunt waterfowl, the licensee must sign the stamp and adhere it to the hunting permit. Each year's stamp is valid from July 1 through June 30 of the following year, when a new stamp must be purchased. (Some collectors collect stamps affixed to licenses, but that is an unusual approach.)

The third most popular form of duck stamp collected is that of plate blocks: four stamps (two by two) from the corner of a sheet, attached to the selvage (edge) with a plate number printed on it. That number is the actual engraving-plate number that is assigned to a sheet of stamps or to an entire printing.

Full sheets are the commodity in the final form of collecting. Because they are expensive, full sheets are the least often collected. For example, the face value of one 1987 stamp was $10, so a full sheet of thirty stamps costs $300.

The condition of a stamp (mint or used; hinged or unhinged; pristine or damaged), the centering of the design on the stamp, and the condition of the gum are the most important factors in determining philatelic value.

Many of the early duck stamps are found today without gum, probably because they were mishandled. Stamp expert Tom Deluca, of the Trenton (N.J.) Stamp and Coin Company, says, "If [a stamp] has no gum, it detracts as much as 60 or 70 percent of the value."

A complete set (1934–1987) of mint stamps can retail in a range of $3000 to $5000, depending on the centering of each stamp's design and on its condition. A complete set of unused, unsigned stamps, in less than mint condition, would cost approximately $1200.

Finally, collectors want either a mint stamp or a signed stamp to accompany their limited-edition print. It is recommended that a mint stamp be part of the collected pair, but often collectors add a signed-by-the-artist stamp with the anticipation that because of the signature, it will become more valuable.

Print Production

Print production has paralleled that of the stamps in that intaglio has been the dominant process. Many of the earlier prints, however, were made by the planographic method, or *lithography* (from the Greek, meaning *drawing in stone*). In this method, the design is drawn by hand or transferred from an original engraving to the surface of a lithographic stone or metal plate in greasy ink. The stone (plate) is made wet with an acid, which causes it to repel the printing ink except on the greasy lines of the design. A fine lithographic print closely resembles an engraving, although the lines are not raised. Offset lithographic reproductions, photographically created, do not produce as fine an image, and they are not valued as highly.

Print Collecting

Duck stamp and print sets were originally collected by hunters and stamp collectors. However, with the increasing quality of the artwork and the escalating value of the sets, their audience has expanded to the general public.

In general, people love owning items that are beautiful, unusual, or available in a limited quantity. There are collectors who buy these art and print sets for art's sake, since they represent the very best in wildlife art. There are duck enthusiasts, hunters, and many others who simply appreciate depictions of the natural world. And many environmentalists have begun collecting them as a means of donating money for the preservation of wildlife habitats. Finally, some purchase duck stamp prints as an investment because, historically, they have been an excellent one.

Value Predictability of Prints

We have already mentioned that many federal duck stamp prints have sharply risen in value. In the future, their value may level off, but so far it has never declined. Furthermore, many state duck stamp prints have experienced even greater appreciation than their federal counterparts. In light of these facts, the question of predictability becomes an important one.

What makes a given federal duck stamp print valuable? Some would argue that the single most important factor is the artist. When a design of a Maynard Reece or a David Maass is selected, it has a promising future. These artists have already proven themselves, they have strong name-recognition, and they have already established a collecting base.

Both the species and the design itself are also important factors, since they are meant to arouse a positive emotional response from the purchaser.

The edition size has a significant effect on the print's value. The edition size is determined by the use of a cut-off date; that is, only orders received by a specified date are honored. In this way, the edition size is determined solely by its immediate demand. Normally, dealers have ninety days to notify collectors and place their orders with a distributor or the publisher. However, in the case of the 1987 work by Arthur Andersen, the edition size was established at 20,000, regardless of the number of potential buyers. This experiment served to test the possibility that an early sellout could affect the appreciation of the print on the secondary, or resale, market.

When the artist, species, and design all contribute to the increased popularity and value of a print, then a small edition size is a further important determinant of its future value. As mentioned earlier, Reece's 1971 depiction of Cinnamon Teal increased in value to more than $6000. In contrast, Edward Bierly's 1970 painting of Ross's Geese—which combined vibrant colors with a delicate, almost Oriental design—increased in value from $75 to $2700, probably because Bierly did not have the name–recognition of Reece. Nevertheless, that represents a 3500 percent increase in just seventeen years.

All in all, the federal duck stamp prints have generally shown steady increases in value. Among recent issues, the 1986 release, depicting a Fulvous Whistling Duck by Burton E. Moore, Jr., increased in value from $142.50 to $190 in just one year. And Phil Scholer's 1983 design of Pintails resting in an early morning setting rose from $142.50 to $500, for a better than 350 percent appreciation in four years.

Artist's and Printer's Proofs

Artist's proofs—identified by *A/P* next to the number on the print—are created for the artist's own use. In the interest of maintaining quality during the printing process, prints are randomly removed and inspected by the artist, usually early in the print run. These prints are considered the very best of the edition because the plate has not yet begun to wear and the images are crisp and clear. The artist numbers these proofs and keeps them, gives them away, or sells them at a premium.

Likewise, in the interest of printing quality, the printer (it may be the artist himself) removes prints during the printing process to be reviewed. These prints are identified by *P/P*, but they are usually not numbered. Their value is considered to be high.

Like ordinary prints, artist's and printer's proofs are more valuable when the prints are original lithos or intaglios, less so when they are photographic lithos.

Remarqued Prints

A *remarque* (a French word meaning *remark*, *note*) is an original work of art: a pencil drawing, watercolor, or acrylic inscription on the border (usually the bottom) of the print. The artist here is combining a limited-edition, signed, and numbered print with an original piece of art. Since remarques are usually done on the plate prior to printing and then cut off, these one-of-a-kind renderings are highly prized, yet affordable, works of art. While few collectors can afford an original Maass or Reece painting, a remarqued print is within the price range of many collectors.

Albert Gilbert's 1978 Hooded Merganser print was one of the last federal to be offered remarqued. The edition sizes and demand for these prints simply got too high for it to be practical for an artist to hand paint or draw remarques.

Medallions

A void was created with the termination of federal remarques in 1978. (This is not to say that an artist could not paint a remarque as a personal favor: Ken Michaelsen offered an original etching with his 1979 design of a Green-Winged Teal.) It was not until 1983 that a replacement for the remarque was found. To commemorate that year's Pintail design by Phil Scholer, a round, gold-plated medallion was offered in a time-limited edition of 6700. Not only did this fill the void left by the cessation of remarques, but it was practical to produce in large numbers in a timely fashion.

Medallions can be formed in a circle, like a coin, or in a rectangular shape, like a stamp. Some medallions, like Gerald Mobley's 1985 design of Cinnamon Teal, even have "perforated" edges.

Like the stamps and prints, the medallions have appreciated considerably in a few years. For example, Scholer's 1983 medallion/stamp/print set was sold for $257.50 and is currently valued at $1300.

Print Editions

Prior to the introduction of lithographic reproduction, second and third print editions were often created because of worn-out plates. From 1934 through approximately 1969, the continuous wear on the plates took their toll on the quality of the prints. The image, particularly the background, began to lose clarity, so new plates were etched. The original plates were defaced or destroyed so that no new prints could be made from them. Generally, on the new plate, as print publisher Burnett Harshman explains, "an artist would etch something into the image to identify which printing, or 'pull,' a particular print came from." A minute change in a leaf or a wing would be enough. "This was done for the artist's own interest and knowledge, so as to identify where a particular print came from, whether from the first 'pull' or from a second or third plate."

The introduction of lithography—where there is virtually no wear on the plates—has reduced the need for second editions of prints. The hundredth print, even the ten-thousandth print, is of the same high quality as the first print created.

Collectors value second and third editions less highly. First editions can bring two—even as high as ten—times more than a third edition! A first edition of Maynard Reece's 1948 Buffleheads is currently valued at $1200, while the fourth edition is valued at $500. Similarly, Leslie Kouba's 1958 first edition of Canada Geese is currently valued at $1100, in contrast to $125 for the third edition.

Signed and Numbered Prints

The limited-edition federal duck stamp prints have always been signed by the artist. But they have been numbered annually only since 1975, when James L. Fisher numbered his edition of 3150 prints. From that year on, the numbering of federal prints has been the norm.

It is now customary for an artist to number a print with two numbers separated by a slash (/). The number at the left is that of the particular print; the second number is the edition size. For example, "1050/3200" means that the print is number 1050 in an edition of 3200.

In 1939, Lynn Hunt numbered his prints, but he did not give a total edition size. In 1945, Owen Gromme numbered his print edition in the lower left-hand corner, but many of these numbers cannot be verified because print framers often trimmed away the number.

The first numbering of an entire edition occurred with Stanley Sterns's set of 300 prints in 1966. The following year, however, Leslie Kouba elected not to number his prints. During the following six years, every edition was numbered. So by 1973, collectors had accepted the numbering of prints as normal. Therefore, when David Maass decided not to number his 1974 edition, it caused quite an uproar among collectors. As a result, all editions from 1975 to the present have been numbered.

There is no added monetary value in having a low-numbered photographically produced print, although original lithographs with low numbers have a slightly higher value.

The signing and numbering of limited-edition duck stamp prints is done with a pencil. This reduces the risk of unauthorized reproductions of these editions because it is more difficult to reproduce pencil than it is ink.

Federal Publishing Rights of the Art Work

The appreciation on federal duck stamp prints has made significant the issue of publishing rights. The design winner retains all publishing rights to his or her design. After winning the competition, the artist receives a mint sheet of stamps with the winning design on it, signed by the Secretary of the Department of the Interior. But the real reward comes with the ability of the artist to market the winning design in other forms. The Department of the Interior receives no financial gain from the reproduction of the federal stamp design as a limited-edition print. Most of the revenues received by the Department of the Interior result from the sale of the stamp.

Traditionally artists have maintained complete control of their publishing rights, but on three occasions artists have apparently relinquished those rights to publishers—in 1979 and 1987, when the artist signed contractual agreements with Petersen Publishing Company of California, and in 1981, when the Minnesota publisher Wild Wings was contracted.

As to whether the licensing procedures will ever change, program coordinator Norma Opgrand has said: "If it ever changed, it would have to be changed by Congress. Last year [1986], there was an effort to change the rights and there was a lot of opposition to this, so the bill never got out of committee. It probably won't surface again for a long time." She added: "My guess is that it is not going to come about. We have had this program for fifty-three years and the tradition is there. People get upset when you change that."

Benefits to Conservation and to Artists

The federal program has sold 90 million duck stamps since 1934, providing more than $300 million for the purchase of 30.5 million acres of wetland habitat for waterfowl. During the 1980-1985 period, an average of $15,336,565 was raised each year. From 1962 through 1986, 526,563 acres of wetlands were acquired, with easements to protect an additional 1,211,167 acres of wetlands, according to the U.S. Fish and Wildlife Service. The total cost for this acreage was $133 million.

In 1987, according to Clyde Schnack, chief of the Branch of Acquisition, there were six major projects being focused on, including those in the Atlantic Coastal Plain, the Gulf Coast, and the Central Valley of California. All fifty states, at one time or another, receive benefits from these funds.

The federal stamp program has also raised the winning artist to instant millionaire status in each of the last few years. According to Norma Opgrand, the staggering windfall reaped by each winning artist has made the federal design competition prize highly coveted. "In the last five to six years, the artists have each had a gain of one million or more dollars, due to the sale of lithographs of the original art works," Opgrand said. "And because the contest is well recognized by the art community, their other works become more and more valuable and in demand."

In the early 1970s, when the federal program began to reach its current highly successful level, the individual states began to look at the program with great interest. They knew that what had been attained by the federal government had been, and could further be, beneficial to the states. But they saw a chance to better control the destinies of their states by conducting programs of their own. As pioneers frequently learn, the early sailing would not be smooth, but the long-term benefits would make it all worthwhile.

The First State Program

In 1971, California issued the nation's first state duck stamp and print combination. Earlier, California officials had decided that they did not want to be tied to the purse strings of the U.S. Department of the Interior so they created a state duck stamp program in their Fish and Wildlife department to generate monies exclusively for in-state conservation.

Californian Paul Johnson was the first artist commissioned to design a state stamp. In fact, California asked him to design the first seven stamps (1971-1977). It was established that Johnson would retain the publishing right to produce prints from his stamp design, the state not sharing the revenue derived from their sale. Instead, California would obtain its revenue solely from state hunting licenses.

Johnson's concept was to create an edition of 500 prints, reproduced in monotone (the first year's print was sepia). The 1971 print sold very briskly, and it appeared that the state duck stamp and print series was going to be successful. This seemed to be confirmed by the sale of the second (1972) stamp. The demand for it exceeded the supply (500), and it has appreciated over the years even more than the 1971 stamp, which has not been typical among second-year releases in other state programs.

When the edition was established—again a fixed-edition size of 500 signed and numbered prints—the stamps that were to accompany these prints were purchased at the end of the hunting season. The decision to do so, it is believed, was made because California had established that after the season ended and that year's stamp was no longer valid, those stamps would remain with the agency

for six more months—after which time they would be shredded. This was a good marketing approach, because it then limited the number of stamps that could be collected, and it could cause serious stamp collectors to increase their purchases. This also tended to increase the revenues for state conservation.

Whether intentional or not, Johnson was to make his purchases of the 500 necessary stamps that he would need for his 1972 edition after the July 31 cut-off date. For from August 1 to December the stamps could be purchased at a reduced rate of 50 percent less than the face value, adding a substantial savings. What Johnson did not know at the time, however, was that an agency clerk mistakenly had taken the balance of the stamps and, instead of storing them, shredded them. Johnson, by going to the individual state offices, tried to collect those stamps that were still available. Instead of having an edition size of 500 with accompanied stamps, in the end the collection consisted of only 166 signed and numbered prints with matching mint stamps.

California is to be commended for its initiative in creating the first state stamp/print program for conservation. Thanks to its pioneering, other states were able to follow with a clear idea of how to conduct their programs.

The Growth of State Programs

As other states began to ponder creating their own duck stamp programs, it became clear from the California experience that there was more to the success of a program than simply creating a stamp and distributing it to state offices for sale with hunting licenses. It took years of detailed planning and cooperation among various state departments.

Since California's trail-blazing duck stamp program, three-quarters of the states have instituted programs of their own, with a great variety of approaches. For instance, Nevada (whose program began in 1979) decided to select its designer through a national competition to ensure the best possible design and to allow new artists to become recognized.

In contrast, the state of Alabama had an in-state competition for its first (1979) design. State officials, with the best intentions, wanted to reward state artists, but unfortunately this greatly limited the range of selections. After Alabama's "first of state" was issued, the edition sizes for succeeding years dropped dramatically.

Nevada, which selected its stamp designers from a national pool, found that the quality of artwork remained at a consistently high level. Consequently, Nevada's edition sizes also remained at a respectable level, resulting in the raising of more money for that state's conservation efforts.

Delaware, also with good intentions, limited its design competition to in-state residents. Consequently, it experienced the same result that other resident-only competitions experienced: Sales after the first year dropped drastically.

Initially, Delaware did not retain the publishing rights, which became part of the award to the winning artist. States that do not choose to retain publishing rights lose out on the considerable amount of revenue that can be earned from the sale of signed and numbered prints. Delaware did not share in any of these proceeds, obtaining revenue only from the stamp's sale.

The Arkansas stamp/print program is an example of one that has put a heavy emphasis on selecting nationally known artists. In the seven years of its program, Arkansas has selected a veritable Who's Who of wildlife artists. Beginning its program in 1981 with Lee LeBlanc, it followed with Maynard Reece in 1982, David Maass in 1983, Larry Hayden in 1984, Ken Carlson in 1985, Jack Cowan in 1986, and Robert Bateman in 1987. (It was Bateman's first state duck stamp design.)

Larry Grishan of Arkansas's Grishan Gallery, publisher of the 1987 print and stamp, felt strongly that in order for the Arkansas program to be successful, he and the members of the Fish and Game Council needed to draw on the national reputation and markets of those artists whom they had selected. They started their successful new series of releases with the 1973 federal winner and mentor to many wildlife artists, Lee LeBlanc.

Grishan felt that to maximize print sales they would have to appeal to people outside of Arkansas. And one way to accomplish this, he believed, was to select active scenes for the state's stamps. Therefore, only two paintings out of seven show tranquil settings, those being the Larry Hayden (1984) and Robert Bateman (1987) paintings.

Perhaps the exemplary Arkansas design was the 1986 Jack Cowan work entitled *Black Swamp Mallards*. Here an active sporting scene was depicted in an Arkansas timber setting. In contrast, Maynard Reece's *Big Lake Wood Ducks* (1982) and David Maass's *Green-Winged Teal* (1983) depict scenes that could be observed in many other regions of the country.

Clearly, designs that are less identifiable with a particular region have a broader appeal. And Grishan believes that paintings with action help stimulate the memories of many collectors who have sporting experience. Waterfowlers, in particular, make up a large portion of the Arkansas collecting base. Nevertheless, the tranquil Hayden design of a pair of Pintail, *Bois D'Arc*, had an impressive edition of 7000 prints. While many of those prints and stamps were sold in Arkansas, Texas, and throughout the Southwest, few were sold in the Northeast.

In contrast, Maynard Reece's 1982 *Big Lake Wood Ducks* achieved good sales throughout the country. And—due to the cooperative efforts of Arkansas and the publisher Mill Pond Press of Florida to broaden the national market to include collectors in regions outside the South and Southwest—Robert Bateman's *Hurricane Lake Wood Ducks* was selected as the 1987 design. Mill Pond's president, Bob Lewin, reasoned that Bateman's recent success with his first National Fish and Wildlife Foundation series, entitled *Pride of Autumn*, would increase his appeal to a national audience.

Bateman's selection was a strong move for Arkansas. While Grishan had aggressively promoted the state's program, his collectors tended to be those active in Arkansas outdoor sporting. The change in the state's marketing approach by the selection of Bateman will eventually alter its program and increase its sales substantially.

The New Jersey Experience

In the spring of 1983, Joe McCaddin was asked to meet with a committee from the Fish, Game and Wildlife Council of New Jersey. They had been considering inaugurating their own stamp/print program. Like other states, New Jersey was considering many options, including either an in-state or a national competition, but not direct commissioning of artists.

McCaddin was hired as an unpaid consultant to the state Division of Fish, Game and Wildlife to work on their program. He recommended that New Jersey commission an artist, rather than hold a competition, and retain all rights to the art. By commissioning an artwork, a state has more control over the species and design of the painting, which increases the potential for a marketable print and reduces the state's financial risk.

It is very important that a stamp design be attractive, for a state has only one opportunity per year to raise the money that it needs for its conservation efforts. And by holding the reprint rights to the art the state can also receive a percentage of the print sales.

McCaddin also suggested that the state select a publisher and have it be responsible for presenting the artwork to the state selection committee. The publisher would be responsible for producing the art prints, setting up a distribution network throughout the country, distributing the prints, and keeping the necessary detailed records on signed and numbered prints.

Equally important, the publisher had to have a specific marketing proposal, including the projected revenue needed for a regional and national marketing effort. McCaddin wanted New Jersey to view its program as a means of raising as much conservation money as possible, and to accomplish this, sound business practices and marketing methods needed to be employed.

McCaddin felt that the one factor that would tie together all the program's different aspects was a successful marketing approach. With a piece of high-quality artwork, one with a design that was stimulating to the collector, a publisher with the ability to set up a national advertising and distribution program could make great strides in the first year.

It was recommended that the committee develop bid specifications. The publishers would be asked to submit to the committee their best proposals, bidding for the right to print and market the New Jersey print. State officials wanted the chosen publisher to represent the program for three years to ensure that the publisher would engage in long-term planning. The state wanted to avoid selecting a publisher that concentrated only on what had traditionally been the easiest year to sell, the first year. The desired publisher would be an equal partner who would share in the success or failure of that three-year program.

"We wanted the publisher's involvement to ensure the success of an ongoing program by their involvement," recalls Fish and Game director Russell Cookingham. And so the committee wanted to learn from each bidder what its national advertising budget would be, whether it had an adequate sales force to properly service existing dealers and to open accounts with new dealers, and whether it could guarantee an accurate count of the number of prints made.

Chairing the committee to review the duck stamp bids was a long-time member of the Fish and Game Council, Jim Craft. On Craft's committee was a spectrum of representatives from conservation and other organizations, such as the Nature Conservancy Foundation, New Jersey State Federation of Sportman's Clubs, League of Women Voters, New Jersey Audubon Society, New Jersey Waterfowlers Association, Natural Areas Council, and the New Jersey Chapter of Ducks Unlimited. Frank Tourine, a member of the New Jersey Division of Fish, Game and Wildlife, was asked to be the coordinator.

The New Jersey Waterfowl Stamp Act was signed by Governor Thomas Kean on January 17, 1984, and it went into effect on July 1, 1984. The law required anyone over the age of sixteen to purchase a stamp prior to hunting waterfowl. Until the June 30, 1985 expiration date, the $2.50 resident stamp would be sold only to persons possessing a valid New Jersey hunting license.

After the expiration date, this stamp would be on sale for six months to anyone wishing to buy one. The $5 nonresident stamp would go on sale to anyone at any time up until six months after the expiration date, at which time all unsold stamps of both denominations would be destroyed.

In the selection process, the names on the paintings were covered so that the committee would select the best one on its artistic merits and not be swayed by the reputation of the artist. The winning design for New Jersey's first duck stamp was created by the state's own Tom Hirata. His painting was one of seventeen submitted by the publisher Mid-West Marketing. In addition to creating the design, Hirata also took an active role in the marketing plan that Mid-West Marketing submitted as a part of its bid to the committee.

The New Jersey duck stamp/print program—while born at a time when successful state programs had become the norm—through its innovations and careful organization has become a model for future state programs.

Ducks Unlimited

In addition to the federal government and thirty-eight individual states generating much-needed monies for wetland conservation, there has been a long history of private funding for the same goal. Such national organizations as the National Audubon Society, Nature Conservancy Foundation, and National Wildlife Federation and local organizations like the Federation of Sportsman's Clubs and New Jersey Waterfowlers have greatly contributed to this end. But one organization that typifies the cooperation of state agencies and private organizations is Ducks Unlimited. Through the years that states have been involved in duck stamp programs, there has been a history of working closely with this national organization. Such states as Illinois, California, South Carolina, and Arkansas, just to name a few, all allocate monies to Ducks Unlimited.

Ducks Unlimited was incorporated on January 29, 1937, in Washington, D.C., and in its golden-anniversary year, it had a national membership of nearly 600,000. The founders were greatly concerned about the future of North America's wild duck and geese populations, so the organization's purpose is to raise funds for developing, preserving, restoring, and maintaining the waterfowl habitat in North America.

With the help of over 3800 local grass-roots organizations, Ducks Unlimited has raised approximately $400 million. Hazard K. Campbell, national president of the organization, has stated: "Raising money is an ever so critical piece of business. But putting the funds to work quickly and efficiently is our bottom line."

Ducks Unlimited has reserved nearly 4,000,000 acres of habitat, constructed over 3000 wetland projects, and carved out more than 16,000 miles of nesting shoreline. According to its 1986 annual report, over $50 million was raised through single volunteer fundraising events held nationwide. In the report, Campbell discusses the spirit of the commitment and enthusiasm of Ducks Unlimited.

The state of New York typifies the cooperation, commitment, and desire of a state to work harmoniously with private conservation organizations. Once New York had established the means for creating a migratory bird stamp and art prints, it included in its state finance law a provision that after payment of administrative costs for the preparation and sale of stamps and art prints, "50 percent of these monies shall be available to the department . . . exclusively for the acquisition, preservation, improvement and development of wetlands and development and maintenance of access sites within the state." The state provided that the remaining 50 percent of the dollars created through the sale of stamps and prints would be distributed "to an appropriate nonprofit organization for the development of waterfowl habitat projects within the domain of Canada, which specifically provides migratory birds for the Atlantic flyway." With this provision, the avenues were established whereby public funds could be used in cooperation with private conservation organizations.

The New York State program's goal is stated in the state finance law: to generate money for the protection and management of wetlands and to improve public access to these areas for a variety of wildlife uses. The developers of this law based their decision on the "scientific knowledge that more than 70 percent of our migratory bird resources originate in Canada." It was in the best interest of the states within the Atlantic flyway to continue the habitat work in Canada in order to create or improve migratory-bird breeding habitats. Canada's portion of the revenue is released only after the Department of Environmental Conservation approves specific Canadian wetland habitat projects within the Atlantic flyway.

Revenues generated from the New York State stamp and print sales for 1985/1986 have been estimated to be $600,000. It is hoped that the sales for 1986/1987 and 1987/1988 will generate an additional $250,000. After administrative costs have been subtracted from those revenues, a substantial amount of money will be made available to Ducks Unlimited so that they can achieve some of their conservation goals.

Bashakil Wildlife Management Area, for instance, is located in the lower Hudson River region of the state of New York. This 1333-acre wetland, owned by the state, was created by a gravel bar deposited at the junction of the Pinekil and Bashakil. Among other things, a dam was built so that the water level could be managed properly.

The money that has been allocated to Ducks Unlimited to be used in Canada has gone to such projects as the Rockland Marsh program in the province of New Brunswick and the Balmoral Marsh program near Lake St. Claire in Ontario. The Canadian chapter of Ducks Unlimited sees the former as an opportunity to protect vital breeding ground. And the Balmoral Marsh, actually a privately owned group of marshes, is in serious jeopardy because of intense economic incentives to drain the marshlands. These represent long-term projects that will require thirty years of cooperation—between private landowners, government officials, and Ducks Unlimited—to salvage the future of these habitats.

The continuing cooperation between state duck stamp programs and Ducks Unlimited (that is, the public and private sectors) represents a third technique for raising money for wetland conservation, one that may well turn out to be as successful as the federal and state duck stamp programs themselves.

A New Type of Duck Stamp Print

The National Fish and Wildlife Foundation was established to create a partnership between public and private foundations to make their conservation efforts more effective. The Foundation was *not* created, says Charles Collins, its executive secretary, "to transfer public responsibilities for managing the nation's fish, wildlife, and plant resources to the private sector. Instead, the Foundation wants to provide a vehicle for private citizens, corporations, and public-spirited institutions to support new and creative programs that will help to meet the changing need in wildlife protection."

President Ronald Reagan signed into law the National Fish and Wildlife Foundation Establishment Act on March 26, 1984. The private, nonprofit Foundation has a nine-member board of directors composed of private citizens experienced in conservation matters; they are appointed by the Secretary of the Interior. With the support of the Executive and the U.S. Congress, the Foundation enjoys a credibility not shared by other private foundations.

The Foundation neither engages in lobbying nor supports any specific activities. Instead, its goal is to be a catalyst in attempts to coordinate the activities of private organizations and public agencies. It encourages and accepts private donations of land, other property, and money for the benefit of programs of the U.S. Fish and Wildlife Service. The Foundation's long-term mission is to preserve the nation's habitat for future generations, to encourage research, and to create public awareness of the Foundation's goals and activities.

With its lofty goals in mind, the National Fish and Wildlife Foundation created its own conservation stamp and print. The internationally renowned Robert Bateman designed *Pride of Autumn—Canada Goose* for the first issue. The Canada Goose was chosen because it inhabits all of North America.

Mill Pond Press's Bob Lewin pointed out that, as a result of sales of the Bateman stamp and print, over $750,000 was transferred to the National Fish and Wildlife Foundation. This money is earmarked for such projects as the restoration of the bald eagle in fourteen states, the Public Education on the Chesapeake Bay Wildlife Restoration Programs, and the development of a permanent River Corridor Protection Program in upstate New York. Among the numerous other projects planned or in progress are satellite tracking of the sea turtle called Kemp's Ridley in the Gulf of Mexico, Striped-Bass stocking and restoration programs in Chesapeake Bay, and public education efforts on behalf of shore birds that nest on sensitive barrier islands and beaches on the Atlantic coast.

Looking Ahead

In the near future, other organizations, such as the National Fish and Wildlife Foundation, will create their own stamp and print programs. And, certainly, the federal and state duck stamp and print programs, after over fifty years of increasing success, will continue to issue original works of art to be cherished by future generations. They will give collectors of limited-edition art an opportunity for a good return on a modest investment. And they will help to ensure the preservation of our nation's natural resources.

In the pages ahead the reader may explore the works and backgrounds of many of the artists who have made this all possible. Let this volume be a grateful tribute to them, for there would be no duck stamp programs without their creative talents.

Joe McCaddin
Marlton, New Jersey
December 1987

The Stamps

FEDERAL 1934–35

FEDERAL 1935–36

FEDERAL 1936–37

FEDERAL 1937–38

FEDERAL 1938–39

FEDERAL 1939–40

FEDERAL 1940–41

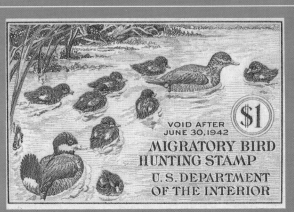

FEDERAL 1941–42

FEDERAL 1942–43

FEDERAL 1943-44

FEDERAL 1944-45

FEDERAL 1945-46

FEDERAL 1946-47

FEDERAL 1947-48

FEDERAL 1948-49

FEDERAL 1949-50

FEDERAL 1950-51

FEDERAL 1951-52

FEDERAL 1952-53

FEDERAL 1953-54

FEDERAL 1954-55

FEDERAL 1955-56

FEDERAL 1956-57

FEDERAL 1957-58

HUNTING STAMP · CANADA GEESE

MIGRATORY BIRD

$2

VOID AFTER JUNE 30, 1959

U.S. DEPARTMENT of the INTERIOR

FEDERAL 1958–59

MIGRATORY BIRD HUNTING STAMP

RETRIEVERS SAVE GAME

VOID AFTER JUNE 30, 1960

$3

U.S. DEPARTMENT OF THE INTERIOR

FEDERAL 1959–60

WILDLIFE NEEDS WATER ★ PRESERVE WETLANDS ★

MIGRATORY BIRD HUNTING STAMP

U.S. DEPARTMENT OF THE INTERIOR

$3

REDHEAD DUCKS

VOID AFTER JUNE 30, 1961

FEDERAL 1960–61

VOID AFTER JUNE 30, 1962

$3

U.S. DEPARTMENT OF THE INTERIOR

MIGRATORY BIRD HUNTING STAMP

MALLARD BROOD

HABITAT PRODUCES DUCKS

FEDERAL 1961–62

PINTAILS

MIGRATORY BIRD HUNTING STAMP

VOID AFTER JUNE 30, 1963

$3

U.S. DEPARTMENT OF THE INTERIOR

FEDERAL 1962–63

$3

U.S. DEPARTMENT OF THE INTERIOR

MIGRATORY BIRD HUNTING STAMP

BRANT

VOID AFTER JUNE 30, 1964

FEDERAL 1963–64

MIGRATORY BIRD HUNTING STAMP

U.S. DEPARTMENT OF THE INTERIOR

$3

VOID AFTER JUNE 30, 1965

NENE GOOSE

FEDERAL 1964–65

$3 MIGRATORY BIRD HUNTING STAMP

VOID AFTER JUNE 30, 1966

CANVASBACKS

U.S. DEPARTMENT OF THE INTERIOR

FEDERAL 1965–66

MIGRATORY BIRD HUNTING STAMP

$3 VOID AFTER JUNE 30, 1967

U.S. DEPARTMENT OF THE INTERIOR

WHISTLING SWANS

FEDERAL 1966–67

MIGRATORY BIRD HUNTING STAMP

$3

U.S. DEPARTMENT OF THE INTERIOR

Old Squaws

VOID AFTER JUNE 30, 1968

FEDERAL 1967–68

VOID AFTER JUNE 30, 1969

$3 MIGRATORY BIRD HUNTING STAMP

Hooded Mergansers

U.S. DEPARTMENT OF THE INTERIOR

FEDERAL 1968–69

U.S. DEPARTMENT OF THE INTERIOR

$3 VOID AFTER JUNE 30, 1970

White-Winged Scoters

MIGRATORY BIRD HUNTING STAMP

FEDERAL 1969–70

MIGRATORY BIRD HUNTING STAMP

$3

VOID AFTER JUNE 30, 1971

ROSS GEESE

U.S. DEPARTMENT OF THE INTERIOR

FEDERAL 1970–71

U.S. DEPARTMENT OF THE INTERIOR

CINNAMON TEAL

VOID AFTER JUNE 30, 1972

$3

MIGRATORY BIRD HUNTING STAMP

FEDERAL 1971–72

CALIFORNIA DUCK STAMP

Pintails

$1.00 Expires 6-30-72   D 0055 -25

CALIFORNIA 1971

FEDERAL 1972-73

CALIFORNIA 1972

IOWA 1972

FEDERAL 1973-74

CALIFORNIA 1973

IOWA 1973

FEDERAL 1974-75

CALIFORNIA 1974

IOWA 1974

MARYLAND 1974

MASSACHUSETTS 1974

FEDERAL 1975-76

CALIFORNIA 1975

ILLINOIS 1975

IOWA 1975

MARYLAND 1975

MASSACHUSETTS 1975

FEDERAL 1976–77

CALIFORNIA 1976

ILLINOIS 1976

INDIANA 1976

IOWA 1976

MARYLAND 1976

MASSACHUSETTS 1976

MICHIGAN 1976

MISSISSIPPI 1976

SOUTH DAKOTA 1976

WOOD DUCKS   EXPIRES FEB. 28, 1979

$1

STATE CONSERVATION COMMISSION

IOWA MIGRATORY WATERFOWL STAMP

IOWA 1978

MIGRATORY WATERFOWL STAMP

Maryland Department of Natural Resources

$1.10

Void After July 31, 1979

MARYLAND 1978

1978 Massachusetts Waterfowl Stamp

$1.25

Black Duck by A. Elmer Crowell

MASSACHUSETTS 1978

1978 MICHIGAN WATERFOWL HUNTING STAMP

$2.10

D   112155

MICHIGAN 1978

1978 MIGRATORY WATERFOWL STAMP

$3

Lesser Scaup

MINNESOTA DEPARTMENT OF NATURAL RESOURCES

MINNESOTA 1978

MISSISSIPPI GAME AND FISH COMMISSION

No 2042485

$2.00

Mississippi Waterfowl Stamp — Expires 6/30/79

MISSISSIPPI 1978

$1   68465

1978

SOUTH DAKOTA RESIDENT MIGRATORY WATERFOWL LICENSE

SOUTH DAKOTA 1978

$3.25

1978 WISCONSIN WATERFOWL STAMP

WISCONSIN 1978

U.S. DEPARTMENT OF THE INTERIOR

GREEN-WINGED TEAL

$7.50

MIGRATORY BIRD HUNTING AND CONSERVATION STAMP

VOID AFTER JUNE 30, 1980

FEDERAL 1979–80

Alabama Department of Conservation & Natural Resources

WATERFOWL STAMP

1979-80 VOID SEPT. 30, 1980

$5   No 02512

ALABAMA 1979

CALIFORNIA DUCK STAMP 1979-80

Wood Ducks

$5   D 01159-15

CALIFORNIA 1979

Green-winged Teal

FLORIDA 1979

1979   **$5.00**

ILLINOIS MIGRATORY WATERFOWL STAMP

Pintail Drake

114380

ILLINOIS 1979

MIGRATORY WATERFOWL STAMP

INDIANA

1979

$5

DEPT. OF NATURAL RESOURCES/DIV. OF FISH AND WILDLIFE

VOID AFTER Dec. 31, 1979

INDIANA 1979

IOWA MIGRATORY WATERFOWL STAMP
EXPIRES FEB. 29, 1980

$5

BUFFLEHEADS
STATE CONSERVATION COMMISSION

IOWA 1979

MARYLAND 1979

MIGRATORY WATERFOWL STAMP
Maryland Department of Natural Resources
Void After July 31, 1980
$1.10

MASSACHUSETTS 1979

1979 Massachusetts Waterfowl Stamp
$1.25
Ruddy Turnstone by Lothrop Holmes

MICHIGAN 1979

MICHIGAN WATERFOWL
1979
HUNTING STAMP 2⁹
R 259 2

MINNESOTA 1979

1979 MIGRATORY WATERFOWL STAMP
Minnesota Department Of Natural Resources
Pintails
$3

MISSISSIPPI 1979

Mississippi Dept. of Wildlife Conservation
No 17212
Canvasback
1980 Waterfowl Stamp
$2

MISSOURI 1979

WATERFOWL 1979
$3.40 FEE
VOID AFTER JANUARY 31, 1980
Missouri Department of Conservation
000643

NEVADA 1979

$2
Nevada Department of Wildlife
Expires 6-30-80
Tule Decoy A.D. 1000
Duck Stamp

TENNESSEE 1979

TENNESSEE WILDLIFE RESOURCES AGENCY
38440
EXPIRES JUNE 30, 1980
RESIDENT $2
MALLARDS
MIGRATORY WATERFOWL STAMP

WISCONSIN 1979

$3.25
EXPIRES AUG. 31, 1980
1979 WISCONSIN WATERFOWL STAMP

FEDERAL 1980–81

VOID AFTER JUNE 30, 1981
MIGRATORY BIRD HUNTING AND CONSERVATION STAMP
U.S. DEPARTMENT OF THE INTERIOR
Mallards
$7.50

ALABAMA 1980

Alabama
VOID SEPT. 30, 1981
1980-81
5
001885
Waterfowl Stamp

CALIFORNIA 1980

CALIFORNIA DUCK STAMP
1980-81
PINTAILS
$5
D 0011 17

DELAWARE 1980

DELAWARE MIGRATORY WATERFOWL STAMP
$5
VOID AFTER JUNE 30, 1981

FLORIDA 1980

Pintails

ILLINOIS 1980

GREEN WINGED TEAL
$5.00
1980 ILLINOIS MIGRATORY WATERFOWL STAMP
000537

MIGRATORY WATERFOWL STAMP
INDIANA
1980
$5
VOID AFTER FEBRUARY 28, 1981
DEPT. OF NATURAL RESOURCES/DIVISION OF FISH AND WILDLIFE

INDIANA 1980

IOWA MIGRATORY WATERFOWL STAMP   Redheads
$5
Expires Feb. 28, 1981
STATE CONSERVATION COMMISSION

IOWA 1980

$1.10
MIGRATORY WATERFOWL STAMP
Maryland Department of Natural Resources
Void After July 31 1981

MARYLAND 1980

1980 Massachusetts Waterfowl Stamp
$1.25
Canvas and slat Oldsquaw by Lothrop Holmes

MASSACHUSETTS 1980

A 2440
MICHIGAN WATERFOWL
1980
HUNTING STAMP $3.75

MICHIGAN 1980

MINNESOTA DEPARTMENT OF NATURAL RESOURCES
1980 MIGRATORY WATERFOWL STAMP
Canvasbacks
$3

MINNESOTA 1980

Mississippi Dept. of Wildlife Conservation
Pintail
No 2013683
$2
Waterfowl Stamp
Void Unless Signed
Void After June 30, 1981

MISSISSIPPI 1980

$3.40 FEE WATERFOWL 1980
VOID AFTER JANUARY 31, 1981
MISSOURI DEPARTMENT OF CONSERVATION
000409

MISSOURI 1980

$2
Nevada Department of Wildlife
Expires 6-30-81
Duck Stamp

NEVADA 1980

$4
OKLAHOMA DEPARTMENT OF WILDLIFE CONSERVATION
1980-81 WATERFOWL HUNTING STAMP
Pintails
Expires June 30, 1981

OKLAHOMA 1980

TENNESSEE WILDLIFE RESOURCES AGENCY MIGRATORY WATERFOWL STAMP
RESIDENT $2
02108
EXPIRES JUNE 30, 1981
CANVASBACKS

TENNESSEE 1980

1980 WISCONSIN WATERFOWL STAMP
$3.25

WISCONSIN 1980

$7.50 MIGRATORY BIRD HUNTING AND CONSERVATION STAMP
VOID AFTER JUNE 30, 1982
Ruddy Ducks
U.S. DEPARTMENT OF THE INTERIOR

FEDERAL 1981–82

Alabama Waterfowl Stamp
02944
VOID AFTER SEPT 30 1982
$5

ALABAMA 1981

ARKANSAS GAME AND FISH COMMISSION WATERFOWL HUNTING AND CONSERVATION STAMP
BAYOU METO MALLARDS
1981-82
$5.50

ARKANSAS 1981

D 00032 11

CANVASBACKS

$5

CALIFORNIA DUCK STAMP

1981-82

CALIFORNIA 1981

DELAWARE MIGRATORY WATERFOWL STAMP

VOID AFTER JUNE 30, 1982

$5

DELAWARE 1981

FLORIDA N° 00512

$3.25

Expires June 30, 1982

American Widgeon

WATERFOWL STAMP

FLORIDA 1981

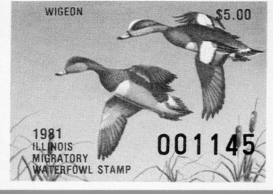

WIGEON

$5.00

1981 ILLINOIS MIGRATORY WATERFOWL STAMP

001145

ILLINOIS 1981

$5

VOID AFTER FEBRUARY 28, 1982

DEPT. OF NATURAL RESOURCES DIVISION OF FISH AND WILDLIFE

1981 INDIANA MIGRATORY WATERFOWL STAMP

INDIANA 1981

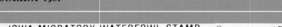

IOWA MIGRATORY WATERFOWL STAMP   Green-winged Teal

$5

Expires Feb 28, 1982

STATE CONSERVATION COMMISSION

IOWA 1981

MIGRATORY WATERFOWL STAMP

$3.00

Maryland Department of Natural Resources

Void After July 31 1982

MARYLAND 1981

1981 Massachusetts Waterfowl Stamp

$1.25   Red-Breasted Merganser by an unknown carver

MASSACHUSETTS 1981

WATERFOWL

MICHIGAN   1981 $3.75

W 004186

MICHIGAN 1981

MINNESOTA DEPARTMENT OF NATURAL RESOURCES

$3

1981 MIGRATORY WATERFOWL STAMP   Giant Canada Geese

MINNESOTA 1981

Mississippi Department of Wildlife Conservation

Expires June 30, 1982

Void Unless Signed

$2

11333

Redheads

Waterfowl Stamp

MISSISSIPPI 1981

Waterfowl 1981   000931

void after January 31, 1982

$3.00 FEE

MISSOURI DEPARTMENT OF CONSERVATION

MISSOURI 1981

Nevada Department of Wildlife

$2

Expires 6-30-82

Duck Stamp

WHISTLING SWAN

NEVADA 1981

OKLAHOMA DEPARTMENT OF WILDLIFE CONSERVATION

Expires June 30, 1982

1981-82 WATERFOWL HUNTING STAMP

$4

OKLAHOMA 1981

SOUTH CAROLINA MIGRATORY WATERFOWL AND HUNTING STAMP

$5.50

EXPIRES JUNE 30, 1982

SOUTH CAROLINA 1981

TENNESSEE WILDLIFE RESOURCES AGENCY
MIGRATORY WATERFOWL STAMP
EXPIRES FEBRUARY 28, 1982
RESIDENT $2
WOOD DUCKS

TENNESSEE 1981

Texas Parks and Wildlife Dept.
Waterfowl Stamp
1981
$5.00

TEXAS 1981

1981 WISCONSIN WATERFOWL STAMP
$3.25

WISCONSIN 1981

VOID AFTER JUNE 30, 1983
MIGRATORY BIRD HUNTING AND CONSERVATION STAMP
$7.50
CANVASBACKS
U.S. DEPARTMENT OF THE INTERIOR

FEDERAL 1982–83

ALABAMA DEPARTMENT OF CONSERVATION AND NATURAL RESOURCES
WATERFOWL STAMP
03217
1982-83
$5.00 VOID SEPTEMBER 30, 1983

ALABAMA 1982

BIG LAKE WOOD DUCKS 1982-83
ARKANSAS GAME AND FISH COMMISSION WATERFOWL HUNTING AND CONSERVATION STAMP $5.50

ARKANSAS 1982

D 00044 -14
$5
CALIFORNIA DUCK STAMP 1982-83

CALIFORNIA 1982

DELAWARE MIGRATORY WATERFOWL STAMP
VOID AFTER JUNE 30, 1983
$5

DELAWARE 1982

FLORIDA Nº 35402
$3.25
Ring-necked Duck
Expires June 30, 1983
WATERFOWL STAMP

FLORIDA 1982

BLACK DUCK $5.00
1982 ILLINOIS MIGRATORY WATERFOWL STAMP
005952

ILLINOIS 1982

1982 INDIANA MIGRATORY WATERFOWL STAMP
$5
VOID AFTER FEB. 28, 1983
DEPARTMENT OF NATURAL RESOURCES - DIVISION OF FISH AND WILDLIFE

INDIANA 1982

IOWA MIGRATORY WATERFOWL STAMP   Snow Geese
$5
Expires Feb. 28, 1983
STATE CONSERVATION COMMISSION

IOWA 1982

MIGRATORY WATERFOWL STAMP
Maryland Department of Natural Resources
$3.00
Void After July 31 1983

MARYLAND 1982

1982 $1.25
Waterfowl Stamp
Massachusetts
Greater Yellowlegs by Fred Nichols

MASSACHUSETTS 1982

WATERFOWL
MICHIGAN
1982 $3.75
Z 076778

MICHIGAN 1982

MINNESOTA 1982

MISSISSIPPI 1982

MISSOURI 1982

NEVADA 1982

NORTH DAKOTA 1982

OHIO 1982

OKLAHOMA 1982

SOUTH CAROLINA 1982

TENNESSEE 1982

TEXAS 1982

WISCONSIN 1982

FEDERAL 1983–84

ALABAMA 1983

ARKANSAS 1983

CALIFORNIA 1983

DELAWARE 1983

FLORIDA 1983

ILLINOIS 1983

INDIANA 1983

IOWA 1983

MARYLAND 1983

MASSACHUSETTS 1983

MICHIGAN 1983

MINNESOTA 1983

MISSISSIPPI 1983

MISSOURI 1983

NEVADA 1983

NEW HAMPSHIRE 1983

1983 NH MIGRATORY WATERFOWL STAMP
007229
$4.00
WOOD DUCKS

NORTH CAROLINA 1983

WATERFOWL CONSERVATION STAMP
1983 NORTH CAROLINA
$5.50

NORTH DAKOTA 1983

1983 No 5866
North Dakota Resident
Small Game & Habitat Stamp
$9.00

OHIO 1983

MALLARD
$5.75
VOID AFTER AUGUST 31, 1984
OHIO WETLANDS HABITAT STAMP

OKLAHOMA 1983

$4
Expires June 30, 1984
1983-84 WATERFOWL HUNTING STAMP
OKLAHOMA DEPARTMENT OF WILDLIFE CONSERVATION

PENNSYLVANIA 1983

1983 Pennsylvania
Save Our Wetlands
$5.50
Void After August 31, 1984
Waterfowl Management Stamp

SOUTH CAROLINA 1983

SOUTH CAROLINA MIGRATORY WATERFOWL & HUNTING STAMP
$5.50
Expires June 30, 1984

TENNESSEE 1983

TENNESSEE WILDLIFE RESOURCES AGENCY
MIGRATORY WATERFOWL STAMP
EXPIRES FEBRUARY 29, 1984
RESIDENT $6.00
01679
PINTAILS

TEXAS 1983

Texas Parks and Wildlife Dept.
1983

WISCONSIN 1983

1983 WISCONSIN WATERFOWL STAMP
$3.25

FEDERAL 1984-85

MIGRATORY BIRD HUNTING AND CONSERVATION STAMP
U.S. DEPARTMENT OF THE INTERIOR $7.50
VOID AFTER JUNE 30, 1985
WIGEON
50TH ANNIVERSARY 1934-1984

ALABAMA 1984

ALABAMA DEPARTMENT OF CONSERVATION AND NATURAL RESOURCES
WATERFOWL STAMP
00389
1984-85
VOID SEPTEMBER 30, 1985
$5.00

ARKANSAS 1984

ARKANSAS GAME AND FISH COMMISSION
BOIS D'ARC PINTAILS $5.50
1984-85
WATERFOWL HUNTING AND CONSERVATION STAMP

CALIFORNIA 1984

D 0122 14
1984-85
$7.50
CALIFORNIA DUCK STAMP

DELAWARE 1984

DELAWARE MIGRATORY WATERFOWL STAMP
VOID AFTER JUNE 30, 1985
$5

FLORIDA No. 019228 $3.25
Hooded Merganser
Expires June 30, 1985
WATERFOWL STAMP
FLORIDA 1984

BLUE-WINGED TEAL $5.00
1984 ILLINOIS MIGRATORY WATERFOWL STAMP
096366
ILLINOIS 1984

$5.00 1984 INDIANA
MIGRATORY WATER FOWL STAMP
Void after Feb. 29, 1985
INDIANA 1984

IOWA MIGRATORY WATERFOWL STAMP
Expires Feb. 28, 1985
$5
STATE CONSERVATION COMMISSION
IOWA 1984

$2.50 Black Ducks
06279
Expires June 30, 1985
1984 MAINE MIGRATORY WATERFOWL STAMP
MAINE 1984

Maryland Department of Natural Resources $6.00
Void After July 31, 1985
MIGRATORY WATERFOWL STAMP
MARYLAND 1984

1984 Massachusetts Waterfowl Stamp
$1.25
White-winged Scoter by S.A. Fabens
MASSACHUSETTS 1984

MICHIGAN WATERFOWL
1984 P 000833 $3.75
MICHIGAN 1984

1984 MIGRATORY WATERFOWL STAMP $3
MINNESOTA DEPARTMENT of NATURAL RESOURCES WOOD DUCKS
MINNESOTA 1984

Mississippi Department of Wildlife Conservation
Waterfowl Stamp
$2
37237
Expires June 30, 1985
Void Unless Signed
Black Duck
MISSISSIPPI 1984

Waterfowl 1984
001335
Void after January 31, 1985
$3.00 Fee
Copyright © 1984 by the Conservation Commission of the State of Missouri
MISSOURI 1984

Nevada Department of Wildlife $2
Expires 6-30-85
PINTAIL
Duck Stamp
NEVADA 1984

1984 NH MIGRATORY WATERFOWL STAMP
000522
$4.00
MALLARD
NEW HAMPSHIRE 1984

• WATERFOWL STAMP •
$2.50 CANVASBACK
047053
NEW JERSEY
VOID AFTER JUNE 30, 1985
1984
NEW JERSEY 1984

WATERFOWL CONSERVATION STAMP
$5.50
1984 NORTH CAROLINA
NORTH CAROLINA 1984

1984   No. 003487
North Dakota Resident Small Game & Habitat Stamp
$9.00
NORTH DAKOTA 1984

OHIO WETLANDS HABITAT STAMP
GREEN-WINGED TEAL
$575
VOID AFTER AUGUST 31, 1985
OHIO 1984

Expires June 30, 1985 $4
1984-85 WATERFOWL HUNTING STAMP
OKLAHOMA DEPARTMENT OF WILDLIFE CONSERVATION
OKLAHOMA 1984

No 062937
Expires 6/30/85
$5
1984 Oregon Waterfowl Stamp
OREGON 1984

1984 Pennsylvania
Save Our Wetlands
Void After August 31, 1985
$5.50
Waterfowl Management Stamp
PENNSYLVANIA 1984

SOUTH CAROLINA MIGRATORY WATERFOWL & HUNTING STAMP
$5.50
EXPIRES JUNE 30, 1985
SOUTH CAROLINA 1984

TENNESSEE WILDLIFE RESOURCES AGENCY
MIGRATORY WATERFOWL STAMP
EXPIRES FEBRUARY 28, 1985. RESIDENT $6.00
BLACK DUCK
TENNESSEE 1984

Texas Parks and Wildlife Dept.
1984
Waterfowl Stamp
$5.00
TEXAS 1984

1984 WISCONSIN WATERFOWL STAMP
$3.25
WISCONSIN 1984

U.S. DEPARTMENT OF THE INTERIOR
$7.50
MIGRATORY BIRD HUNTING AND CONSERVATION STAMP
CINNAMON TEAL · VOID AFTER JUNE 30, 1986
FEDERAL 1985–86

ALABAMA DEPARTMENT OF CONSERVATION AND NATURAL RESOURCES
WATERFOWL STAMP
05735
$5.00
1985-86 VOID SEPTEMBER 30, 1986
ALABAMA 1985

$5
expires 1-31-86
1985 Alaska Waterfowl Stamp
ALASKA 1985

ARKANSAS GAME AND FISH COMMISSION
BAYOU DE VIEW MALLARDS 1985-86
$5.50
WATERFOWL HUNTING AND CONSERVATION STAMP
ARKANSAS 1985

$7.50   CALIFORNIA DUCK STAMP
1985-86
D 0029 23
CALIFORNIA 1985

DELAWARE MIGRATORY WATERFOWL STAMP
$5
VOID AFTER JUNE 30, 1986
DELAWARE 1985

FLORIDA № 000042
$3.25
Wood Duck
Expires June 30, 1986
WATERFOWL STAMP

FLORIDA 1985

1985 FIRST GEORGIA WATERFOWL CONSERVATION STAMP
$5.50

GEORGIA 1985

RED HEAD $5.00
1985 ILLINOIS MIGRATORY WATERFOWL STAMP
090645

ILLINOIS 1985

1985 Indiana Migratory Water Fowl Stamp—$5.00 Void after Feb. 28, 1986

INDIANA 1985

IOWA MIGRATORY WATERFOWL STAMP
$5
Expires Feb. 28, 1986
STATE CONSERVATION COMMISSION

IOWA 1985

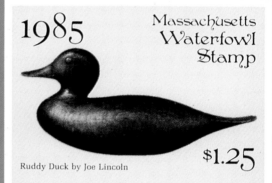

1985 KENTUCKY WATERFOWL STAMP
09258
$5.25

KENTUCKY 1985

Common Eiders
$2.50
Expires June 30, 1986
02221
1985 MAINE MIGRATORY WATERFOWL STAMP

MAINE 1985

Maryland Department of Natural Resources
$6.00
Void After July 31, 1986
MIGRATORY WATERFOWL STAMP

MARYLAND 1985

1985 Massachusetts Waterfowl Stamp
Ruddy Duck by Joe Lincoln
$1.25

MASSACHUSETTS 1985

1985 U 003570 $3.75
MICHIGAN WATERFOWL
Issued Mo. _____ Day _____

MICHIGAN 1985

• **MINNESOTA DEPARTMENT of NATURAL RESOURCES**
$3
1985 MIGRATORY WATERFOWL STAMP
WHITE FRONTED GEESE

MINNESOTA 1985

Waterfowl Stamp
$2
Expires June 30, 1986
Void Unless Signed
Mallards
33794
Mississippi Department of Wildlife Conservation

MISSISSIPPI 1985

Waterfowl
1985

000090

$3.00
Fee

Void after January 31, 1986

Copyright © 1985 by the Conservation Commission of the State of Missouri

MISSOURI 1985

Nevada Department of Wildlife

$2

Expires 6-30-86

Duck Stamp

LESSER
CANADA GOOSE

NEVADA 1985

1985 NH MIGRATORY WATERFOWL STAMP

005827

$4.00

BLUE WINGED TEAL

NEW HAMPSHIRE 1985

• WATERFOWL STAMP •

NEW JERSEY

$5.00

1985 039999

MALLARDS

VOID AFTER
JUNE 30, 1986

NEW JERSEY 1985

1985 NEW YORK
MIGRATORY BIRD STAMP

$5.50

CANADA GEESE

NEW YORK 1985

WATERFOWL CONSERVATION STAMP

NORTH CAROLINA

1985 NORTH CAROLINA

$5.50

NORTH CAROLINA 1985

North Dakota Resident
Small Game & Habitat Stamp

1985

Nº 018105

$9.00

NORTH DAKOTA 1985

OHIO WETLANDS HABITAT STAMP

REDHEADS

$5.75

VOID AFTER AUGUST 31, 1986

OHIO 1985

Expires
June 30, 1986

$4

1985-86 WATERFOWL HUNTING STAMP

OKLAHOMA DEPARTMENT OF
WILDLIFE CONSERVATION

OKLAHOMA 1985

29166

Expires
6/30/86

$5

1985 Oregon Waterfowl Stamp

OREGON 1985

1985 Pennsylvania

Save Our Wetlands

Void After August 31, 1986

$5.50

© PA Game Commission

Waterfowl Management Stamp

PENNSYLVANIA 1985

SOUTH CAROLINA MIGRATORY
WATERFOWL & HUNTING STAMP

$5.50

EXPIRES
JUNE 30, 1986

SOUTH CAROLINA 1985

TENNESSEE WILDLIFE RESOURCES AGENCY
MIGRATORY
WATERFOWL
STAMP

EXPIRES FEBRUARY 28, 1986   RESIDENT $6.00

BLUE-WINGED TEAL

TENNESSEE 1985

Texas Parks and Wildlife Dept.

Waterfowl Stamp

1985

$5.00

TEXAS 1985

$3.25

1985
WISCONSIN WATERFOWL STAMP

WISCONSIN 1985

No 006794   **WYOMING 1985** Conservation Stamp

Expires December 31, 1985 $5.00

SIGNATURE

WYOMING 1985

MIGRATORY BIRD HUNTING AND CONSERVATION STAMP
$7.50
VOID AFTER JUNE 30, 1987

Fulvous Whistling Duck

U.S. DEPARTMENT OF THE INTERIOR

FEDERAL 1986–87

WATERFOWL STAMP
$5.00
ALABAMA DEPARTMENT OF CONSERVATION AND NATURAL RESOURCES
03492
1986-87   VOID SEPT. 30, 1987

ALABAMA 1986

$5
expires 1-31-87
1986 Alaska Waterfowl Stamp

ALASKA 1986

ARKANSAS GAME AND FISH COMMISSION
BLACK SWAMP MALLARDS 1986-1987
$5.50
WATERFOWL HUNTING AND CONSERVATION STAMP

ARKANSAS 1986

$7.50   CALIFORNIA DUCK STAMP
1986-87
000021 14

CALIFORNIA 1986

DELAWARE MIGRATORY WATERFOWL STAMP
$5
VOID AFTER JUNE 30, 1987

DELAWARE 1986

FLORIDA NO.   0584   -00
$3.00
Canvasbacks
Expires June 30, 1987
WATERFOWL STAMP

FLORIDA 1986

$5.50
1986 WATERFOWL
CONSERVATION STAMP
GEORGIA

GEORGIA 1986

1986 ILLINOIS MIGRATORY WATERFOWL STAMP
$5.00
GADWALL   000792

ILLINOIS 1986

1986 Indiana Migratory Waterfowl Stamp—$5.00
Void after Feb. 28, 1987   No 32131

INDIANA 1986

IOWA MIGRATORY WATERFOWL STAMP
$5
Expires Feb. 28, 1987
STATE CONSERVATION COMMISSION

IOWA 1986

KENTUCKY 1986

1986 MAINE MIGRATORY WATERFOWL STAMP

MAINE 1986

MARYLAND 1986

MASSACHUSETTS 1986

MICHIGAN 1986

MINNESOTA 1986

MISSISSIPPI 1986

MISSOURI 1986

MONTANA 1986

NEVADA 1986

NEW HAMPSHIRE 1986

NEW JERSEY 1986

NEW YORK 1986

NORTH CAROLINA 1986

NORTH DAKOTA 1986

VOID AFTER AUGUST 31, 1987

CANVASBACK

$5⁷⁵

OHIO WETLANDS—HABITAT STAMP

OHIO 1986

OKLAHOMA DEPARTMENT OF WILDLIFE CONSERVATION
Expires June 30, 1987

1986-87 WATERFOWL HUNTING STAMP

$4

DU-50 YEARS

OKLAHOMA 1986

Expires
6/30/87

$5

Nº 15949

1986 Oregon Waterfowl Stamp

OREGON 1986

1986 Pennsylvania

$5.50

Save Our Wetlands

Void After August 31, 1987

PA Game Commission

Waterfowl Management Stamp

PENNSYLVANIA 1986

SOUTH CAROLINA MIGRATORY
WATERFOWL & HUNTING STAMP

$5.50

EXPIRES
JUNE 30, 1987

SOUTH CAROLINA 1986

1986

$2

75745

SOUTH DAKOTA WATERFOWL RESTORATION STAMP

SOUTH DAKOTA 1986

TENNESSEE WILDLIFE RESOURCES AGENCY
MIGRATORY
WATERFOWL
STAMP

EXPIRES FEBRUARY 28, 1987   RESIDENT $6.00

MALLARD

TENNESSEE 1986

1986

Waterfowl Stamp

Texas Parks and Wildlife Dept.

$5.00

TEXAS 1986

$3.30

UTAH

074852

Waterfowl Stamp

FIRST OF STATE 1986   Exp. 6-30-87

UTAH 1986

MIGRATORY WATERFOWL STAMP
VERMONT

1986

$5

VERMONT 1986

020260

Expires
3/1/87

$5

1986 Washington Waterfowl Stamp

WASHINGTON 1986

$3.25

1986
WISCONSIN WATERFOWL STAMP

WISCONSIN 1986

MIGRATORY BIRD HUNTING AND CONSERVATION STAMP
VOID AFTER JUNE 30, 1988
$10

US DEPARTMENT OF INTERIOR

REDHEAD DUCKS

FEDERAL 1987–88

ALABAMA DEPARTMENT OF CONSERVATION
AND NATURAL RESOURCES
1987 - 88

WATERFOWL
STAMP

$5.00   VOID SEPTEMBER 30, 1988
DU-50 YEARS

ALABAMA 1987

Expires 1-31-88

$5

1987 Alaska Waterfowl Stamp

ALASKA 1987

ARIZONA 1987

ARKANSAS 1987

CALIFORNIA 1987

DELAWARE 1987

FLORIDA 1987

GEORGIA 1987

IDAHO 1987

ILLINOIS 1987

INDIANA 1987

IOWA 1987

KANSAS 1987

KENTUCKY 1987

MAINE 1987

$2.50 Buffleheads
Expires June 30, 1988
00897
1987 MAINE MIGRATORY WATERFOWL STAMP

MARYLAND 1987

MIGRATORY WATERFOWL STAMP
Maryland Department of Natural Resources
$6.00
Void After July 31 1988
DUCKS UNLIMITED LEADERS IN WETLANDS CONSERVATION 50 YEARS

MASSACHUSSETS 1987

Massachusetts Waterfowl Stamp
1987
$1.25
American Wigeon Drake – Carver: Joe Lincoln

MICHIGAN 1987

1987 T 001692 $3.85
MICHIGAN WATERFOWL
Issued Mo. _____ Day _____

MINNESOTA 1987

COMMON GOLDENEYE
1987 MIGRATORY WATERFOWL STAMP
MINNESOTA DEPARTMENT OF NATURAL RESOURCES
$5

MISSISSIPPI 1987

Mississippi Department of Wildlife Conservation
Waterfowl Stamp
$2
Void Unless Signed
Expires June 30, 1988
Ring-necked Ducks
DU 50 YEARS
000456

MISSOURI 1987

Waterfowl 1987 $3.00
002433
Void after January 31, 1988
50th ANNIVERSARY 1937 through 1987
Copyright © 1987 by the Conservation Commission of the State of Missouri.

MONTANA 1987

29- 012390
1987 MONTANA Waterfowl Stamp • Exp. 2-29-88
$5.00

NEVADA 1987

Nevada Department of Wildlife
$2
Expires 6-30-88
BUFFLEHEAD
Duck Stamp

NEW HAMPSHIRE 1987

1987 NH MIGRATORY WATERFOWL STAMP
006273
$4.00
CANADA GEESE

NEW JERSEY 1987

• WATERFOWL STAMP •
NEW JERSEY
$5.00
1987 041216
CANADA GEESE
VOID AFTER JUNE 30, 1988

NEW YORK 1987

1987 NEW YORK MIGRATORY BIRD STAMP
WOOD DUCKS
$5.50

NORTH CAROLINA 1987

WATERFOWL CONSERVATION STAMP
$5.50
1987 NORTH CAROLINA
N.C. SALUTES DUCKS UNLIMITED, 1937-1987

NORTH DAKOTA 1987

1987 No. 003450
North Dakota Resident Small Game & Habitat Stamp
$9.00

OHIO 1987

VOID AFTER AUGUST 31, 1988
$6.00
BLUE-WINGED TEAL
OHIO WETLANDS HABITAT STAMP

$4

1987-88 WATERFOWL HUNTING STAMP

Expires June 30, 1988

OKLAHOMA DEPARTMENT OF WILDLIFE CONSERVATION

OKLAHOMA 1987

Expires
6/30/88

№ 69130

$5

1987 Oregon Waterfowl Stamp

OREGON 1987

1987 Pennsylvania

$5.50

Save Our Wetlands

© Pa Game Commission

Waterfowl Management Stamp

Void After August 31, 1988

PENNSYLVANIA 1987

SOUTH CAROLINA MIGRATORY WATERFOWL & HUNTING STAMP

DUCKS UNLIMITED 1937-1987

$5.50

EXPIRES JUNE 30, 1988

SOUTH CAROLINA 1987

3872

1987

$2

SOUTH DAKOTA WATERFOWL RESTORATION STAMP

SOUTH DAKOTA 1987

TENNESSEE WILDLIFE RESOURCES AGENCY

MIGRATORY WATERFOWL STAMP

EXPIRES FEBRUARY 29, 1988   RESIDENT $6.00

TENNESSEE 1987

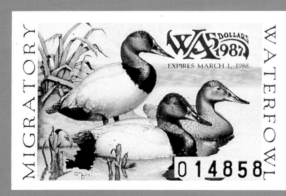

50 Years of Conservation

Texas Parks and Wildlife Dept.

Waterfowl Stamp

1987

$5.00

Ducks Unlimited 1937-1987

TEXAS 1987

$3.30

UTAH 00 1229

1987 Waterfowl Stamp

Exp. 6-30-88

UTAH 1987

MIGRATORY WATERFOWL STAMP

1987

VERMONT

$5

VERMONT 1987

MIGRATORY

WAS DOLLARS 1987

EXPIRES MARCH 1, 1988

WATERFOWL

0 14858

WASHINGTON 1987

WEST VIRGINIA

CONSERVATION STAMP   RESIDENT $5.00

WATERFOWL 1987

WEST VIRGINIA 1987

$3.25

WISCONSIN WATERFOWL STAMP   1987

WISCONSIN 1987

The Prints

1934–35
FIRST FEDERAL DUCK STAMP

Mallards Dropping In
Jay Norwood Darling

The original art, a brush and ink design, measures 10″ x 14″. How the work was chosen is not known today.

The stamp is printed in blue ink and sold for $1.00. The first day of sale was August 14, 1934; 635,001 were sold.

The print was made by an etching process from a 5¾″ x 8½″ plate. The first edition probably numbers about 300. It was printed on white paper by Gordon Meaney from plates by René Lundgren. The first edition is not numbered, and it is unknown if there is a second edition.

1935–36
SECOND FEDERAL DUCK STAMP

Untitled (Canvasbacks)
Frank Weston Benson

The original art is a watercolor wash depicting Canvasbacks. It measures 5″ x 7″ and was chosen by the request of Jay N. Darling.

The stamp was printed in rose lake ink and sold for $1.00. The first day of sale was July 1, 1935. There were 448,204 sold.

The print was made by a hand-pulled etching process from a 3″ x 5″ plate. The first edition numbers 100, and was printed on light cream Shogun paper by John Peterson and Son Co. from plates by Frank Weston Benson. The first edition is not numbered. This print is the rarest and most valuable in the entire collection. There are believed to be imitations of this print that are slightly larger than the original.

1936–37
THIRD FEDERAL DUCK STAMP

Coming In
Richard E. Bishop

The original art is a drypoint etching of Canada Geese. It measures 9″ x 14⅞″ and was executed in 1931. It was chosen by the honorary request of Jay N. Darling.

The stamp was printed in black ink and sold for $1.00. The first day of sale was July 1, 1936; 603,623 were sold.

The print was made from a 5″ x 8″ plate created by the artist, who hand-pulled the prints on cream paper. To prevent wear from the printing process, Bishop used a chrome-faced plate. The prints are in an unnumbered edition.

1937–38
FOURTH FEDERAL DUCK STAMP

Untitled (Greater Scaup)
Joseph D. Knap

The original art, a watercolor wash in brown, depicting Greater Scaup in flight, measures 10½″ x 14½″. The work was chosen in an honorary limited competition.

The stamp was printed in light green ink and sold for $1.00. The first day of sale was July 1, 1937. There were 783,039 sold.

The print was made by fine-grained gravure from a 5¾″ x 8⅝″ plate and printed on off-white paper. There were 260 unnumbered first edition prints and there is probably not a second edition. The platemaker and printer are unknown. Above the image is the legend *Published and Copyrighted by the Sporting Gallery & Bookshop, Inc. Edition limited to 260 proofs.*

1938–39
FIFTH FEDERAL DUCK STAMP

Untitled (Pintails)
Roland H. Clark

The original art depicted five Pintails, but the plate was cut down and the artist's design altered, eliminating three birds. The work was chosen in an honorary limited competition.

The stamp was printed in light violet ink and sold for $1.00. The first day of sale was July 1, 1938; 1,002,715 were sold.

The print was made on off-white paper from a 6⅞″ x 11″ drypoint etching and the unnumbered first edition consists of about 300 prints. It is doubtful that a second edition was produced, and the design is out of print today. The printer is unknown; the plates were made by the artist.

1939–40
SIXTH FEDERAL DUCK STAMP

Untitled (Green-Winged Teal)
Lynn Bogue Hunt, Sr.

The original art, size unknown, depicts Green-Winged Teal. The medium of the original art is graphite pencil. It was chosen in an honorary limited competition.

The stamp was printed in chocolate brown and sold for $1.00. The first day of sale was July 1, 1939; 1,111,561 were sold.

The print, measuring 7¾″ x 11″, is a stone lithograph, using brownish black ink on white stock. The platemaker and printer are unknown. The first edition is signed and numbered, but the total is unknown. There is a second edition, quantity unknown, but prints marked *2nd E* are only a second state of the first edition.

1940–41
SEVENTH FEDERAL DUCK STAMP

Untitled (Black Ducks)
Francis Lee Jaques

The original art is a wash painting of two Black Ducks in flight. Its measurements are unknown. It was chosen in an honorary limited competition.

The stamp was printed in sepia and sold for $1.00. The first day of sale was July 1, 1940; 1,260,810 were sold

The print is a stone lithograph; the actual image of the vignette is about 7¼″ x 10″ with the matted area about 9½″ x 12½″. The black ink is printed on white, probably Curtis, stock. The first and second edition stones were made by the artist and the third edition stone by Ellison Hoover, artist and cartoonist. The three editions totaled around 260 prints.

1941–42
EIGHTH FEDERAL DUCK STAMP

Ruddy Ducks
Edwin Richard Kalmbach

The original art is a wash with some gouache details, but its size is unknown. It was chosen in an honorary limited competition.

The stamp was printed in brown carmine and sold for $1.00. The first day of sale was July 1, 1941; 1,439,967 were sold.

The print in its second edition was handled by the artist. The medium of this 7″ x 9″ print is possibly fine-grain gravure, using black ink on white stock. The platemaker and printer was Bradford-Robinson Printing Co. The quantity of both editions is unknown. The first edition print, titled *Migratory Bird Hunting Stamp, 1941–42* and signed E. R. Kalmbach, was flopped left to right.

1942–43
NINTH FEDERAL DUCK STAMP

American Widgeon
Alden Lassell Ripley

The original art, size unknown, comprises sketches in pencil and pen of Widgeon in the water and landing. It was chosen in an honorary limited competition.

The stamp was printed in brown and sold for $1.00. The first day of sale was July 1, 1942; 1,383,629 were sold.

The print, measuring 6″ x 8½″, is a drypoint etching, using warm black ink on white stock. The artist made the plates, and the printer was John Peterson & Son Company. The quantity of the first editon is unknown. It is signed A. Lassell Ripley. This *artist's original print* is both aesthetically and technically a fine example of drypoint.

1943–44
TENTH FEDERAL DUCK STAMP

Untitled (Wood Ducks)
Walter E. Bohl

The original art is a 5″ (shy) x 7″ drypoint etching on copper of Wood Ducks in flight. It was chosen in an honorary limited competition.

The stamp was printed in Indian red and sold for $1.00. The first day of sale was July 1, 1943; 1,169,352 were sold.

The print, measuring 5″ (shy) x 7″ is a drypoint etching on copper, using black ink on white Rives stock. The first edition numbers 290 and is signed Walter E. Bohl. The second edition is in two states: the first state is not labelled; the second state is labelled *II*. Since the artist made the plate and did the printing, this is an *artist's original print*.

1944–45
ELEVENTH FEDERAL DUCK STAMP

White-Fronted Geese
Walter A. Weber

The original art is a 5″ x 7″ wash showing the birds in flight. It was chosen in an honorary limited competition.

The stamp was printed in orange and sold for $1.00. The first day of sale was July 1, 1944; 1,487,029 were sold.

The print is a stone lithograph; the vignette at the bottom has an actual image of 6½″ x 9½″. It was printed with black and sepia inks on white Rives Heavy stock. The platemaker is unknown; the printer was Geo. C. Miller & Son, Inc. The first edition consists of 100 flopped prints that are unnumbered but signed Walter A. Weber. The second and third editions are right-reading.

1945–46
TWELFTH FEDERAL DUCK STAMP

Shovelers
Owen J. Gromme

The original art is a 5″ x 7″ wash showing Shovelers in flight. It was chosen in an honorary limited competition.

The stamp was printed in black and white and sold for $1.00. The first day of sale was July 1, 1945; 1,725,505 were sold.

The print is a 5″ x 7″ fine-grain gravure, using black ink on white stock. The platemaker is unknown and the printer was possibly Beck Engraving Company. The first edition is 250. They are signed Owen J. Gromme. This is a *printer's print* since it was transferred photographically, and it bears the legend *Copyright 1945 by the F. H. Bresler Co., Milwaukee* over the image at the left. The print is very difficult to obtain today.

1946–47
THIRTEENTH FEDERAL DUCK STAMP

Redheads
Robert W. Hines

The original art, size and medium unknown, was chosen in an honorary limited competition.

The stamp was printed in brown and black and sold for $1.00. The first day of sale was July 1, 1946; 2,016,841 were sold.

The print is a 8⅛″ x 11″ stone lithograph, printed with black ink on white stock. The platemaker was the artist and the printer is unknown. The quantity of the first edition is unknown, possibly 300. It was signed Bob Hines 1946; it is not known if it is numbered. There is a second edition of 385. This *artist's original print* is notated B-31 in pencil.

1947–48
FOURTEENTH FEDERAL DUCK STAMP

From Beyond the North Wind
Jack Murray

The original art is 14″ x 18½″ in what appears to be wash and gouache. It shows two Snow Geese in flight. It was chosen in an honorary limited competition.

The stamp was printed in black and sold for $1.00. The first day of sale was July 1, 1947; 1,722,677 were sold.

The print is an 8⅛″ x 11⅜″ fine-grain gravure, black ink on off-white stock. The platemaker and printer was Thomas J. Foley. The first edition is 300, unnumbered, and signed Jack Murray © 1947. This is a *printer's print* since it was photographically transferred.

1948–49
FIFTEENTH FEDERAL DUCK STAMP

Buffleheads Aloft
Maynard Reece

The original art is a 5″ x 7″ wash and gouache painting of the birds in flight. It was chosen in an honorary invitational competition with some freely submitted designs.

The stamp was printed in brilliant light blue and sold for $1.00. The first day of sale was July 1, 1948; 2,127,603 were sold.

The print is a 6¾″ x 9⅛″ stone lithograph, black ink on white Rives Heavy stock. The platemaker for the first edition was C. W. Anderson; for the second edition it was the artist. The printer was Geo. C. Miller & Son, Inc. The first edition is 200 prints; they are unnumbered and signed Maynard Reece. There is a second edition of 150 plus 25 artist's proofs, a third edition of 400, and a fourth edition of 350. The fourth edition was printed in full color using offset lithography.

1949–50
SIXTEENTH FEDERAL DUCK STAMP

American Goldeneyes
Roger E. Preuss

The original art is a 5″ x 7″ wash of the birds in flight and in the water. It was chosen in honorary invitational competition plus some freely submitted designs.

The stamp was printed in brilliant green and sold for $2.00. The first day of sale was July 1, 1949; 1,954,734 were sold.

The print is a 6⅝″ x 9⅛″ stone lithograph, black ink on white Rives Heavy stock. The platemaker was C. W. Anderson and the printer was Geo. C. Miller & Son, Inc. The first edition is 250 unnumbered prints, signed Rog [or Roger] E. Preuss. Some bear the date 1949. The artist remarqued in pencil eight of the prints from the edition.

1950-51
SEVENTEENTH FEDERAL DUCK STAMP

Trumpeter Swans
Walter A. Weber

The original art is a 5″ x 7″ wash and gouache painting of the birds in flight. It was chosen in open national competition (this was the first open national competition). The design was chosen from 88 designs by 65 artists.

The stamp was printed in brilliant bluish purple and sold for $2.00. The first day of sale was July 1, 1950; 1,903,644 were sold.

The print is a 5″ x 7″ fine-grain gravure, blue-gray ink on white stock. The platemaker and printer was Beck Engraving Company. For the first edition 500 were made, about 250 (possibly fewer) signed, and the balance lost. It is signed Walter A. Weber. There is a second edition of 300 numbered and signed 7″ x 10⅛″ prints. This is a *printer's print*, transferred photographically. *Copyright 1950 Walter A. Weber* appears in the margin at the upper left.

1951–52
EIGHTEENTH FEDERAL DUCK STAMP

Gadwalls
Maynard Reece

The original art is a 5″ x 7″ wash and gouache painting of Gadwalls taking off. It was chosen in open national competition from 74 designs by 51 artists.

The stamp was printed in dark or smoke gray and sold for $2.00. The first day of sale was July 1, 1951; 2,167,767 were sold.

The print is a 6¾″ x 9⅛″ stone lithograph, black ink on white Rives Heavy stock. The platemaker was the artist and the printer was Geo. C. Miller & Son, Inc. The first edition comprises 250 unnumbered prints, signed Maynard Reece. There is a second edition of 400. This is an *artist's original print* since Mr. Reece made the drawing on the stone. The second edition carries the notation *2nd ed*.

1952–53
NINETEENTH FEDERAL DUCK STAMP

Untitled (Harlequins)
John Henry Dick

The original art is a 5″ x 7″ wash of Harlequins in flight. It was chosen in open national competition from an unknown number of entries.

The stamp was printed in a reduced red shade of blue, or lilac blue, and sold for $2.00. The first day of sale was July 1, 1952; 2,296,628 were sold.

The print is a 7⅛″ x 9⅜″ stone lithograph, black ink on white Curtis stock. The platemaker was possibly C. W. Anderson and the printer was Geo. C. Miller & Son, Inc. The quantity of the first edition is not known (possibly 250). It is unnumbered and is signed John H. Dick. There is a second edition of 300.

1953–54
TWENTIETH FEDERAL DUCK STAMP

Early Express
Clayton B. Seagears

The original art is a 5″ x 7″ India ink wash drawing of Blue-Winged Teal in flight. It was chosen in open national competition from 92 entries by 53 artists.

The stamp was printed in maroon and sold for $2.00. The first day of sale was July 1, 1953; 2,268,446 were sold.

The print is a 6¾″ x 9″ stone lithograph, black ink on white stock. The platemaker was C. W. Anderson and the printer was Geo. C. Miller & Son, Inc. The quantity of the first edition is possibly 250. It is signed Clayt Seagears. The second edition, using offset lithography, is 1500.

1954–55
TWENTY-FIRST FEDERAL DUCK STAMP

Ring-Necks
Harvey Dean Sandstrom

The original art is a 5″ x 7″ gouache drawing of the birds in flight. It was chosen in open national competition from 114 entries by 87 artists.

The stamp was printed in black and white and sold for $2.00. The first day of sale was July 1, 1954; 2,184,550 were sold.

The print is a 5″ x 7″ stone lithograph, black ink on white stock. The platemaker was C. W. Anderson and the printer was Geo. C. Miller & Son, Inc. The first edition comprises 250 unnumbered prints, signed Harvey D. Sandstrom. There is a second edition of 400.

1955–56
TWENTY-SECOND FEDERAL DUCK STAMP

Blue Geese
Stanley Stearns

The original art is a 5″ x 7″ ink and pencil drawing on scratchboard of Blue Geese in flight. It was chosen in open national competition from 93 designs by 66 artists.

The stamp was printed in a warm, medium dark blue and sold for $2.00. The first day of sale was July 1, 1955; 2,369,940 were sold.

The print is a 7½″ x 10½″ etching and aquatint on a chrome-faced copper plate made by the artist. The first edition comprises 250 unnumbered signed prints from two printings. The first was in warm black ink. The second is in brown ink and carries the mark *ST*.

1956–57
TWENTY-THIRD FEDERAL DUCK STAMP

American Mergansers
Edward J. Bierly

The original art is a 5″ x 7″ gouache drawing showing the birds in flight. It was chosen in open national competition from 64 designs by 42 artists.

The stamp was printed in blue-black and sold for $2.00. The first day of sale was July 1, 1956; 2,332,014 were sold.

The print is a 5″ x 7″ etching and aquatint, steel-faced, using black ink on ivory finish Rives for the first printing and white Linweave stock for the second. The platemaker was the artist and the printer was Andersen-Lamb Photogravure Corporation. The first edition comprises 450 unnumbered signed prints.

1957–58
TWENTY-FOURTH FEDERAL DUCK STAMP

American Eiders
Jackson Miles Abbott

The original art is a 5″ x 7″ gouache drawing of the birds in flight. It was chosen in open national competition from 106 entries by 60 artists.

The stamp was printed in a medium yellowish green and sold for $2.00. The first day of sale was July 1, 1957; 2,355,353 were sold.

The print is a 7½″ x 9¾″ stone lithograph, black ink on white stock. The platemaker was C. W. Anderson and the printer was Geo. C. Miller & Son, Inc. The first edition comprises 250 unnumbered prints, signed Jackson M. Abbott. There is a second edition of 500 and a third of 1500.

1958–59
TWENTY-FIFTH FEDERAL DUCK STAMP

Canada Geese
Leslie C. Kouba

The original art is a 5″ x 7″ wash of the birds landing and on the ground. It was chosen in open national competition over 96 entries by 55 artists.

The stamp was printed in midnight black and sold for $2.00. The first day of sale was July 1, 1958; 2,176,425 were sold.

The print is a 6 ⅞″ x 9 ¼″ stone lithograph for the first edition; the second edition is a 7″ x 9″ drypoint etching and aquatint. The ink is black on white stock in the first edition and black on off-white Early American stock in the second edition. The platemaker for the first edition was C. W. Anderson and for the second edition was the artist.

1959–60
TWENTY-SIXTH FEDERAL DUCK STAMP

King Buck
Maynard Reece

The original art is a 5″ x 7″ wash and gouache painting of a Labrador Retriever, King Buck, retrieving a Mallard. It was chosen in open national competition from 110 entries by 64 artists.

The stamp was printed in black, blue, and yellow and sold for $3.00. The first day of sale was July 1, 1959; 1,626,115 were sold.

The print, a best-seller, is a 6⅝″ x 9⅛″ stone lithograph, black ink on white Rives heavy stock. The platemaker was the artist, and the printer was Geo. C. Miller & Son, Inc. The first edition comprises 400 unnumbered signed prints. There is a second edition of 300 and a third of 400.

1960–61
TWENTY-SEVENTH FEDERAL DUCK STAMP

Redhead Ducks
John A. Ruthven

The original art is a 5″ x 7″ gouache drawing of Redheads in water. It was chosen in open national competition over an unknown number of entries.

The stamp was printed in yellow, crimson-brown, and bonnie blue and sold for $3.00. The first day of sale was July 1, 1960; 1,725,634 were sold.

The print, 6¾″ x 9¼″, was hand-painted on grained zinc plate (lithograph), using black ink on off-white stock. The platemaker was the artist and the printer was Strobridge Litho Company. The first edition comprises 400 unnumbered signed prints.

1961–62
TWENTY-EIGHTH FEDERAL DUCK STAMP

Nine Mallards
Edward A. Morris

The original art is a 5″ x 7″ wash of a family of Mallards in water. It was chosen in open national competition from 100 entries from an unknown number of artists.

The stamp was printed in red-brown, yellow-brown, and light blue and sold for $3.00. The first day of sale was July 1, 1961; 1,344,236 were sold.

The print is a 6⅝″ x 5¼″ drypoint etching and aquatint, using black ink on antique white English Text stock. The platemaker and the printer was Cornelis A. Bartels. The first edition comprises 250 unnumbered prints, signed Edward A. Morris.

1962–63
TWENTY-NINTH FEDERAL DUCK STAMP

Pintails
Edward A. Morris

The original art is a 5″ x 7″ wash of the birds landing. It was chosen in open national competition from an unknown number of entries.

The stamp was printed in black, purple-blue, and red-brown and sold for $3.00. The first day of sale was July 1, 1962; 1,147,212 were sold.

The print is a 6½″ x 9″ drypoint etching and aquatint, using black ink on antique white English Text stock. The platemaker and printer was Cornelis A. Bartels. The first edition comprises 250 unnumbered signed prints. This is the only time an artist has won the federal competition twice in a row.

1963–64
THIRTIETH FEDERAL DUCK STAMP

American Brant
Edward J. Bierly

The original art is a 5″ x 7″ gouache of the birds about to land. It was chosen in open national competition from 161 designs by 87 artists.

The stamp was printed in pale blue, orange-yellow, and black and sold for $3.00. The first day of sale was July 1, 1963; 1,448,191 were sold.

The print is a 7″ x 9″ etching and aquatint, steel faced, using warm black ink on white Rives stock for the first printing and white Linweave stock for the second. The platemaker was the artist and the printer was Andersen-Lamb Photogravure Corp. The first edition comprises 675 unnumbered signed prints.

1964–65
THIRTY-FIRST FEDERAL DUCK STAMP

Nene High Among the Lava Flows
Stanley Stearns

The original art is a 5″ x 7″ wash and gouache drawing of Nene Geese. It was chosen in open national competition from 158 entries by 87 artists.

The stamp was printed in blue, khaki, yellow, and black and sold for $3.00. The first day of sale was July 1, 1964; 1,573,155 were sold.

The print is a 7½″ x 10½″ stone lithograph, black ink on white Rives Heavy stock. The platemaker was the artist and the printer was Geo. C. Miller & Son, Inc. The first edition comprises 665 unnumbered signed prints. There is a second edition of 100; numbers 1 through 10 are hand-colored.

1965–66
THIRTY-SECOND FEDERAL DUCK STAMP

Canvasbacks
Ron Jenkins

The original art is a 5″ x 7″ gouache (with photo-retouch grays) of the birds in flight. It was chosen in open national competition from 138 entries by 85 artists.

The stamp was printed in two browns and two greens and sold for $3.00. The first day of sale was July 1, 1965; 1,558,197 were sold.

The print is a 5¼″ x 9½″ stone lithograph, black ink on white Rives Heavy stock. The platemaker was the artist and the printer was Geo. C. Miller & Son, Inc. The first edition comprises 700 unnumbered signed prints. Numbers 1 through 9 were hand-colored by the artist.

1966–67
THIRTY-THIRD FEDERAL DUCK STAMP

Whistling Swans
Stanley Stearns

The original art is a 5″ x 7″ wash and gouache (polymer) drawing of the birds in flight over the water. It was chosen from 181 designs by 105 artists.

The stamp was printed in black, blue, and green and sold for $3.00. The first day of sale was July 1, 1966; 1,805,341 were sold.

The print is a 7½″ x 10½″ stone lithograph, black ink on white Rives Heavy stock. The platemaker was the artist and the printer was Geo. C. Miller & Son, Inc. The first edition comprises 300 numbered, unsigned prints. There is a second edition of 300.

1967–68

THIRTY-FOURTH FEDERAL DUCK STAMP

Old Squaw — Tree River, N.W.T.
Leslie C. Kouba

The original art is a 5″ x 7″ wash and gouache drawing of the birds on the ground. It was chosen in open national competition from 170 entries.

The stamp was printed in blue, brown, and yellow and sold for $3.00. The first day of sale was July 1, 1967; 1,934,697 were sold.

The print is a 6¾″ x 9¼″ drypoint and aquatint, using black ink on antique white English Text stock. The platemaker and the printer was Cornelis A. Bartels. The first edition comprises 250 (to date) unnumbered signed prints. Changes were made to the sky during printing, so there are two states of this print.

1968–69

THIRTY-FIFTH FEDERAL DUCK STAMP

Poised
Claremont Gale Pritchard

The original art is a 5″ x 7″ wash of Hooded Mergansers at rest. There are two copies: (1) a 7″ x 11″ pastel and (2) a large painting in Pioneer Village, Minden, Nebraska. It was chosen in open national competition from 184 entries.

The stamp was printed in black, brown, and green and sold for $3.00. The first day of sale was July 1, 1968; 1,837,139 were sold.

The print is a 6⅝″ x 9¼″ stone lithograph, black ink on white Rives Heavy stock. The platemaker was Stanley Malzman and the printer was Geo. C. Miller & Son, Inc. The first edition comprises 750 numbered prints.

1969–70

THIRTY-SIXTH FEDERAL DUCK STAMP

White-Winged Scoters
Maynard Reece

The original art is a 5″ x 7″ wash of the birds taking off. It was chosen in open national competition from 218 entries.

The stamp was printed in red, brown, slate blue, and black and sold for $3.00. The first day of sale was July 1, 1969; 2,072,108 were sold.

The print is a 6½″ x 9¼″ stone lithograph, black ink on white Rives Heavy stock. The platemaker was the artist and the printer was Geo. C. Miller & Son, Inc. The first edition comprises 750 numbered prints.

1970–71
THIRTY-SEVENTH FEDERAL DUCK STAMP

Ross's Geese
Edward J. Bierly

The original art is a 5" x 7" watercolor of the birds in the water. It was chosen in open national competition from 148 entries.

The stamp was printed in yellow-red, blue, green, and black and sold for $3.00. The first day of sale was July 1, 1970; 2,420,244 were sold.

The print is a 7" x 9¾" four-color photolithograph, using unknown inks with special fade-resistant coating on white Weyerhauser 80-lb. Carousel Cover stock. The separation negative maker and the printer was Edmund A. Loper. The first edition comprises 300 remarqued prints (numbered 1–300) and 700 regular prints (numbered 1–700). There is only one printing of the first edition, and it is not known if the separation negatives were destroyed. There is a second edition of 2150. This is the first year the print was in full color.

1971–72
THIRTY-EIGHTH FEDERAL DUCK STAMP

Cinnamon Teal
Maynard Reece

The original art is a 5″ x 7″ full-color wash of the birds coming in to land. It was chosen in open national competition from 191 entries.

The stamp was printed in full color and sold for $3.00. The first day of sale was July 1, 1971; 2,445,977 were sold.

The print is a 6⅝″ x 9¼″ stone lithograph, hand-pulled, printed with black and tan inks on white Rives Heavy stock. The platemaker was the artist and the printer was Geo. C. Miller & Son, Inc. The first edition comprises 950 numbered prints. Each print carries the initials of the person who hand-colored it: June, Mark, or Brad Reece.

1971
FIRST CALIFORNIA DUCK STAMP

Pintails
Paul B. Johnson

The original art depicts a pair of Pintails in flight. Mr. Johnson was commissioned by the California Department of Fish and Game to design the artwork for the first state waterfowl stamp.

The stamp is numbered on the front. It sold for $1.00. Of the 400,000 stamps that were printed, 178,245 were sold.

The print is 5¾″ x 7½″. The edition consists of 500 signed and numbered and 150 Executive Series prints.

1972–73
THIRTY-NINTH FEDERAL DUCK STAMP

Emperor Geese
Arthur M. Cook

The original art is a 5″ x 7″ watercolor of the birds about to land. It was chosen in open national competition from 213 entries.

The stamp was printed in full color and sold for $5.00. The first day of sale was July 1, 1972; 2,184,343 were sold.

The print is a 6⅜″ x 9″ photolithograph (five-color process), using an unknown ink on white Strathmore Beau Brilliant stock. The separation negative maker and the printer was R.R. Donnelly & Sons, Inc. The first edition comprises 950 numbered prints. The first 200 are remarqued. There is a second edition of 900, of which 400 have remarques.

1972
SECOND CALIFORNIA DUCK STAMP

Canvasbacks
Paul B. Johnson

The original art, a pair of Canvasbacks in flight, is featured on the second California stamp.

The stamp is numbered on the front. It sold for $1.00. Of the 400,000 stamps that were printed, 160,256 were sold. In early 1973, the remaining unsold stamps of both 1971 and 1972 were accidentally destroyed. Because the collecting aspect of state waterfowl stamps was virtually nonexistent at that time, only a very few of the 1971 and 1972 stamps were purchased by collectors.

The print is 6½" x 9". The edition consists of 40 signed and numbered and 150 Executive Series prints. The small size of the edition reflects the destruction of the stamps.

1972
FIRST IOWA DUCK STAMP

Mallards
Maynard Reece

The original art depicts three Mallards in flight. Mr. Reece, a renowned wildlife artist, was commissioned by the Iowa Conservation Commission to design the artwork for the initial Iowa waterfowl stamp.

The stamp is not numbered. It sold for $1.00. Of the 125,000 stamps that were printed, 70,446 were sold. The remainders were sold until June 1978.

The print is 6⁷⁄₁₆" x 11". The edition consists of 500 signed and numbered prints.

1973–74
FORTIETH FEDERAL DUCK STAMP

Steller's Eiders
Lee LeBlanc

The original art is a 5" x 7" opaque watercolor painting of the birds at rest. It was chosen in open national competition from 249 entries.

The stamp was printed in full color and sold for $5.00. The first day of sale was July 1, 1973; 2,094,414 were sold.

The print is a 6½" x 9" four-color photolithograph, using Sleight-Hellmuth inks on 100-lb. Curtis Stoneridge Menu Cover stock. The separation negative maker was Colorcraft, Inc. and the printer was NAPCO Graphic Arts, Inc. The first edition comprises 1000 numbered prints. There is a second edition of 600 signed and numbered prints and 300 remarqued.

1973
THIRD CALIFORNIA DUCK STAMP

Mallards
Paul B. Johnson

The original art depicts a pair of Mallards in flight.

The stamp is numbered on the front. It sold for $1.00. All of the 375,000 stamps that were printed were sold.

The print is 6½″ x 9″. The edition consists of 500 signed and numbered and 150 Executive Series prints.

1973
SECOND IOWA DUCK STAMP

Pintails
Thomas Murphy

The original art depicts Pintails in flight. The design was chosen from 41 entries in the first open Iowa competition. (The contest is open to Iowa residents only.)

The stamp is not numbered. It sold for $1.00. Of the 125,000 stamps that were printed, 67,323 were sold. The remainders were on sale until June 1978.

The print is 6⅜″ x 11″. The edition consists of 500 signed and numbered prints.

1974–75
FORTY-FIRST FEDERAL DUCK STAMP

Wood Ducks
David A. Maass

The original art is a 5″ x 7″ oil painting; a larger oil painting was done for the print. It was chosen in open national competition from 291 entries.

The stamp was printed in full color and sold for $5.00. The first day of sale was July 1, 1974; 2,214,056 were sold.

The print is a 6½″ x 9″ four-color photolithograph, using specially compounded lite-fast inks on 100-lb. Warrens Lustro Dull, Saxony Finish Cover stock. The separation negative maker and the printer was Johnson Printing, Inc. The first edition was not limited to a specific number, and the prints are unnumbered.

1974
FOURTH CALIFORNIA DUCK STAMP

White-Fronted Geese
Paul B. Johnson

The original art depicts three White-Fronted Geese in flight.

The stamp is numbered on the front. It sold for $1.00. There were 375,000 stamps printed.

The print is 6½″ x 9″. The edition consists of 500 signed and numbered and 150 Executive Series prints.

1974
THIRD IOWA DUCK STAMP

Gadwalls
James F. Landenberger

The original art depicts a pair of Gadwalls landing. The design was chosen from 79 entries.

The stamp is not numbered. It sold for $1.00. Of the 125,000 stamps printed, 70,953 were sold. The remainders were on sale until June 1978.

The print is 6⁷/₁₆″ x 11″. The edition consists of 500 signed and numbered prints.

1974
FIRST MARYLAND DUCK STAMP

Mallards
John W. Taylor

The original art depicts a pair of Mallards in the snow. Mr. Taylor was commissioned by the Maryland Department of Natural Resources to design this first Maryland State Waterfowl Stamp.

The stamp is numbered on an attached tab. It sold for $1.10. All 90,000 stamps that were printed were sold.

The print is 6⅜″ x 9″. The edition consists of 500 signed and numbered prints plus artist's proofs.

1974
FIRST MASSACHUSETTS DUCK STAMP

Wood Duck Decoy
Milton C. Weiler

The original art was commissioned from Mr. Weiler by the Massachusetts Division of Fisheries and Wildlife. It was the state's first waterfowl stamp. The design features a Wood Duck drake decoy carved by Joe Lincoln.

The stamp is not numbered. It sold for $1.25. All of the 50,400 stamps that were printed were sold.

The print size of 7″ x 9″ refers to the later print published by Mr. Weiler's heirs. That edition consists of 600 prints. There is also a larger print published by Ducks Unlimited that is a reproduction of the stamp itself. Neither of the editions is signed.

1975–76
FORTY-SECOND FEDERAL DUCK STAMP

Canvasback
James P. Fisher

The original art is a 5″ x 7″ watercolor of a Canvasback decoy. It was chosen in open national competition from 268 entries.

The stamp was printed in full color and sold for $5.00. The first day of sale was July 1, 1975; 2,237,126 were sold.

The print is 6½″ x 9″, a combination of offset lithograph and collotype (using seven colors). The stock is Arches 88 (100% rag content), and the separation negative maker and the printer was Triton Press, Inc. The first edition numbers 3150, and the prints are numbered and untitled. This is the first and only federal design to feature a decoy.

1975
FIFTH CALIFORNIA DUCK STAMP

Green-Winged Teal
Paul B. Johnson

The original art depicts a pair of Green-Winged Teal in flight.

The stamp is numbered on the front. It sold for $1.00. All of the 375,000 stamps that were printed were sold.

The print is 5″ x 7¼″. The edition consists of 500 signed and numbered and 150 Executive Series prints.

1975
FIRST ILLINOIS DUCK STAMP

Mallard
Robert Eschenfeldt

The original art depicts a Mallard drake in flight. The Illinois Department of Conservation commissioned the artist to design the first state waterfowl stamp.

The stamp is numbered on the front. It sold for $5.25. Of the 200,000 stamps that were printed, 60,377 were sold. All remainders were destroyed on June 30, 1982.

The print is 7″ x 9″. The edition consists of 500 signed and numbered prints.

1975
FOURTH IOWA DUCK STAMP

Canada Geese
Mark Reece

The original art, by the son of the renowned wildlife artist Maynard Reece, depicts a pair of Canada Geese. The design was chosen from 100 entries.

The stamp is not numbered. It sold for $1.00. Of the 125,000 stamps that were printed, 70,756 were sold. The remainders were on sale until June 1978.

The print is 6⅜″ x 10⅞″. The edition consists of 900 signed and numbered prints.

1975
SECOND MARYLAND DUCK STAMP

Canada Geese
Stanley Stearns

The original art depicts Canada Geese in flight. The design was chosen from 38 entries in the first open competition of the Maryland Duck Stamp contest. (The contest is open to Maryland residents only.)

The stamp is numbered on an attached tab. It sold for $1.10. All of the 90,000 stamps that were printed were sold.

The print is 6½″ x 9¹/₁₆″. The first edition consists of 650 signed and numbered prints, 65 artist's proofs, and 10 remarqued proofs. There is a second edition of 300 prints and 30 artist's proofs.

1975

SECOND MASSACHUSETTS DUCK STAMP

Pintail Decoy
Tom Hennessey

The original art depicts a Pintail drake decoy carved by Elmer Crowell. The design was chosen from six entries in the first open contest for the state's duck stamp. (Residents of any state may enter the Massachusetts contest, but artwork is restricted to designs of decoys carved by New England decoy carvers.)

The stamp is not numbered. It sold for $1.25. All of the 50,400 stamps that were printed were sold.

The print is 7″ x 10″. The edition consists of 500 signed and numbered prints. Many collectors regard this as the "first-of-state" print because the 1974 print is unsigned.

1976–77

FORTY-THIRD FEDERAL DUCK STAMP

Canada Geese
Alderson Magee

The original art is a 5″ x 7″ scratchboard rendering of Canada Geese in the water. There is one copy at a 6½″ x 9″ size. It was chosen in open national competition from 264 entries.

The stamp was printed in black and light green and sold for $5.00. The first day of sale was July 1, 1976; 2,170,194 were sold.

The print is a 6½″ x 9″ photolithograph in a three-plate process, using special lite-fast inks. The stock is Triton 100-lb. cover, neutral pH. The separation negative maker and the printer was Triton Press, Inc. The first edition consists of 3600 signed and numbered prints and 1000 with companion pieces.

1976

SIXTH CALIFORNIA DUCK STAMP

Widgeon
Paul B. Johnson

The original art depicts three Widgeon in flight. This was the sixth consecutive duck stamp design that Mr. Johnson was commissioned to do by the California Fish and Game Department.

The stamp is numbered on the front. It sold for $1.00. All of the 375,000 stamps that were printed were sold.

The print is 5″ x 8¼″. The edition consists of 500 signed and numbered and 150 Executive Series prints.

1976
SECOND ILLINOIS DUCK STAMP

Wood Ducks
Robert G. Larson

The original art depicts a pair of Wood Ducks
sitting on a log. The design was chosen from
100 entries in the first open competition for
state duck stamp design in Illinois. (The contest is open only to Illinois residents.)

The stamp is numbered on the front. It sold
for $5.25. Of the 165,000 stamps that were
printed, 66,038 were sold. All remainders were
destroyed on June 30, 1982.

The print is 14″ x 19½″. This print is unique,
being the largest of the state prints issued thus
far. It also is, along with the 1976 South Dakota print, one of the first state prints to be
issued with a matching numbered stamp. The
edition consists of 500 signed and numbered
prints.

1976
FIRST INDIANA DUCK STAMP

Green-Winged Teal
Sonny Bashore

The original art depicts a Green-Winged Teal drake in flight. The Indiana Department of Natural Resources commissioned the artist to design the artwork for the state's first waterfowl stamp.

The stamp is numbered on the front. It sold for $5.00. There were 70,000 stamps printed.

The print is 6″ x 9″. The edition consists of 500 signed and numbered prints. This is the only stamp print in the Indiana series that was offered for sale nationally. All reproduction rights regarding sales of prints after 1976 were retained by the Department of Natural Resources, according to the rules of the contest.

1976
FIFTH IOWA DUCK STAMP

Canvasbacks
Nick Klepinger

The original art depicts two Canvasbacks in flight. The design was chosen from 100 entries.

The stamp is not numbered. It sold for $1.00. Of the 125,000 stamps that were printed, 66,120 were sold. The remainders were on sale until June 1978.

The print is 6⅜″ x 10⅞″. The edition consists of 560 signed and numbered prints.

1976
THIRD MARYLAND DUCK STAMP

Canvasbacks
Louis Frisino

The original art depicts Canvasbacks in flight. The design was chosen from 61 entries.

The stamp is numbered on an attached tab. It sold for $1.10. All of the 90,000 stamps that were printed were sold.

The print is 6½″ x 9″. The edition consists of 500 signed and numbered prints. Added to this were 200 remarques and 70 artist's proofs.

1976
THIRD MASSACHUSETTS DUCK STAMP

Canada Goose Decoy
William P. Tyner

The original art depicts a Canada Goose decoy carved by Captain Osgood. The design was chosen from 20 entries.

The stamp is not numbered. It sold for $1.25. All of the 50,400 stamps that were printed were sold.

The print is 6½" x 9". The edition consists of 500 signed and numbered prints.

1976
FIRST MICHIGAN DUCK STAMP

Wood Duck
Oscar Warbach

The original art depicts a Wood Duck drake. The Michigan Department of Natural Resources commissioned the artist to design the artwork for Michigan's initial duck stamp.

The stamp is numbered on the front. It sold for $2.10. Of the 250,000 stamps that were printed, 92,802 were sold. The remainders were disposed of in July 1978.

The print is 4¹¹/₁₆" x 8". The edition consists of 500 signed and numbered prints.

1976
FIRST MISSISSIPPI DUCK STAMP

Wood Duck
Carroll J. and Gwen K. Perkins

The original art for the first Mississippi required waterfowl stamp is a photograph of a Wood Duck swimming in calm water. It was taken from a blind on the shore of a small pond. The artists were commissioned to design this initial stamp by the Mississippi Game and Fish Commission.

The stamp is numbered on the front. It sold for $2.00. There were 50,000 stamps printed.

The print is 6½" x 9⅜". The edition consists of 500 signed and numbered prints.

1976

FIRST SOUTH DAKOTA DUCK STAMP

Mallards
Robert Kusserow

The original art depicts a pair of Mallards, one in the water and one coming in for a landing. This was the first required waterfowl stamp contest for South Dakota. (Only residents of South Dakota are eligible to enter the contest.)

The stamp is numbered on the front. It sold for $1.00. Of the 89,000 stamps that were printed, 38,788 were sold.

The print is 6½″ x 9″. The edition consists of 500 signed and numbered prints. Matching numbered stamps were offered with each print in the edition for the first time.

1977–78

FORTY-FOURTH FEDERAL DUCK STAMP

Ross's Geese
Martin R. Murk

The original art is a 5″ x 7″ acrylic rendering of Ross's Geese in flight. It was chosen in open national competition from 264 entries.

The stamp was printed in full color and sold for $5.00. The first day of sale was July 1, 1977; 2,196,774 were sold.

The print is a 6 ½″ x 9″ photolithograph in six colors, using permanent, lite-fast inks. The stock is Gallery 100 plate finish (100% rag), and the separation negative maker and printer was Wetzel Brothers, Inc. The first edition consists of 5800 numbered prints. The image's subtlety was enhanced by the addition of a fifth and sixth color in printing.

1977

SEVENTH CALIFORNIA DUCK STAMP

Cinnamon Teal
Paul B. Johnson

The original art depicts three Cinnamon Teal in flight.

The stamp: two were issued in 1977 due to a fee increase that went into effect on January 1, 1978, while the hunting season went to the end of January. All of the 375,000 stamps in the first issue were sold, and all of the 75,000 in the second were sold.

The print is 5½″ x 8¼″. The edition consists of 500 signed and numbered and 150 Executive Series prints. There was also an Executive Series of 150 prints and stamps from each of the seven California designs by Mr. Johnson.

1977
THIRD ILLINOIS DUCK STAMP

Canada Goose
Richard Lynch

The original art depicts a lone Canada Goose sitting in the rushes. The design was chosen from 136 entries.

The stamp is numbered on the front. It sold for $5.25. Of the 165,000 stamps that were printed, 65,241 were sold. All remainders were destroyed on June 30, 1982.

The print is 9″ x 11″. The edition consists of 500 signed and numbered prints.

1977
SECOND INDIANA DUCK STAMP

Pintail
Sonny Bashore

The original art depicts a Pintail standing in a marsh. The Indiana Department of Natural Resources again commissioned the artist to design the artwork for the waterfowl stamp and print. The 1976 and 1977 designs were done in 1976 due to the split season January duck hunting in Indiana.

The stamp is numbered on the front. It sold for $5.00. There were 70,000 stamps printed.

The print is 17″ x 21″. The edition consists of 18 signed and numbered prints. Beginning with this edition, the state of Indiana decided to issue series of the prints of the stamp design in edition sizes comparable to the number of Indiana Ducks Unlimited chapters.

1977
SIXTH IOWA DUCK STAMP

Lesser Scaup
Maynard Reece

The original art depicts three Lesser Scaup flying low over rough water. The design was chosen from 100 entries. This marked Mr. Reece's sixth win in open competition and his seventh design overall, since he was commissioned to do Iowa's initial stamp.

The stamp is not numbered. It sold for $1.00. Of the 125,000 stamps that were printed, 69,179 were sold. The remainders were on sale until June 1978.

The print is 6⁹/₁₆″ x 11″. The edition consists of 900 signed and numbered prints.

1977
FOURTH MARYLAND DUCK STAMP

Bluebills at Sunset
Jack Schroeder

The original art depicts two Greater Scaup in flight. The design was chosen from 50 entries.

The stamp is numbered on an attached tab. It sold for $1.10. All of the 90,000 stamps that were printed were sold.

The print is 6⁷⁄₁₆″ x 9″. The edition consists of 850 signed and numbered prints. There are also 85 artist's proofs.

1977
FOURTH MASSACHUSETTS DUCK STAMP

Goldeneye Decoy
William P. Tyner

The original art depicts a Goldeneye drake decoy carved by an unknown artist. The design was chosen from twelve entries. Mr. Tyner's win marks the first time that any artist won two consecutive state duck stamp contests in the same state.

The stamp is not numbered. It sold for $1.25. All of the 50,400 stamps that were printed were sold.

The print is 6½″ x 9″. The edition consists of 137 signed and numbered prints. Separately, there are 30 remarqued artist's proofs. A second edition issued by Ducks Unlimited is recognizable by the wording *2nd edition*.

1977
SECOND MICHIGAN DUCK STAMP

Canvasbacks
Larry Hayden

The original art depicts a pair of Canvasbacks swimming, with a group flying in the background. It was chosen from 56 entries in the first open competition in Michigan to determine the design of the state duck stamp. (The contest is open only to residents of Michigan.)

The stamp is numbered on an attached sheet. It sold for $2.10. Of the 250,000 stamps that were printed, 83,885 were sold. The remainders were disposed of in July 1978.

The print is 6½″ x 9″. The edition consists of 650 signed and numbered prints.

1977
FIRST MINNESOTA DUCK STAMP

Mallards
David Maass

The original art depicts three Mallards taking flight. The Minnesota Department of Natural Resources commissioned the artist to design the artwork for the first state waterfowl stamp and print. This design is the official logo of the Minnesota Waterfowl Association; the department selected it in recognition of the efforts of the Waterfowl Association.

The stamp is numbered on the back. It sold for $3.50. There were 300,000 stamps printed.

The print is 6½″ x 9″. This was a time-limited edition taken to order. The quantity has never been officially published, but it is believed to be approximately 3300 signed but unnumbered prints.

1977
SECOND MISSISSIPPI DUCK STAMP

Mallards
Allen Hughes

The original art depicts a pair of Mallards in flight. The artist was commissioned by the Mississippi Game and Fish Commission to provide the artwork design for the second Mississippi State Waterfowl Stamp.

The stamp is numbered on the front. It sold for $2.00. There were 50,000 stamps printed.

The print is 6½″ x 9″. The edition consists of 500 signed and numbered prints.

1977
SECOND SOUTH DAKOTA DUCK STAMP

Pintails
Don Steinbeck

The original art depicts a pair of Pintails in flight.

The stamp is numbered on the front. It sold for $1.00. All of the 80,000 stamps that were printed were sold.

The print is 4⅛″ x 5⅞″. The first edition consists of 150 signed and numbered prints. Because the quantity was not sufficient to fulfill the demand, a second edition, also consisting of 150 signed and numbered prints, was issued. This is the first time that a second edition was issued on a state duck stamp print.

1978–79
FORTY-FIFTH FEDERAL DUCK STAMP

Hooded Merganser
Albert Earl Gilbert

The original art is a 5″ x 7″ opaque watercolor. It was chosen in open national competition from 296 entries.

The stamp was printed in full color and sold for $5.00. The first day of sale was July 1, 1978; 2,206,421 were sold.

The print is a 7″ x 9⅞″ photolithograph in six colors, using lite-fast inks. The stock is 100% rag Mont-Lith Vellum 140 lb, and the separation negative maker and printer was Litho-Craft of New England. The first edition is 5800 regular plus 1350 remarqued. The edition is numbered and is the first federal print to have watercolor remarques.

1978
EIGHTH CALIFORNIA DUCK STAMP

Hooded Mergansers
Ken Michaelsen

The original art, a full-color painting, depicts Hooded Mergansers in the water. This was the first open competition of the California Duck Stamp contest. (The contest is open to California residents only.)

The stamp was printed in the two-color process, despite the choice of a full-color art design and print. The stamp is numbered on the front. It sold for $5.00. All of the 325,000 stamps that were printed were sold.

The print, California's first full-color print, is 6⁹⁄₁₆″ x 9³⁄₁₆″. The edition consists of 500 signed and numbered and 150 Executive Series prints.

1978
FOURTH ILLINOIS DUCK STAMP

Canvasbacks
Everett Staffeldt

The original art depicts a pair of Canvasbacks flying over rough water. The design was chosen from 93 entries.

The stamp is numbered on the front. It sold for $5.25. Of the 165,000 stamps that were printed, 66,240 were sold. All remainders were destroyed on June 30, 1982.

The print is 7½″ x 11″. The edition consists of 500 signed and numbered prints.

1978
THIRD INDIANA DUCK STAMP

Canada Geese
Carl "Spike" Knuth

The original art depicts a pair of Canada Geese in flight. The design was chosen from 89 entries in the first open competition to determine the design for the Indiana State Waterfowl Stamp. (The contest is open to artists from any state.)

The stamp is numbered on the front. It sold for $5.00. There were 70,000 stamps printed.

The print is 7⅝″ x 10¾″. The edition consists of 18 signed and numbered prints.

1978
SEVENTH IOWA DUCK STAMP

Wood Ducks
Nick Klepinger

The original art depicts Wood Ducks in flight. The design, chosen from 80 entries, marked the artist's second Iowa win.

The stamp is not numbered. It sold for $1.00. Of the 125,000 stamps that were printed, 60,041 were sold. The remainders were on sale until March 1979.

The print is 6½″ x 11″. The edition consists of 600 signed and numbered prints. Added to this were 50 prints remarqued with woodcuts and numbered 1 to 50.

1978
FIFTH MARYLAND DUCK STAMP

Redheads
Stanley Stearns

The original art depicts Redheads coming in for a landing. The design was chosen from 96 entries.

The stamp is numbered on an attached tab. It sold for $1.10. All of the 90,000 stamps that were printed were sold.

The print is 6½″ x 9″. The edition consists of 1200 signed and numbered prints. Added to this were 120 artist's proofs and 10 remarques, 10 Special Edition gold medallions, and 100 Special Edition silver medallions.

1978

FIFTH MASSACHUSETTS DUCK STAMP

Black Duck Decoy
William P. Tyner

The original art depicts a Black Duck decoy carved by Elmer Crowell. The design was chosen from 22 entries. Mr. Tyner became the first artist to win three consecutive state waterfowl stamp contests.

The stamp is not numbered. It sold for $1.25. All of the 50,400 stamps that were printed were sold.

The print is 6½″ x 10″. The edition consists of 175 signed and numbered prints. There are also 100 remarqued artist's proofs.

1978

THIRD MICHIGAN DUCK STAMP

Mallards
Richard Timm

The original art depicts a pair of Mallards coming in for a landing. The design was chosen from 74 entries.

The stamp is numbered on the front. It sold for $2.10. Of the 200,000 stamps that were printed, 73,046 were sold. The remainders were disposed of in August 1979.

The print is 6½″ x 9″. The edition consists of 700 signed and numbered prints.

1978

SECOND MINNESOTA DUCK STAMP

Lesser Scaup
Leslie C. Kouba

The original art depicts Lesser Scaup in flight. The design was chosen from 45 entries in the first open competition for the state duck stamp design. (The Minnesota contest is open to residents of Minnesota only.) The design includes a "Kouba trademark" of 13 ducks.

The stamp is numbered on the back. It sold for $3.50. There were 300,000 stamps printed.

The print is 6⁹⁄₁₆″ x 9¼″. The edition consists of 3500 signed and numbered prints. There are also three medallion editions.

1978
THIRD MISSISSIPPI DUCK STAMP

Green-Winged Teal
John Reimers

The original art depicts a pair of Green-Winged Teal in flight. This was the first of the open competitions for the Mississippi Waterfowl Stamp design. (The contest is open to residents of Mississippi only.) Mr. Reimer's design was chosen from 35 entries.

The stamp is numbered on the front. It sold for $2.00. There were 50,000 stamps printed.

The print is 6½″ x 9″. The edition consists of 500 signed and numbered prints.

1978
THIRD SOUTH DAKOTA DUCK STAMP

Canvasbacks
John Moisan

The original art depicts Canvasbacks in flight. The design was chosen from 20 entries.

The stamp is numbered on the front. It sold for $1.00. Of the 70,000 stamps that were printed, 15,831 were sold.

The print is 6½″ x 8⅞″. The edition consists of 300 signed and numbered prints. The print is entitled *Behold the King*.

1978

FIRST WISCONSIN DUCK STAMP

Wood Ducks
Owen J. Gromme

The original art depicts three Wood Ducks in flight. The Wisconsin Department of Natural Resources commissioned Mr. Gromme to design the artwork for this initial state waterfowl stamp.

The stamp is numbered on an attached tab. It sold for $3.25. All of the 280,000 stamps that were printed were sold.

The print is 6½″ x 9″. The edition consists of 5800 signed and numbered prints.

1979–80

FORTY-SIXTH FEDERAL DUCK STAMP

Green-Winged Teal
Lawrence K. Michaelson

The original art is a 5″ x 7″ gouache painting of Green-Winged Teal in the water. It was chosen in open national competition from 374 entries.

The stamp was printed in full color and sold for $7.50. The first day of sale was July 1, 1979; 2,090,155 were sold.

The print is a 7″ x 9⅞″ four-color photolithograph, using Jefferies Custom Made Inks on Jefferies Archival 100 stock. The separation negative maker was Color Service (Los Angeles, CA), and the printer was Jefferies Bank Note Company. The first edition is 7000 regular plus 1500 with companion piece. The prints are numbered. In lieu of remarques, the artist here chose to produce miniature etchings the same size as the stamp, which can be framed alongside the stamp underneath the print.

1979
FIRST ALABAMA DUCK STAMP

Wood Ducks
Barbara Keel

The original art depicts a pair of Wood Ducks standing on a log. The Alabama Department of Conservation commissioned the artist to design the artwork for this initial Alabama State Waterfowl Stamp.

The stamp is numbered on the front. It sold for $5.25. There were 35,000 stamps printed.

The print is 6½″ x 9″. The edition consists of 1750 signed and numbered prints. There are also 250 watercolor remarques.

1979
NINTH CALIFORNIA DUCK STAMP

Wood Ducks
Walter Wolfe

The original art, depicting Wood Ducks standing in a white alder tree, was done in casein watercolor. The design was chosen from 45 entries.

The stamp is numbered on the front. It sold for $5.00. All of the 325,000 stamps that were printed were sold.

The print is a 6⅝″ x 9¹⁄₁₆″ four-color photolithograph with five impressions using Gans fade-resistant inks on Rising Gallery 100, a pH-neutral 100% rag paper. The edition consists of 500 signed and numbered and 150 Executive Series prints. There are 70 painted remarques and 40 pencil remarques, which are part of the signed and numbered edition.

1979
FIRST FLORIDA DUCK STAMP

Green-Winged Teal
Bob Binks

The original art depicts a pair of Green-Winged Teal in flight. The Florida Game Commission commissioned the artist to design the artwork for this initial Florida State Duck Stamp.

The stamp is numbered on the front. It sold for $3.25. All of the 72,875 stamps that were printed were sold.

The print is 6″ x 9″. The edition consists of 1000 signed and numbered prints. There are, separately, also 250 watercolor remarques.

1979
FIFTH ILLINOIS DUCK STAMP

Pintail
John Eggert

The original art depicts a lone Pintail drake swimming next to the ice. The design was chosen from 116 entries.

The stamp is numbered on the front. It sold for $5.25. Of the 140,000 stamps that were printed, 64,699 were sold. All remainders were destroyed on June 30, 1982.

The print is 7¾″ x 11″. The edition consists of 500 signed and numbered prints.

1979
FOURTH INDIANA DUCK STAMP

Canvasbacks
Diane Pierce

The original art depicts three Canvasbacks in flight. The design was chosen from 52 entries. The artist is the first woman ever to win a duck stamp competition.

The stamp is numbered on the back. It sold for $5.00. There were 60,000 stamps printed.

The print is 7⅝″ x 10¾″. The edition consists of 20 signed and numbered prints.

1979
EIGHTH IOWA DUCK STAMP

Buffleheads
Andrew Peters

The original art depicts three Buffleheads in flight. The design was chosen from 90 entries.

The stamp is not numbered. It sold for $5.00. Of the 125,000 stamps that were printed, 52,865 were sold. The remainders were taken off sale in April 1980.

The print is 6½″ x 11″. The edition consists of 750 prints.

1979
SIXTH MARYLAND DUCK STAMP

Wood Ducks
John W. Taylor

The original art depicts a pair of Wood Ducks on the ground. The design was chosen from 126 entries.

The stamp is numbered on an attached tab. It sold for $1.10. All of the 90,000 stamps that were printed were sold.

The print is 6½″ x 9″. The edition consists of 950 signed and numbered prints. There are, separately, also 200 remarques and 115 artist's proofs.

1979
SIXTH MASSACHUSETTS DUCK STAMP

Ruddy Turnstone Decoy
Randy Julius

The original art depicts a Ruddy Turnstone decoy carved by Lothrop Holmes. The design was chosen from 17 entries. The Ruddy Turnstone is the first shorebird to appear on a waterfowl stamp.

The stamp is not numbered. It sold for $1.25. All of the 50,400 stamps that were printed were sold.

The print is 8″ x 9″. The edition consists of 175 signed and numbered prints. There are also 125 remarqued artist's proofs.

1979
FOURTH MICHIGAN DUCK STAMP

Canada Geese
Andrew Kurzmann

The original art depicts a pair of Canada Geese in a cornfield. The design was chosen from 82 entries.

The stamp is numbered on the front. It sold for $2.10. All of the 160,000 stamps that were printed were sold.

The print is 6½″ x 9″. The edition consists of 700 signed and numbered prints.

1979
THIRD MINNESOTA DUCK STAMP

Pintails
David Maass

The original art depicts Pintails coming in for a landing. The design was chosen from 68 entries.

The stamp is numbered on the back. It sold for $3.50. There were 300,000 stamps printed.

The print is 6½″ x 9″. The edition consists of 3800 signed and numbered prints.

1979
FOURTH MISSISSIPPI DUCK STAMP

Canvasbacks
Carole Pigott Hardy

The original art depicts a pair of Canvasbacks in flight. The design was chosen from 35 entries.

The stamp is numbered on the front. It sold for $2.00. There were 50,000 stamps printed.

The print is 6⅝" x 9¾". The edition consists of 500 signed and numbered prints.

1979
FIRST MISSOURI DUCK STAMP

Giant Canada Geese
Charles W. Schwartz

The original art depicts three Giant Canada Geese coming in for a landing. The Missouri Department of Conservation commissioned the artist to design the artwork for the state's first waterfowl stamp.

The stamp is numbered on the front. It sold for $3.40. Of the 160,000 stamps that were printed, 56,694 were sold. The remainders were taken off sale on May 1, 1980.

The print is 6½" x 9". The edition consists of 2000 signed and numbered prints, 200 of which are remarques.

1979
FIRST NEVADA DUCK STAMP

Tule Canvasback Decoy
Larry Hayden

The original art depicts an ancient Tule Canvasback decoy used by the Northern Paiute Indians nearly 1000 years ago. The design was chosen from 32 entries in the open contest to determine the artwork for the state's first duck stamp. (The Nevada contest is open to residents of any state.)

The stamp is numbered on an attached booklet tab. It sold for $2.00. All of the 24,000 stamps that were printed were sold.

The print is 6½" x 9". The edition consists of 1990 signed and numbered prints, plus 500 pencil remarques.

1979
FIRST TENNESSEE DUCK STAMP

Mallards
Dick Elliott

The original art depicts three Mallards landing. The design was chosen from eleven entries in the state's open competition to choose a design for its initial waterfowl stamp. (The contest is open to residents of Tennessee only.)

The stamp is numbered on the front. It sold for $2.30 resident and $5.30 nonresident. The numbers printed were 60,000 resident and 20,000 nonresident. The numbers sold were 19,580 resident and 1491 nonresident. All remainders were taken off sale on June 30, 1981.

The print is 6⁷/₁₆″ x 8¹⁵/₁₆″. The edition consists of 1979 signed and numbered prints, 200 of which are remarques.

1979
SECOND WISCONSIN DUCK STAMP

Buffleheads
Rockne Knuth

The original art depicts a pair of Buffleheads swimming in calm water. The design was chosen from 133 entries in the first open contest for the Wisconsin Duck Stamp design. (The contest is open only to residents of Wisconsin.)

The stamp is numbered on an attached tab. It sold for $3.25. All of the 240,000 stamps that were printed were sold.

The print is 6½″ x 9″. The edition consists of 1700 signed and numbered prints.

1980–81
FORTY-SEVENTH FEDERAL DUCK STAMP

Mallards
Richard W. Plasschaert

The original art is a 5″ x 7″ rendering in acrylic of Mallards in flight. It was chosen in open national competition from 1329 entries.

The stamp was printed in full color and sold for $7.50. The first day of sale was July 1, 1980; 2,045,114 were sold.

The print is a 6½″ x 9″ four-color photolithograph, using special lite-fast inks on Rising Mirage stock. The separation negative maker and the printer was Johnson Printing, Inc. The first edition is 12,950 numbered prints.

1980
SECOND ALABAMA DUCK STAMP

Mallards
Wayne Spradley

The original art depicts a pair of Mallards swimming. The Alabama Department of Conservation commissioned the artist to design the artwork.

The stamp is numbered on the front. It sold for $5.25. There were 20,000 stamps printed.

The print is 6½" x 9". The edition consists of 1000 signed and numbered prints, 100 of which are remarques.

1980
TENTH CALIFORNIA DUCK STAMP

Pintails
Walter Wolfe

The original art, a casein watercolor painting, depicts a pair of Pintails in flight. The design was chosen from 75 entries, marking Mr. Wolfe's second consecutive win.

The stamp is numbered on the front. It sold for $5.00. All of the 325,000 stamps that were printed were sold.

The print is a 6½" x 9¹/₁₆" color photolithograph, using Acme fade-resistant inks on Rising Mirage 100% rag pH-neutral stock. The edition consists of 700 signed and numbered and 200 Executive Series prints. There are also 81 painted remarques and 46 pencil remarques, which are part of the signed and numbered edition.

1980
FIRST DELAWARE DUCK STAMP

Black Ducks
Ned Mayne

The original art depicts a pair of Black Ducks in flight. The design was chosen from 35 entries in the open contest to determine the artwork for the state's first duck stamp. (The Delaware contest is open to residents of Delaware and also to residents of states that allow Delaware residents to enter their state contests.)

The stamp is not numbered (sheets were). It sold for $5.00. Of the 30,000 stamps that were printed, 17,510 were sold. The remainders were sold until July 1, 1983.

The print is 6½" x 9". The edition consists of 1980 signed and numbered prints, some of which have remarques in pencil.

1980
SECOND FLORIDA DUCK STAMP

Pintails
Ernest Simmons

The original art depicts a pair of Pintails flying through the cypress. The design was chosen from 87 entries in the first open contest held in Florida to determine the state's waterfowl stamp artwork. (The Florida contest is open to residents of any state.)

The stamp is numbered on the front. It sold for $3.25. There were 70,000 stamps printed.

The print is 6½" x 9". The edition consists of 1000 signed and numbered prints, 250 of which have remarques in pencil.

1980

SIXTH ILLINOIS DUCK STAMP

Green-Winged Teal
Bart Kassabaum

The original art depicts a pair of Green-Winged Teal drakes in flight. The design was chosen from 79 entries.

The stamp is numbered on the front. It sold for $5.50. Of the 126,000 stamps that were printed, 61,813 were sold. All remainders were destroyed on June 30, 1982.

The print is 7¾″ x 11″. The edition consists of 500 signed and numbered prints.

1980

FIFTH INDIANA DUCK STAMP

Mallard Ducklings
Dean "Rocky" Barrick

The original art depicts a clutch of Mallard ducklings in the nest. The design was chosen from 37 entries.

The stamp is numbered on the back. It sold for $5.00. There were 60,000 stamps printed.

The print is 7⅝″ x 10 ¾″. The edition consists of 24 signed and numbered prints.

1980

NINTH IOWA DUCK STAMP

Redheads
Paul Bridgford

The original art depicts a pair of Redheads in flight. The design was chosen from 100 entries.

The stamp is not numbered. It sold for $5.00. Of the 100,000 stamps that were printed, 49,913 were sold. The remainders were taken off sale on March 31, 1981.

The print is 6½″ x 10 ¾″. The edition consists of 850 signed and numbered prints.

1980

SEVENTH MARYLAND DUCK STAMP

The Ward Brothers/Decoy
Jack Schroeder

The original art depicts the two Ward brothers—decoy carvers of Maryland's famed Eastern Shore—and one of their decoys. The design was chosen from 129 entries.

The stamp is numbered on an attached tab. It sold for $1.10. All of the 90,000 stamps that were printed were sold.

The print is 6½″ x 9″. The edition consists of 1175 signed and numbered prints. There are also 125 artist's proofs and a Special Edition of 480 prints.

1980

SEVENTH MASSACHUSETTS DUCK STAMP

Old Squaw Decoy
John Eggert

The original art depicts an Old Squaw drake decoy constructed of canvas and slats by Lothrop Holmes. The design was chosen from 43 entries, representing 30 artists from 14 different states.

The stamp is not numbered. It sold for $1.25. All of the 50,400 stamps that were printed were sold.

The print is 8½″ x 12″. The edition consists of 600 signed and numbered prints.

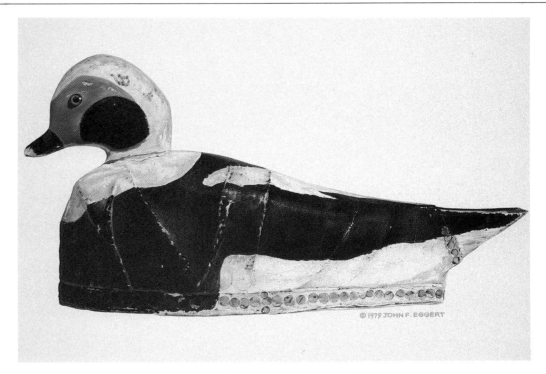

1980

FIFTH MICHIGAN DUCK STAMP

Lesser Scaup
Larry Hayden

The original art depicts a pair of Lesser Scaup swimming in calm water. The design was chosen from 73 entries. This was the artist's second win in the Michigan contest.

The stamp is numbered on the front. It sold for $3.75. All of the 150,000 stamps that were printed were sold.

The print is 6½″ x 9″. The edition consists of 900 signed and numbered prints.

1980
FOURTH MINNESOTA DUCK STAMP

Canvasbacks
James Meger

The original art depicts a pair of Canvasbacks coming in for a landing with one in the water. The design was chosen from 109 entries.

The stamp is numbered on the back. It sold for $3.50. There were 250,000 stamps printed.

The print is 6½″ x 9″. The edition consists of 3500 prints.

1980
FIFTH MISSISSIPPI DUCK STAMP

Pintails
Bob Tompkins

The original art depicts a pair of Pintails in flight. The design was chosen from 45 entries.

The stamp is numbered on the front. It sold for $2.00. There were 50,000 stamps printed.

The print is 6½″ x 9″. The edition consists of 500 signed and numbered prints.

1980
SECOND MISSOURI DUCK STAMP

Wood Ducks
David Plank

The original art depicts a pair of Wood Ducks swimming next to a log. The design was chosen from 41 entries. This was the first open competition to determine the artwork for the state's duck stamp. (The contest is open to Missouri residents only.)

The stamp is numbered on the front. It sold for $3.40. Of the 130,000 stamps that were printed, 48,224 were sold. The remainders were taken off sale on May 1, 1981.

The print is 6⅛″ x 9⅛″. The edition consists of 1250 signed and numbered prints, 250 of which are remarques.

1980
SECOND NEVADA DUCK STAMP

Cinnamon Teal
Dick McRill

The original art depicts a pair of Cinnamon Teal on the water. The design was chosen from 64 entries.

The stamp is numbered on an attached booklet tab. It sold for $2.00. There were 26,000 stamps printed. This stamp is unique since the ducks face opposite the way they face on the original painting and on the prints.

The print is 6⁷⁄₁₆″ x 9″. The edition consists of 1990 signed and numbered prints.

1980

FIRST OKLAHOMA DUCK STAMP

Pintails
Patrick Sawyer

The original art depicts a pair of Pintails in flight. The design was chosen from 89 entries in the open contest to determine the artwork for the state's first waterfowl stamp. (The contest is open to residents of Oklahoma only.)

The stamp is numbered on the back. It sold for $4.00. There were 60,000 stamps printed. Any remainders were sold until July 1, 1985.

The print is 6½" x 9". The edition consists of 1980 signed and numbered prints, some of which have remarques in color and some in pencil.

1980

SECOND TENNESSEE DUCK STAMP

Canvasbacks
Thompson Phillip Crowe IV

The original art depicts a pair of Canvasbacks in flight. The design was chosen from 15 entries. The drake in the painting wears a leg band; this marks the first state waterfowl stamp design to depict a bird with an identification band.

The stamp is numbered on the front. It sold for $2.30 resident and $5.30 nonresident. The numbers printed were 60,000 resident and 20,000 nonresident. The numbers sold were 17,423 resident and 1368 nonresident. All remainders were destroyed on June 30, 1981.

The print is 6½" x 9". The edition consists of 1000 signed and numbered prints. There is, separately, an Artist's Proof Edition of 250, including remarques.

1980

THIRD WISCONSIN DUCK STAMP

Widgeon
Martin Murk

The original art depicts a pair of Widgeon standing. The design was chosen from 83 entries.

The stamp is numbered on an attached tab. It sold for $3.25. There were 180,000 stamps printed.

The print is 6½" x 9". The edition consists of 1250 signed and numbered prints.

1981–82
FORTY-EIGHTH FEDERAL DUCK STAMP

Ruddy Ducks
John S. Wilson

The original art is a 5″ x 7″ gouache painting of the birds in the water. It was chosen in open national competition from 1507 entries.

The stamp was printed in full color and sold for $7.50. The first day of sale was July 1, 1981; 1,907,120 were sold. Note that individual stamps are separated only by the perforations in this unbordered design.

The print is a 6½″ x 9″ four-color photolithograph, using special lite-fast inks on Rives Offset stock. The separation negative maker and the printer was Johnson Printing, Inc. The first edition is 16,000 numbered prints.

1981
THIRD ALABAMA DUCK STAMP

Canada Geese
Jack DeLoney

The original art depicts three Canada Geese in flight. The design was chosen from 39 entries in the first open contest to determine the artwork for the state's waterfowl stamp. (The contest is open to residents of Alabama only.)

The stamp is numbered on the front. It sold for $5.25. There were 20,000 stamps printed.

The print is 6½″ x 9″. The edition consists of 950 signed and numbered prints, 100 of which are remarques.

1981
FIRST ARKANSAS DUCK STAMP

Mallards
Lee LeBlanc

The original art, entitled *Mallards in Flooded Timber*, depicts a flock of Mallards coming in for a landing. The Arkansas Fish and Game Department commissioned the artist to do the artwork for the state's initial waterfowl stamp. (No contests were held to determine artwork for later Arkansas designs.)

The stamp is numbered on the back. It sold for $5.50. Of the 200,000 stamps that were printed, 51,041 were sold. The remainders were sold until July 1, 1984.

The print is 6″ x 9″. The edition consists of 7200 signed and numbered prints. There are a separate Executive Edition of 500 and a remarqued edition of 600.

1981
ELEVENTH CALIFORNIA DUCK STAMP

Canvasbacks
Robert Steiner

The original art depicts a pair of Canvasbacks landing. The design was chosen from 78 entries.

The stamp is numbered on the front. It sold for $5.00. There were 325,000 stamps printed.

The print is 6⅝″ x 9⅛″. The edition consists of 1150 signed and numbered and 300 Executive Series prints.

1981
SECOND DELAWARE DUCK STAMP

Snow Geese
Charles Rowe

The original art depicts a pair of Snow Geese in flight. The design was chosen from 53 entries.

The stamp is not numbered (sheets were). It sold for $5.00. Of the 30,000 stamps that were printed, 15,423 were sold. The remainders were sold until July 1, 1984.

The print is 6″ x 9″. The edition consists of 1981 signed and numbered prints, some of which have remarques in pencil and some in color.

1981
THIRD FLORIDA DUCK STAMP

Widgeon
Clark Sullivan

The original art depicts a Widgeon drake swimming in calm water. The design was chosen from 87 entries.

The stamp is numbered on the front. It sold for $3.25. There were 50,000 stamps printed.

The print is 6½″ x 9″. The edition consists of 1000 signed and numbered prints, 250 of which have remarques in pencil.

1981
SEVENTH ILLINOIS DUCK STAMP

Widgeon
Jim Trandel

The original art depicts a pair of Widgeon in flight. The design was chosen from 67 entries.

The stamp is numbered on the front. It sold for $5.50. Of the 123,000 stamps that were printed, 62,297 were sold. The remainders were on sale until April 1, 1983.

The print is 8⅞″ x 11″. The edition consists of 500 signed and numbered prints.

1981
SIXTH INDIANA DUCK STAMP

Hooded Mergansers
Rodney Crossman

The original art depicts two Hooded Mergansers swimming. The design was chosen from 61 entries. Mr. Crossman is the first native Indianan to win the contest.

The stamp is numbered on the back. It sold for $5.00. There were 60,000 stamps printed.

The print is 7⅝″ x 10 ¾″. The edition consists of 30 signed and numbered prints.

1981
TENTH IOWA DUCK STAMP

Green-Winged Teal
Brad Reece

The original art depicts three Green-Winged Teal in flight. The design was chosen from 100 entries. The artist is the son of the renowned wildlife artist Maynard Reece and the brother of the 1975 Iowa contest winner, Mark Reece.

The stamp is numbered. It sold for $5.00. Of the 100,000 stamps that were printed, 45,751 were sold. The remainders were sold until April 1, 1982.

The print is 6½″ x 11″. The edition consists of 900 signed and numbered prints.

1981
EIGHTH MARYLAND DUCK STAMP

Widgeon
Arthur R. Eakin

The original art depicts a Widgeon drake in flight. The design was chosen from 135 entries. Mr. Eakin used the same painting that he had entered in a recent federal duck stamp contest in which he had finished very high.

The stamp is numbered on an attached tab. It sold for $3.00. All of the 90,000 stamps that were printed were sold.

The print is 6½" x 9". The edition consists of 1250 signed and numbered prints. There are, separately, 125 remarques and 150 artist's proofs.

1981
EIGHTH MASSACHUSETTS DUCK STAMP

Red-Breasted Merganser Decoy
Randy Julius

The original art depicts a Red-Breasted Merganser decoy carved by an unknown artist. The design was chosen from 59 entries.

The stamp is not numbered. It sold for $1.25. All of the 50,400 stamps that were printed were sold.

The print is 8" x 10½". The edition consists of 250 signed and numbered prints. There are also 125 remarqued artist's proofs.

1981
SIXTH MICHIGAN DUCK STAMP

Buffleheads
Dietmar Krumrey

The original art depicts a pair of Buffleheads at rest. The design was chosen from 80 entries.

The stamp is numbered on the front. It sold for $3.75. All of the 150,000 stamps that were printed were sold.

The print is 6¹¹⁄₁₆" x 9¼". The edition consists of 1200 signed and numbered prints, including remarques in watercolor and in pencil.

1981
FIFTH MINNESOTA DUCK STAMP

Giant Canada Geese
Terry Redlin

The original art depicts two Giant Canada Geese, one with a neck collar and a leg band, standing on the shore. The design was chosen from 168 entries.

The stamp is numbered on the back. It sold for $3.50. There were 250,000 stamps printed.

The print is 6″ x 9″. The edition consists of 7800 signed and numbered prints.

1981
SIXTH MISSISSIPPI DUCK STAMP

Redheads
John Reimers

The original art depicts a pair of Redheads in shallow water. The design was chosen from 60 entries. This marks the second win for the artist in the Mississippi contest.

The stamp is numbered on the front. It sold for $2.00. There were 50,000 stamps printed.

The print is 6½″ x 9″. The edition consists of 500 signed and numbered prints.

1981
THIRD MISSOURI DUCK STAMP

Lesser Scaup
Tom Crain

The original art depicts a single Lesser Scaup swimming in calm water. The design was chosen from 54 entries.

The stamp is numbered on the front. It sold for $3.00. All of the 130,000 stamps that were printed were sold.

The print is 6½″ x 9″. The edition consists of 1000 signed and numbered prints, 150 of which have pencil remarques and 50 of which have color remarques.

1981
THIRD NEVADA DUCK STAMP

Whistling Swans
Phil Scholer

The original art depicts a pair of Whistling Swans swimming in calm water. The design was chosen from 111 entries.

The stamp is numbered on an attached booklet tab. It sold for $2.00. There were 25,000 stamps printed.

The print is 6½″ x 9″. The edition consists of 2025 signed and numbered prints.

1981

SECOND OKLAHOMA DUCK STAMP

Canada Goose
Hoyt Smith

The original art depicts a single Canada Goose swimming in calm water. The design was chosen from 31 entries.

The stamp is numbered on the back. It sold for $4.00. There were 60,000 stamps printed. Any remainders were sold until July 1, 1986.

The print is 6½" x 9". The edition consists of 1980 signed and numbered prints, some of which have remarques in color and some in pencil.

1981

FIRST SOUTH CAROLINA DUCK STAMP

Wood Ducks
Lee LeBlanc

The original art depicts a pair of Wood Ducks standing on a log. The design was chosen from 56 entries in the open competition to determine the artwork for the state's first waterfowl stamp. (The South Carolina contest is open to residents of any state.)

The stamp is not numbered. It sold for $5.50. Of the 105,000 stamps that were printed, 36,022 were sold. The remainders were destroyed in April 1982.

The print is 6½" x 9". The edition consists of 4500 signed and numbered prints.

1981

THIRD TENNESSEE DUCK STAMP

Wood Ducks
Bob Gillespie

The original art depicts a pair of Wood Ducks on a log. The design was chosen from 31 entries.

The stamp is numbered on the front. It sold for $2.30. Of the 60,000 stamps that were printed, 21,389 were sold. Remainders were destroyed on November 30, 1982.

The print is 6½" x 9". The edition consists of 1200 signed and numbered prints, 250 of which have color remarques.

1981
FIRST TEXAS DUCK STAMP

Mallards
Larry Hayden

The original art depicts a pair of Mallards swimming. The artist was state-appointed.

The stamp is numbered on the front. It sold for $5.00. Of the 300,000 stamps that were printed, 136,553 were sold. The remainders were destroyed on January 1, 1983.

The print is 6½" x 9". The edition consists of 16,500 signed and numbered prints.

1981
FOURTH WISCONSIN DUCK STAMP

Lesser Scaup
Timothy C. Schultz

The original art depicts a pair of Lesser Scaup in flight. The design was chosen from 114 entries.

The stamp is numbered on an attached tab. It sold for $3.25. There were 180,000 stamps printed.

The print is 6½″ x 9″. The edition consists of 1700 signed and numbered prints.

1982–83
FORTY-NINTH FEDERAL DUCK STAMP

Canvasbacks
David Maass

The original art is a 5″ x 7″ oil-on-board painting of Canvasbacks in flight. It was chosen in open national competition from 2099 entries.

The stamp was printed in full color and sold for $7.50. The first day of sale was July 1, 1982; 1,926,253 were sold.

The print is a 6½″ x 9″ four-color photolithograph, using special lite-fast inks on Rag-Cote stock. The separation negative maker and the printer was Johnson Lithographics. The first edition comprises 22,250 numbered but untitled prints. There are also about 800 signed and numbered conservation prints that were donated to nonprofit wildlife-oriented organizations.

1982
FOURTH ALABAMA DUCK STAMP

Green-Winged Teal
Joe Michelet

The original art depicts a pair of Green-Winged Teal in flight. The design was chosen from 28 entries.

The stamp is numbered on the front. It sold for $5.25. There were 20,000 stamps printed.

The print is 6″ x 8″. The edition consists of 850 signed and numbered prints. There are, separately, 100 color remarques.

1982
SECOND ARKANSAS DUCK STAMP

Big Lake
Maynard Reece

The original art depicts a pair of Wood Ducks in flight. The renowned wildlife artist Maynard Reece was commissioned to do the design.

The stamp is numbered on the back. It sold for $5.50. There were 175,000 stamps printed. The remainders were sold until July 1, 1985.

The print is 6½″ x 9¾″. The edition consists of 7440 signed and numbered prints. There are, separately, an Executive Edition of 500 and a remarqued edition of 600, each including hand-colored stone lithographs.

1982
TWELFTH CALIFORNIA DUCK STAMP

Widgeon
Robert Richert

The original art depicts a pair of Widgeon swimming in calm water. The design was chosen from 89 entries.

The stamp is numbered on the front. It sold for $5.00. There were 250,000 stamps printed.

The print is 6⅝″ x 9⅛″. The edition consists of 950 signed and numbered and 300 Executive Series prints.

1982
THIRD DELAWARE DUCK STAMP

Canada Geese
Lois Butler

The original art depicts a pair of Canada Geese in calm water. The design was chosen from 64 entries.

The stamp is not numbered (sheets were). It sold for $5.00. There were 35,000 stamps printed. The remainders were sold until July 1, 1985.

The print is 6½″ x 9″. The edition consists of 1982 signed and numbered prints, some of which have remarques in color and some in pencil.

1982
FOURTH FLORIDA DUCK STAMP

Ring-Necked Ducks
Lee Cable

The original art depicts three Ring-Necked Ducks in flight. The design was chosen from 146 entries.

The stamp is numbered on the front. It sold for $3.25. There were 50,000 stamps printed.

The print is 6½″ x 9″. The edition consists of 1250 signed and numbered prints, some of which have remarques in pencil.

1982
EIGHTH ILLINOIS DUCK STAMP

Black Ducks
Art Sinden

The original art depicts two Black Ducks swimming in calm water. The design was chosen from 98 entries.

The stamp is numbered on the front. It sold for $5.50. Of the 125,000 stamps that were printed, 57,957 were sold. The remainders were on sale until April 1, 1984.

The print is 9″ x 11″. The edition consists of 600 signed and numbered prints.

1982
SEVENTH INDIANA DUCK STAMP

Blue-Winged Teal
George Metz

The original art depicts two Blue-Winged Teal in flight. The design was chosen from 102 entries.

The stamp is numbered on the back. It sold for $5.00. There were 51,000 stamps printed.

The print is 7⅝″ x 10¾″. The edition consists of 50 signed and numbered prints.

1982
ELEVENTH IOWA DUCK STAMP

Snow Geese
Tom Walker

The original art depicts two Snow Geese in flight. The design was chosen from 50 entries.

The stamp is not numbered. It sold for $5.00. Of the 100,000 stamps that were printed, 43,152 were sold. The remainders were on sale until March 1, 1983.

The print is 6½″ x 11″. The edition consists of 600 signed and numbered prints.

1982
NINTH MARYLAND DUCK STAMP

Loafing Along
Roger Bucklin

The original art depicts a lone Canvasback drake swimming in calm water. The design was chosen from 184 entries.

The stamp is numbered on an attached tab. It sold for $3.00. All of the 80,000 stamps that were printed were sold.

The print is 6½″ x 9″. The edition consists of 1575 signed and numbered prints, including remarques in color and in pencil. An Executive Edition of 100 prints, including remarques, was also available.

1982
NINTH MASSACHUSETTS DUCK STAMP

Greater Yellowlegs Decoy
John Eggert

The original art depicts a Greater Yellowlegs decoy. The design was chosen from 64 entries.

The stamp is not numbered. It sold for $1.25. There were 50,400 stamps printed. The remainders were on sale until January 1, 1986.

The print is 6½″ x 10½″. The edition consists of 400 signed and numbered prints. There are, separately, remarques in pencil and in color.

1982
SEVENTH MICHIGAN DUCK STAMP

Redheads
Gijsbert van Frankenhuyzen

The original art depicts a pair of Redheads swimming through the shallows. The design was chosen from 122 entries.

The stamp is numbered on the front. It sold for $3.75. All of the 150,000 stamps that were printed were sold.

The print is 6½″ x 9″. The edition consists of 1200 signed and numbered prints, including remarques in color and in pencil.

1982
SIXTH MINNESOTA DUCK STAMP

Redheads
Phil Scholer

The original art depicts a pair of Redheads swimming in calm water. The design was chosen from 171 entries.

The stamp is numbered on the back. It sold for $3.75. There were 250,000 stamps printed.

The print is 6½″ x 9″. The edition consists of 6500 signed and numbered prints.

1982
SEVENTH MISSISSIPPI DUCK STAMP

Canada Geese
Jerry Johnson

The original art depicts a pair of Canada Geese in flight. The design was chosen from 61 entries.

The stamp is numbered on the front. It sold for $2.00. There were 50,000 stamps printed.

The print is 6″ x 9″. The edition consists of 500 signed and numbered prints.

1982
FOURTH MISSOURI DUCK STAMP

Buffleheads
Gary Lucy

The original art depicts two Buffleheads in flight. The design was chosen from 59 entries.

The stamp is numbered on the front. It sold for $3.00. Of the 130,000 stamps that were printed, 52,382 were sold. The remainders were sold until December 31, 1983.

The print is 6½″ x 9⅞″. The edition consists of 1800 signed and numbered prints.

1982
FOURTH NEVADA DUCK STAMP

Shovelers
Richard Timm

The original art depicts a pair of Shovelers in the water. The design was chosen from 163 entries.

The stamp is numbered on an attached tab. It sold for $2.00. There were 26,000 stamps printed.

The print is 6½″ x 9″. The edition consists of 2200 signed and numbered prints, some of which have color and pencil remarques.

1982
FIRST NORTH DAKOTA DUCK STAMP

Giant Canada Geese
Richard Plasschaert

The original art depicts three Giant Canada Geese in flight. The North Dakota Game and Fish Department commissioned the artist to design the state's first annual stamp print. (In the future, the state will continue to commission only top-name artists to enhance the collectability of the stamps and prints.)

The stamp is numbered on the front. It sold for $9.00. There were 160,050 stamps printed. The remainders were sold until January 1, 1986.

The print is 6½″ x 9″. The edition consists of 9939 signed and numbered prints. There are also 250 artist's proofs.

1982
FIRST OHIO DUCK STAMP

Wood Ducks
John Ruthven

The original art depicts a pair of Wood Ducks in flight. The Ohio Fish and Game Department commissioned the artist to design the artwork for the first state waterfowl stamp.

The stamp is not numbered. It sold for $5.75. Of the 100,000 stamps that were printed, 41,309 were sold. The remainders were sold until January 1, 1984.

The print is 6½″ x 9″. The edition consists of 9000 signed and numbered prints. There are, separately, 530 pencil remarques and 300 color remarques.

1982
THIRD OKLAHOMA DUCK STAMP

Green-Winged Teal
Jeffrey Frey

The original art depicts a pair of Green–Winged Teal standing along the shoreline. The design was chosen from 34 entries.

The stamp is numbered on the back. It sold for $4.00. There were 60,000 stamps printed. Any remainders were sold until July 1, 1987.

The print is 6½″ x 9″. The edition consists of 1980 signed and numbered prints, some of which have remarques in pencil and some in color.

1982
SECOND SOUTH CAROLINA DUCK STAMP

Mallards
Bob Binks

The original art depicts a pair of Mallards in flight. The design was chosen from 106 entries.

The stamp is not numbered. It sold for $5.50. Of the 100,000 stamps that were printed, 29,783 were sold. The remainders were sold until April 1, 1983.

The print is 6½″ x 9″. The edition consists of 4000 signed and numbered prints, some of which have remarques in color.

1982
FOURTH TENNESSEE DUCK STAMP

Canada Geese
Ken Schulz

The original art depicts a flock of Canada Geese in flight. The design was chosen from 20 entries.

The stamp is numbered on the front. It sold for $6.50. Of the 60,000 stamps that were printed, 17,531 were sold. The remainders were sold until November 30, 1983.

The print is 6½″ x 9″. The edition consists of 1250 signed and numbered prints, including 250 remarques.

1982
SECOND TEXAS DUCK STAMP

Pintails
Ken Carlson

The original art depicts a pair of Pintails in the water. The artist was selected by bid proposal.

The stamp is numbered on the front. It sold for $5.00. There were 320,000 stamps printed.

The print is 6½″ x 9″. The edition consists of 9500 signed and numbered prints.

1982

FIFTH WISCONSIN DUCK STAMP

Pintails
William Koelpin

The original art depicts a pair of Pintails standing along a shoreline. The design was chosen from 142 entries.

The stamp is numbered on an attached tab. It sold for $3.25. There were 165,000 stamps printed.

The print is 6½″ x 9″. The edition consists of 2300 signed and numbered prints.

1983–84

FIFTIETH FEDERAL DUCK STAMP

Untitled (Pintails)
Phil Scholer

The original art is a 5″ x 7″ rendering in acrylic of Pintails in the water. It was chosen in open national competition from 1564 entries.

The stamp was printed in full color and sold for $7.50. The first day of sale was July 1, 1983; 1,867,998 were sold.

The print is a 6½″ x 9″ photolithograph, in five colors, using special lite-fast inks on Rising Mirage stock. The separation negative maker and the printer was Mueller-Krus. The first edition consists of 17,400 regular prints and a separately numbered edition of 6700 prints accompanying a gold-plated medallion commemorating the fiftieth duck stamp.

1983

FIFTH ALABAMA DUCK STAMP

Widgeon
John Lee

The original art depicts a pair of Widgeon swimming in calm water. The design was chosen from 24 entries.

The stamp is numbered on the front. It sold for $5.25. There were 20,000 stamps printed.

The print is 7″ x 9″. The edition consists of 1000 signed and numbered prints, including 100 color remarques.

1983
THIRD ARKANSAS DUCK STAMP

Green-Winged Teal
David Maass

The original art depicts three Green-Winged Teal in flight.

The stamp is numbered on the back. It sold for $5.50. There were 160,000 stamps printed. The remainders were sold until July 1, 1986.

The print, entitled *Black River Green-Winged Teal*, is 6½″ x 9″. The edition consists of 7200 signed and numbered prints. There are also an Executive Edition of 500 and a Special Edition of 600. The latter two were offered with a silver or gold medallion.

1983
THIRTEENTH CALIFORNIA DUCK STAMP

Green-Winged Teal
Charles Allen

The original art depicts two Green-Winged Teal in flight. The design was chosen from 96 entries.

The stamp is numbered on the front. It sold for $5.00. There were 250,000 stamps printed.

The print is 6⅝″ x 9⅛″. The edition consists of 750 signed and numbered prints, plus 250 Executive Series prints. Some of the signed and numbered prints have pencil and color remarques.

1983
FOURTH DELAWARE DUCK STAMP

Riding the Waves
John Green

The original art depicts a pair of Canvasbacks swimming in rough water. The design was chosen from 132 entries.

The stamp is not numbered (sheets were). It sold for $5.00. There were 35,000 stamps printed. The remainders were sold until July 1, 1986.

The print is 6½″ x 9″. The edition consists of 1983 signed and numbered prints, some of which have remarques in color and some in pencil. There are, separately, 200 artist's proofs.

1983

FIFTH FLORIDA DUCK STAMP

The Squadron
Heiner Hertling

The original art depicts three Buffleheads in flight. The design was chosen from 158 entries.

The stamp is numbered on the front. It sold for $3.25. There were 38,000 stamps printed.

The print is 6½″ x 9″. The edition consists of 1000 signed and numbered prints, some of which have remarques in color and some in pencil.

1983

NINTH ILLINOIS DUCK STAMP

Bluebills
Bart Kassabaum

The original art depicts two Lesser Scaup in flight. The design was chosen from 83 entries.

The stamp is numbered on the front. It sold for $5.50. There were 125,010 stamps printed. The remainders were on sale until March 31, 1985.

The print is 8″ x 10″. The edition consists of 600 signed and numbered prints, some of which have pencil remarques.

1983

EIGHTH INDIANA DUCK STAMP

Snow Geese
Keith Freeman

The original art depicts three Snow Geese in flight over water. The design was chosen from 123 entries.

The stamp is numbered on the back. It sold for $5.00. There were 50,000 stamps printed.

The print is 9″ x 12″. The edition consists of 60 signed and numbered prints. The print is entitled *Sunset Flight*.

1983
TWELFTH IOWA DUCK STAMP

Sunset Widgeon
Tom Bridgford

The original art depicts three Widgeon in flight. The design was chosen from 37 entries.

The stamp is not numbered. It sold for $5.00. Of the 100,000 stamps that were printed, 42,981 were sold. The remainders were sold until April 1, 1984.

The print is 6½" x 11". The edition consists of 600 signed and numbered prints, some of which have pencil remarques.

1983
TENTH MARYLAND DUCK STAMP

Wood Duck
Roger Lent

The original art depicts a Wood Duck drake sitting on a tree branch. The design was chosen from 209 entries.

The stamp is numbered on an attached tab. It sold for $3.00. All of the 80,000 stamps that were printed were sold.

The print, entitled *Holly Swamp*, is 6½" x 9". The edition consists of 1200 signed and numbered prints, some of which have pencil remarques. There are also 175 signed and numbered color remarques.

1983
TENTH MASSACHUSETTS DUCK STAMP

Redhead Decoy
Randy Julius

The original art depicts a Redhead decoy carved by H. Keyes Chadwick. The design was chosen from 63 entries.

The stamp is not numbered. It sold for $1.25. There were 40,800 stamps printed. The remainders were on sale until January 1, 1986.

The print is 4¼" x 8⅞". The edition consists of 250 signed and numbered prints. There are also 125 separately numbered and remarqued color artist's proofs.

1983
EIGHTH MICHIGAN DUCK STAMP

Wood Ducks
Rod Lawrence

The original art depicts a pair of Wood Ducks on calm water. The design was chosen from 101 entries.

The stamp is numbered on the front. It sold for $3.75. There were 130,000 stamps printed. The remainders were sold until December 31, 1984.

The print is 6½″ x 9″. The edition consists of 950 signed and numbered prints, some of which have remarques in pencil and some in color.

1983
SEVENTH MINNESOTA DUCK STAMP

Blue Geese—Snow Goose
Gary Moss

The original art depicts the geese standing in water close to shore. The design was chosen from 202 entries.

The stamp is numbered on the back. It sold for $3.75. There were 250,000 stamps printed.

The print is 6½″ x 9″. The edition consists of 5000 signed and numbered prints.

1983
EIGHTH MISSISSIPPI DUCK STAMP

Lesser Scaup
Jerrie Glasper

The original art depicts a pair of Lesser Scaup swimming in calm water. The design was chosen from 53 entries.

The stamp is numbered on the front. It sold for $2.00. There were 50,000 stamps printed.

The print is 6½″ x 10″. The edition consists of 500 signed and numbered prints, some of which have remarques in color and in pencil.

1983
FIFTH MISSOURI DUCK STAMP

Blue-Winged Teal
Doug Ross

The original art depicts a pair of Blue-Winged Teal, one in the water and one on a sunken branch. It was chosen from 64 entries.

The stamp is numbered on the front. It sold for $3.00. There were 130,000 stamps printed. The remainders were sold until December 31, 1984.

The print is 6½″ x 9″. The edition consists of 1000 signed and numbered prints, some of which are remarqued in color and some in pencil.

1983
FIFTH NEVADA DUCK STAMP

Gadwalls
Charles Allen

The original art depicts a pair of Gadwalls in flight. The design was chosen from 156 entries. Mr. Allen also won the California Duck Stamp contest in 1983, making him the first artist to win two different state waterfowl contests in the same year.

The stamp is numbered on the front. It sold for $2.00. There were 25,000 stamps printed.

The print is 6½″ x 9″. The edition consists of 1990 signed and numbered prints, some of which have remarques in color and some in pencil.

1983
FIRST NEW HAMPSHIRE DUCK STAMP

Wood Ducks
Richard Plasschaert

The original art depicts a pair of Wood Ducks in flight. Mr. Plasschaert became the first artist to design three "first-of-state" waterfowl stamp prints when he was commissioned to do this design.

The stamp is numbered on the front. It sold for $4.00. There were 100,000 printed. The remainders were destroyed on April 1, 1984.

The print is 6½" x 9". The edition consists of 5507 signed and numbered prints. There are, separately, 400 artist's proofs.

1983
FIRST NORTH CAROLINA DUCK STAMP

Mallards
Richard Plasschaert

The original art depicts a pair of Mallards landing on the water. The artist was selected by bid proposal to design the state's initial stamp.

The stamp is not numbered. It sold for $5.50. There were 100,000 stamps printed. The remainders were sold until June 30, 1984.

The print is 6½" x 9". The edition consists of 13,652 signed and numbered prints.

1983
SECOND NORTH DAKOTA DUCK STAMP

Mallards
Terry Redlin

The original art depicts a pair of Mallards in flight.

The stamp is numbered on the front. It sold for $9.00. There were 160,000 stamps printed. The remainders were sold until December 31, 1986.

The print is 6½″ x 9″. The edition consists of 3438 signed and numbered prints.

1983
SECOND OHIO DUCK STAMP

In for the Evening
Harry Antis

The original art depicts a pair of Mallards preparing to land. The state of Ohio invited 25 selected artists to participate in the first contest to determine artwork for the waterfowl stamp. Six artists participated.

The stamp is not numbered. It sold for $5.75. There were 100,000 stamps printed. The remainders were sold until December 31, 1984.

The print is 6½″ x 9″. The edition consists of 1350 signed and numbered prints.

1983
FOURTH OKLAHOMA DUCK STAMP

Wood Ducks
Gerald Mobley

The original art depicts a pair of Wood Ducks swimming. The design was chosen from 31 entries.

The stamp is numbered on the back. It sold for $4.00. There were 40,000 stamps printed.

The print is 6½″ x 9″. The edition consists of 1980 signed and numbered prints, some of which have remarques in pencil and some in color.

1983

FIRST PENNSYLVANIA DUCK STAMP

Sycamore Creek Woodies
Ned Smith

The original art depicts a pair of Wood Ducks in flight. The artist was commissioned to design the artwork.

The stamp is not numbered. It sold for $5.50. There were 55,000 stamps printed. The remainders were sold until December 31, 1984.

The print is 6½" x 9". The edition consists of 7380 signed and numbered prints. There are also 625 gold medallions.

1983

THIRD SOUTH CAROLINA DUCK STAMP

Pintails
Jim Killen

The original art depicts two Pintails in flight. The design was chosen from 136 entries.

The stamp sold to hunters is numbered on the back; the stamp sold to collectors is not numbered. Of the 99,960 stamps that were printed, 29,117 were sold. The remainders were sold until April 1, 1984.

The print is 6⅜" x 9". The edition consists of 4000 signed and numbered prints, some of which have remarques in color and some in pencil.

1983

FIFTH TENNESSEE DUCK STAMP

Pintails on the Water
Thompson Phillip Crowe IV

The original art depicts a pair of Pintails swimming in calm water. The design was chosen from 37 entries.

The stamp is numbered on the front. It sold for $6.50. There were 50,000 stamps printed. The remainders were sold until November 30, 1984.

The print is 6½" x 9". The edition consists of 1000 signed and numbered prints. There are, separately, 250 color remarques as well as artist's proofs.

1983
THIRD TEXAS DUCK STAMP

American Widgeon
Maynard Reece

The original art depicts a pair of American Widgeon in flight. The artist was selected by bid proposal.

The stamp is numbered on the front. It sold for $5.00. There were 250,000 stamps printed.

The print is 6½" x 9". The edition consists of 7700 signed and numbered prints.

1983
SIXTH WISCONSIN DUCK STAMP

Blue-Winged Teal
Rockne Knuth

The original art depicts a pair of Blue-Winged Teal swimming in calm water. The design was chosen from 154 entries. Mr. Knuth is the state's first two-time winner of the annual waterfowl stamp contest.

The stamp is numbered on an attached tab. It sold for $3.25. There were 160,000 stamps printed.

The print is 6½" x 9". The edition consists of 1550 signed and numbered prints, some of which have remarques in pencil and some in watercolor.

1984–85
FIFTY-FIRST FEDERAL DUCK STAMP

Untitled (Widgeon)
William C. Morris

The original art is a 5" x 7" acrylic watercolor painting of Widgeon in the water. It was chosen in open national competition from 1582 entries.

The stamp was printed in full color and sold for $7.50. The first day of sale was July 2, 1984; 1,913,509 were sold.

The print is a 6½" x 9" four-color photolithograph, using special lite-fast inks on Rising Mirage stock. The separation negative maker and the printer was Mueller-Krus. The first edition consists of 20,400 regular and 11,500 with companion piece. The prints are numbered.

1984
SIXTH ALABAMA DUCK STAMP

Buffleheads
William Morris

The original art depicts a pair of Buffleheads
swimming. The design was chosen from 36
entries.

The stamp is numbered on the front. It sold
for $5.25. There were 18,000 stamps printed.

The print is 6½″ x 9″. The edition consists of
1500 signed and numbered prints, some of
which have pencil remarques.

1984
FOURTH ARKANSAS DUCK STAMP

Pintails
Larry Hayden

The original art depicts a pair of Pintails swimming gracefully on the water. The artwork was selected by bid proposal.

The stamp is numbered on the back. It sold for $5.50. There were 100,000 stamps printed. The remainders were sold until July 1, 1987.

The print is 6½″ x 9″. The edition consists of 7200 signed and numbered prints. There are also an Executive Edition of 500 and a Special Edition of 600. The latter two editions were offered with gold medallions.

1984
FOURTEENTH CALIFORNIA DUCK STAMP

Golden State Decoy
Robert Montanucci

The original art depicts a Mallard decoy. The design was chosen from 114 entries.

The stamp is numbered on the front. It sold for $7.50. There were 200,000 stamps printed.

The print is 6½″ x 9″. The edition consists of 950 signed and numbered and 250 Executive Series prints. In addition, 375 gold medallions were struck and numbered 1 to 375. The medallions were available for all editions.

1984
FIFTH DELAWARE DUCK STAMP

Mallards
Nolan Haan

The original art depicts a pair of Mallards in the water. The design was chosen from 144 entries.

The stamp is not numbered (sheets were). It sold for $5.00. There were 35,000 stamps printed. The remainders were sold until July 1, 1987.

The print is 6½″ x 9″. The edition consists of 1980 signed and numbered prints, some of which have pencil remarques.

1984
SIXTH FLORIDA DUCK STAMP

Hooded Merganser
John Taylor

The original art depicts a single Hooded Merganser swimming in calm water. The design was chosen from 180 entries.

The stamp is numbered on the front. It sold for $3.25. There were 38,000 stamps printed.

The print is 6½″ x 9″. The edition consists of 1000 signed and numbered prints, some of which have remarques in pencil.

1984
TENTH ILLINOIS DUCK STAMP

Blue-Winged Teal
George Kieffer

The original art depicts a pair of Blue-Winged Teal on the water. The design was chosen from 71 entries.

The stamp is numbered on the front. It sold for $5.50. There were 105,000 stamps printed. The remainders were on sale until April 1, 1986.

The print is 8″ x 10″. The edition consists of 600 signed and numbered prints, some of which have color remarques.

1984
NINTH INDIANA DUCK STAMP

Windy Retreat
Lyn Briggs

The original art depicts a pair of Redheads coming in to land on rough water. The design was chosen from 134 entries.

The stamp is numbered on the back. It sold for $5.00. There were 51,000 stamps printed.

The print is 7″ x 10″. The edition consists of 70 signed and numbered prints.

LARRY ZACH 1983

1984
THIRTEENTH IOWA DUCK STAMP

Wood Ducks
Larry Zach

The original art depicts a pair of Wood Ducks in the water. The design was chosen from 38 entries.

The stamp is not numbered. It sold for $5.00. There were 100,000 stamps printed. The remainders were sold until March 1, 1985.

The print is 6½" x 11". The edition consists of 600 signed and numbered prints, 60 of which have pencil remarques.

1984
FIRST MAINE DUCK STAMP

Black Ducks
David Maass

The original art depicts a pair of Black Ducks in flight. The artist was selected by bid proposal.

The stamp is numbered on the front. It sold for $2.50. There were 60,000 stamps printed. The remainders were sold until July 1, 1985.

The print is 6½" x 9". The edition consists of 11,115 signed and numbered prints and 1730 gold medallions.

1984
ELEVENTH MARYLAND DUCK STAMP

Black Duck
Carla Huber

The original art depicts a single Black Duck in flight. The design was chosen from 213 entries.

The stamp is numbered on an attached tab. It sold for $6.00. There were 80,000 stamps printed. The remainders were on sale until November 28, 1985.

The print is 6½" x 9". The edition consists of 1400 signed and numbered prints, some of which have remarques in pencil and some in color.

1984
ELEVENTH MASSACHUSETTS DUCK STAMP

Scoter Decoy
Joseph Cibula

The original art depicts a White-Winged Scoter decoy carved by S.A. Fabens. The design was chosen from 67 entries.

The stamp is not numbered. It sold for $1.25. There were the 40,800 stamps printed. The remainders were on sale until January 1, 1987.

The print is 4½" x 9". The edition consists of 420 signed and numbered prints, 120 of which are color remarques.

1984
NINTH MICHIGAN DUCK STAMP

Pintails
Larry Cory

The original art depicts Pintails in flight. The design was chosen from 90 entries.

The stamp is numbered on the front. It sold for $3.75. There were 110,000 stamps printed. The remainders were sold until December 31, 1985.

The print is 6½" x 9". The edition consists of 950 signed and numbered prints, some of which have remarques in pencil and some in watercolor.

1984
EIGHTH MINNESOTA DUCK STAMP

Wood Ducks
Thomas Gross

The original art depicts three Wood Ducks on the water. The design was chosen from 173 entries.

The stamp is numbered on the back. It sold for $3.75. There were 250,000 stamps printed.

The print is 5⅞" x 8⅞". The edition consists of 4200 signed and numbered prints, some of which have pencil remarques.

1984
NINTH MISSISSIPPI DUCK STAMP

Two Black Ducks Flying
Tommy Goodman

The original art depicts a pair of Black Ducks in flight. The design was chosen from 65 entries.

The stamp is numbered on the front. It sold for $2.00. There were 45,000 stamps printed.

The print is 6½" x 9". The edition consists of 500 signed and numbered prints, some of which have pencil and color remarques.

1984
SIXTH MISSOURI DUCK STAMP

Mallards
Glenn Chambers

The original art depicts a pair of Mallards swimming in calm water. The design was chosen from 44 entries.

The stamp is numbered on the front. It sold for $3.00. There were 130,000 stamps printed. The remainders were sold until December 31, 1985.

The print is 6½″ x 9″. The edition consists of 1000 signed and numbered prints, some of which are remarques in color and some in pencil.

1984
SIXTH NEVADA DUCK STAMP

Pintails at Stillwater
Robert Steiner

The original art depicts a pair of Pintails in flight. The design was chosen from 314 entries.

The stamp is numbered on the front. It sold for $2.00. There were 25,000 stamps printed.

The print is 6½″ x 9″. The edition consists of 1990 signed and numbered prints, some of which have remarques in color and some in pencil.

1984
SECOND NEW HAMPSHIRE DUCK STAMP

Mallards
Phillip Crowe

The original art depicts a pair of Mallards in flight. The artist was selected by bid proposal.

The stamp is numbered on the front. It sold for $4.00. There were 51,000 stamps printed. The remainders were sold until March 31, 1985.

The print is 6½″ x 9″. The edition consists of 5507 signed and numbered prints. There are also 200 color artist's proofs numbered separately.

1984
FIRST NEW JERSEY DUCK STAMP

Canvasbacks
Tom Hirata

The original art depicts a pair of Canvasbacks swimming in calm water. The artist was chosen by bid competition.

The stamp is numbered on the front. It sold for $2.50 resident and $5.00 nonresident. The number of stamps printed was 102,000 resident and 102,000 nonresident. The remainders were sold until December 31, 1985.

The print is 6½″ x 9″. The edition consists of 10,011 signed and numbered prints with 1210 gold medallions. There is an Executive Edition with 650 color remarques and gold medallions. There are 150 artist's proofs, numbered separately, with color remarques and gold medallions.

1984
SECOND NORTH CAROLINA DUCK STAMP

Wood Ducks
Jim Killen

The original art depicts a pair of Wood Ducks in flight. The artist was selected by bid proposal.

The stamp is not numbered. It sold for $5.50. There were 100,050 stamps printed. The remainders were sold until December 31, 1985.

The print is 6½″ x 9″. The edition consists of 5020 signed and numbered prints, some of which have color remarques.

1984
THIRD NORTH DAKOTA DUCK STAMP

Canvasbacks
David Maass

The original art depicts Canvasbacks in flight over water.

The stamp is numbered on the front. It sold for $9.00. There were 160,000 stamps printed.

The print is 6½″ x 9″. The edition consists of 3438 signed and numbered prints. There are, separately, 340 artist's proofs.

1984
THIRD OHIO DUCK STAMP

Green-Winged Teal
Harold Roe

The original art depicts a pair of Green-Winged Teal on the water. The design was chosen from 28 entries.

The stamp is not numbered. It sold for $5.75. There were 100,000 stamps printed. The remainders were sold until December 31, 1985.

The print is 6½" x 9". The edition consists of 2000 signed and numbered prints, 100 color remarques, and 200 pencil remarques.

1984
FIFTH OKLAHOMA DUCK STAMP

Ring-Necked Ducks
Hoyt Smith

The original art depicts a pair of Ring-Necked Ducks swimming in calm water. The design was chosen from 39 entries.

The stamp is numbered on the back. It sold for $4.00. There were 40,000 stamps printed.

The print is 6½″ x 9″. The edition consists of 1980 signed and numbered prints, some of which have remarques in pencil and some in color.

1984
FIRST OREGON DUCK STAMP

Canada Geese
Michael Sieve

The original art depicts Canada Geese in flight.

The stamp is numbered on the front. It sold for $5.00. There were 120,000 stamps printed. The remainders were sold until June 30, 1985.

The print, entitled *Dusky Canada Geese,* is 6½″ x 9″. The edition consists of 11,825 signed and numbered prints. There are also 2975 silver medallions.

1984

SECOND PENNSYLVANIA DUCK STAMP

Canada Geese
Jim Killen

The original art depicts three Canada Geese swimming in calm water. The artist was commissioned.

The stamp is not numbered. It sold for $5.50. There were 40,000 stamps printed. The remainders were sold until December 31, 1986.

The print is 6½" x 9". The edition consists of 7380 signed and numbered prints. There is also a series of 625 gold/silver medallions.

1984

FOURTH SOUTH CAROLINA DUCK STAMP

Canada Geese
Al Dornisch

The original art depicts a flock of Canada Geese in flight. The design was chosen from 238 entries.

The stamp sold to hunters is numbered on the back; the stamp sold to collectors is not numbered. There were 99,960 stamps printed. The stamps were sold until April 1, 1985.

The print is 6½" x 9". The edition consists of 4000 signed and numbered prints, some of which have color remarques.

1984
SIXTH TENNESSEE DUCK STAMP

Black Ducks
Allen Hughes

The original art depicts a pair of Black Ducks in flight. The design was chosen from 37 entries.

The stamp is numbered on the front. It sold for $6.50. There were 50,000 stamps printed. The remainders were sold until November 30, 1985.

The print is 6½" x 9". The edition consists of 1250 signed and numbered prints, some of which are pencil remarques. There are 250 color artist's proofs in a separate edition.

1984
FOURTH TEXAS DUCK STAMP

Wood Ducks
David Maass

The original art depicts a pair of Wood Ducks in flight. The artist was commissioned.

The stamp is numbered on the front. It sold for $5.00. There were 210,000 stamps printed.

The print is 6½" x 9". The edition consists of 9400 signed and numbered prints.

1984
SEVENTH WISCONSIN DUCK STAMP

Hooded Mergansers
Michael J. Riddet

The original art depicts a pair of Hooded Mergansers swimming in calm water. The design was chosen from 44 entries.

The stamp is numbered on an attached tab. It sold for $3.25. There were 160,000 stamps printed.

The print is 6½″ x 9″. The edition consists of 1500 signed and numbered prints. There are separate editions of 100 watercolor and 200 pencil remarques.

1985–1986
FIFTY-SECOND FEDERAL DUCK STAMP

Untitled (Cinnamon Teal)
Gerald Mobley

The original art is a 5″ x 7″ opaque watercolor painting of a Cinnamon Teal drake in its spring plumage gliding on calm water. It was chosen in open national competition from 1515 entries.

The stamp was printed in full color and sold for $7.50. The first day of sale was July 1, 1985; 1,779,299 were sold.

The print is a 6½″ x 9″ four-color photolithograph, using special lite-fast inks on acid-free Rising Mirage stock. The separation negative maker and the printer was Mueller-Krus. The first edition consists of 18,200 regular prints and 6650 with companion piece. The prints are signed and numbered but not titled. A Medallion Edition of 6650, consisting of a matching numbered print and a gold-plated medallion, were also made available.

1985
SEVENTH ALABAMA DUCK STAMP

Wood Ducks
Larry Martin

The original art depicts a pair of Wood Ducks in a unique bi-level design (the first time a bi-level design appears in a stamp print). It was chosen from 52 entries.

The stamp is numbered on the front. It sold for $6.00. There were 18,000 stamps printed.

The print is 6½″ x 9″. The edition consists of 1280 signed and numbered and a separate Executive Edition of 380 14½″ x 18″ prints. Porcelain and bronze sculptures were also made available.

1985
FIRST ALASKA DUCK STAMP

Emperor Geese
Daniel Smith

The original art depicts a trio of Emperor Geese standing in the snow. For this first–of–state Alaska Duck Stamp, the Alaska Fish and Game Department selected Mr. Smith to create the design.

The stamp is numbered on the back. It sold for $5.00. There were 130,020 stamps printed.

The print is 6½″ x 9″. The edition consists of 14,650 signed and numbered prints and 2450 gold-plated medallions with prints. Also available was an Executive Edition of 250, consisting of print with color remarque and medallion.

1985
FIFTH ARKANSAS DUCK STAMP

Bayou DeView Mallards
Ken Carlson

The original art depicts Mallard ducks. The artist was selected to create this stamp/print design. The publisher issued two duck leg bands with each stamp and print set. This was to recognize the country's bird-banding program.

The stamp is numbered on the back. It sold for $5.50. There were 100,000 stamps printed.

The print is 6½″ x 9″. The edition consists of 7200 signed and numbered prints, 600 Special Series prints, and 500 Executive Series prints. A color etching accompanies each print in the latter two series.

1985

FIFTEENTH CALIFORNIA DUCK STAMP

Ring-Necks
Richard L. Wilson

The original art depicts a Ring-Necked drake and hen swimming. The design was chosen from 109 entries.

The stamp is numbered on the front. It sold for $7.50. There were 200,000 stamps printed.

The print is 6½" x 9". The edition was time-limited, with a minimum number of 950 signed and numbered prints. In addition, there were 250 Executive Edition prints and 350 silver medallions. Pencil and color re-marques were also available.

1985

SIXTH DELAWARE DUCK STAMP

Pintail
Don Breyfogle

The original art depicts a Pintail drake. The design was chosen from 139 entries.

The stamp is not numbered (sheets were). It sold for $5.00. There were 35,000 stamps printed.

The print, entitled *Autumn Song,* is 6½" x 9". The edition consists of 1980 signed and num-bered prints, some of which have pencil or color remarques.

1985

SEVENTH FLORIDA DUCK STAMP

Wood Ducks
Bob Binks

The original art was chosen from more than 40 entries. Mr. Binks is the first two-time win-ner of the Florida contest.

The stamp is numbered on the front. It sold for $3.25. There were 45,000 stamps printed.

The print is 6½" x 9". The edition consists of 1000 signed and numbered prints; pencil re-marques were available with this edition.

1985

FIRST GEORGIA DUCK STAMP

Wood Ducks
Daniel Smith

The original art was chosen from 37 entries. Mr. Smith, who also won the 1985 Alaska competition, is the first artist to win two first-of-state competitions in the same year.

The stamp is not numbered. It sold for $5.50. There were 105,020 stamps printed.

The print is 6½″ x 9″. The edition consists of 14,100 signed and numbered prints. Also available were a Medallion Edition of 1460 and an Executive Edition of 250, consisting of print, medallion, and color remarque.

1985

ELEVENTH ILLINOIS DUCK STAMP

Redheads
Bart Kassabaum

The original art depicts a pair of Redheads in flight over a marsh. The design was chosen from 66 entries.

The stamp is numbered on the front. It sold for $5.50. There were 177,450 stamps printed.

The print is 8″ x 10″. The edition consists of 600 signed and numbered prints; pencil remarques were available with this edition.

1985

TENTH INDIANA DUCK STAMP

Pintail
Rick Pas

The original art depicts a lone Pintail drake. The design was chosen from 274 entries.

The stamp is numbered on the back. It sold for $5.00. There were 51,000 stamps printed.

The print is 9¾″ x 7″. The edition consists of 95 signed and numbered prints.

1985
FOURTEENTH IOWA DUCK STAMP

The Drake Decoy
Jack C. Hahn

The original art depicts a Mallard drake and an antique wooden decoy. The design was chosen from 37 entries.

The stamp is not numbered. It sold for $5.00. There were 80,000 stamps printed.

The print is 6½″ x 11″. The edition consists of 600 signed and numbered prints; pencil remarques were available with this edition.

1985
FIRST KENTUCKY DUCK STAMP

Mallards
Ray Harm

The original art for this first-of-state stamp/print design depicts a pair of Mallards coming in for a landing over the trees. The design was commissioned from the artist.

The stamp is numbered on the front. It sold for $5.25. There were 45,000 stamps printed.

The print is 6½″ x 9″. The edition consists of 8189 signed and numbered prints. Added to this were 566 signed and numbered prints with gold medallion, 60 signed and numbered prints with medallion and pencil remarque, and 273 signed and numbered prints with medallion and color remarque.

1985
SECOND MAINE DUCK STAMP

Common Eiders
David Maass

The original art depicts a trio of Common Eiders, sea ducks, in flight over open water with the famous Pemaquid Lighthouse in the background. The artist was commissioned to design the state's duck stamp for the second consecutive year.

The stamp is numbered on the front. It sold for $2.50. There were 60,000 stamps printed.

The print is 6½″ x 9″. The edition consists of 2330 signed and numbered prints. Also available were 270 gold-plated bronze medallions.

1985
TWELFTH MARYLAND DUCK STAMP

Canada Geese
David Turnbaugh

The original art depicts a scene of Canada Geese in a snowstorm. The design was chosen from 183 entries.

The stamp is numbered on an attached tab. It sold for $6.00. There were 85,000 stamps printed.

The print is 6½" x 9". The edition consists of 1400 signed and numbered prints; pencil and color remarques were available with this edition.

1985
TWELFTH MASSACHUSETTS DUCK STAMP

Ruddy Duck Decoy
Randy Julius

The original art depicts a Ruddy Duck decoy carved by Joe Lincoln. The design was chosen from 56 entries.

The stamp is not numbered. It sold for $1.25. There were 40,800 stamps printed.

The print is 4¾" x 10³⁄₁₆". The edition consists of 250 signed and numbered prints; 125 separately numbered color remarques were also available.

1985
TENTH MICHIGAN DUCK STAMP

Ring-Necks
Robert Steiner

The original art depicts Ring-Necks in flight. The design was chosen from 150 entries.

The stamp is numbered on the front. It sold for $3.75. There were 110,000 printed.

The print is 6½" x 9". The edition consists of 980 signed and numbered prints; pencil and color remarques were available with this edition. Also available was an Executive Edition of 10, consisting of print, gold-plated medallion, and color remarque.

1985
NINTH MINNESOTA DUCK STAMP

White-Fronted Geese
Terry Redlin

The original art depicts a pair of White-Fronted Geese feeding on the shore. The design was chosen from 172 entries.

The stamp is numbered on the back. It sold for $3.75. There were 250,000 stamps printed.

The print is 6½″ x 9″. The edition consists of 4385 signed and numbered prints.

1985
TENTH MISSISSIPPI DUCK STAMP

Mallards
Lottie Fulton

The original art was chosen from 50 entries.

The stamp is numbered on the front. It sold for $2.00. There were 50,000 stamps printed.

The print is 6½″ x 9″. The edition consists of 500 signed and numbered prints; pencil and color remarques were available with this edition.

1985
SEVENTH MISSOURI DUCK STAMP

Widgeon
Ron Clayton

The original art depicts a scene of Widgeon. The design was chosen from 49 entries.

The stamp is numbered on the front. It sold for $3.00. There were 130,000 stamps printed.

The print is 6½″ x 9″. The edition consists of 1000 signed and numbered prints; pencil and color remarques were available with this edition.

1985
SEVENTH NEVADA DUCK STAMP

Lesser Canada Geese
Richard Wilson

The original art depicts a pair of Lesser Canada Geese. The design was chosen from 218 entries.

The stamp is numbered on the front. It sold for $2.00. There were 25,000 stamps printed.

The print is 6½" x 9". The edition consists of 2000 signed and numbered prints, some of which have pencil or color remarques. Available also were 300 silver medallions.

1985
THIRD NEW HAMPSHIRE DUCK STAMP

Blue-Winged Teal
Tom Hirata

The original art was chosen by bid proposal.

The stamp is numbered on the front. It sold for $4.00. There were 51,000 stamps printed.

The print is 6½" x 9". The edition consists of 5507 signed and numbered prints. Added to this were 250 artist's proofs and color remarques.

1985
SECOND NEW JERSEY DUCK STAMP

Mallards
David Maass

The original art depicts a pair of Mallards rising from a marsh. The design was commissioned from the artist.

The stamp is numbered on the front. It sold for $2.50 ($5.00 nonresident). There were 162,000 stamps printed.

The print is 6½" x 9". The edition consists of 10,011 signed and numbered prints; the Medallion Edition comprises 1210 prints and medallions. Also available were an Executive Edition of 650 consisting of an embossed print and medallion and an Artist's-Proof Edition of 150 consisting of embossed print, medallion, and remarque.

1985
FIRST NEW YORK DUCK STAMP

Canada Geese
Larry Barton

The original art depicts a flock of Canada Geese in flight. The artist was selected to create the design.

The stamp is numbered on the front. It sold for $5.50. There were 200,010 stamps printed.

The print is 6½″ x 9″. The edition consisted of 14,040 signed and numbered prints; 1035 silver medallions were also available. Also available were an Executive Edition of 580, consisting of print, medallion, and remarque, and an Artist's Proof Edition of 250, consisting of artist's proof print, medallion, and remarque.

1985

THIRD NORTH CAROLINA DUCK STAMP

Canvasbacks
Tom Hirata

The original art was chosen from 12 bid proposals.

The stamp is not numbered. It sold for $5.50. There were 100,050 stamps printed.

The print is 6½″ x 9″. The edition consists of 5020 signed and numbered prints; 100 gold-plated medallions were also available. Also available was an Artist's Proof Edition of 150, consisting of artist's proof print, medallion, and color remarque.

1985

FOURTH NORTH DAKOTA DUCK STAMP

Lesser Scaup
Leslie C. Kouba

The original art depicts a scene with Lesser Scaup. The artist was commissioned to create the design.

The stamp is numbered on the front. It sold for $9.00. There were 160,000 stamps printed.

The print is 6½″ x 9″. The edition consists of 3438 signed and numbered prints. Also available were 340 artist's proof prints.

1985
FOURTH OHIO DUCK STAMP

Redheads
Ronald J. Louque

The original art was chosen from 37 entries.

The stamp is not numbered. It sold for $5.75. There were 75,000 stamps printed.

The print is 6½" x 9". The edition consists of 2000 signed and numbered prints. An additional 200 pencil and 100 color remarques were also available.

1985
SIXTH OKLAHOMA DUCK STAMP

Mallards
Gerald Mobley

The original art depicts a pair of Mallards swimming in calm water. The design was chosen from 33 entries.

The stamp is numbered on the back. It sold for $4.00. There were 40,000 stamps printed.

The print is 6½" x 9". The edition consists of 1980 signed and numbered prints.

1985
SECOND OREGON DUCK STAMP

Snow Geese
Michael Sieve

The original art depicts a trio of Snow Geese in flight. The design was chosen from 49 entries.

The stamp is numbered on the front. It sold for $5.00. There were 120,000 stamps printed.

The print is 6½" x 9". The edition consists of 11,825 signed and numbered prints. Also available were 2975 silver medallions and 500 bronze sculptures designed by George Northup.

1985
THIRD PENNSYLVANIA DUCK STAMP

Mallards
Ned Smith

The original art depicts a pair of Mallards rising into flight. The artist was commissioned to create the design.

The stamp is not numbered. It sold for $5.50. There were 40,000 stamps printed.

The print is 6½" x 9". The edition consists of 7380 signed and numbered prints. Also available were 625 gold-plated silver medallions.

1985
FIFTH SOUTH CAROLINA DUCK STAMP

Green-Winged Teal
Rosemary Millette

The original art was chosen from 188 entries.

The stamp sold to hunters is numbered on the back; the stamp sold to collectors is not numbered. In either case, it sold for $5.50. There were 99,960 stamps printed.

The print is 6½" x 9". The edition consists of 4000 signed and numbered prints; pencil remarques were available with this edition.

1985
SEVENTH TENNESSEE DUCK STAMP

Blue-Winged Teal
Jimmy Stewart

The original art depicts a pair of Blue-Winged Teal in calm water. The design was chosen from 35 entries.

The stamp is numbered on the front. It sold for $6.50. There were 50,000 stamps printed.

The print is 6½" x 9". The edition consists of 1000 signed and numbered prints and 250 artist's proof prints with color remarques.

1985
FIFTH TEXAS DUCK STAMP

Blue Geese
John Cowan

The original art depicts Blue Geese in a rice field. The artist was commissioned to create the design.

The stamp is numbered on the front. It sold for $5.00. There were 210,000 stamps printed.

The print is 6½" x 9". The edition consists of 11,300 signed and numbered prints. Also available were 1200 medallions.

1985
EIGHTH WISCONSIN DUCK STAMP

Lesser Scaup
Greg Alexander

The original art depicts a pair of Lesser Scaup, or Bluebills. The design was chosen from 76 entries.

The stamp is numbered on an attached tab. It sold for $3.25. There were 160,000 stamps printed.

The print is 6½" x 9". The edition consists of 1250 signed and numbered prints. Also available were a pencil remarque edition of 100 and a watercolor remarque edition of 50, both separately numbered.

1985
FIRST WYOMING DUCK STAMP

Canada Geese
Robert Kusserow

The original art depicts three Canada Geese by the water's edge. It was chosen from 30 entries.

The stamp, printed in full color, is numbered on the front and sold for $5.00. There were 450,000 printed.

The print measures 6½″ x 9″. The edition consists of 4,750 signed and numbered prints. In addition there is an Executive edition of 250 prints plus 250 artist's proofs with remarques.

1986–87

FIFTY-THIRD FEDERAL DUCK STAMP

Fulvous Whistling Duck
Burton E. Moore, Jr.

The original art is an acrylic-on-Masonite paint-ing of a Fulvous Whistling Duck in the water. ("Fulvous" refers to the duck's deep yellow or tawny color.) The design was chosen from 1242 entries.

The stamp, which was unnumbered, was printed in full color and sold for $7.50. The first day of sale was July 1, 1986. Four mil-lion were printed; it is not known how many were sold.

The print, 6½″ x 9″, is acrylic on Masonite, using fade-resistant inks on 100% acid-free rag stock. The separation negative maker and printer was Mueller-Krus. The first edition consists of 16,310. Also available was a Me-dallion Edition of 4,670.

1986

EIGHTH ALABAMA DUCK STAMP

Canada Geese
Danny W. Dorning

The original art, depicting a pair of Canada Geese, was chosen from 74 entries.

The stamp is numbered on the front. It sold for $6.00. There were 18,000 stamps printed.

The print is 6½″ x 9″. The edition consists of 1200 signed and numbered prints and a sepa-rate Executive Edition of 450 14″ x 18″ prints. Some of the signed and numbered and Exec-utive Edition sets have color remarques.

1986

SECOND ALASKA DUCK STAMP

Steller's Eiders
James Merger

The original art depicts a pair of Steller's Eider ducks in flight over water. The design was chosen from 27 entries.

The stamp is numbered on the back. It sold for $5.00. There were 81,000 stamps printed.

The print is 6½″ x 9″. The edition consists of 3665 signed and numbered prints and 1075 gold-plated medallions with prints. Also avail-able was an Executive Edition of 250, con-sisting of the print with hand-colored remarque and medallion.

1986

SIXTH ARKANSAS DUCK STAMP

Black Swamp Mallards
John P. Cowan

The original art was commissioned by the Arkansas Game and Fish Commission.

The stamp is numbered on the back. It sold for $5.50. There were 100,000 stamps printed.

The print is 6½" x 9". The edition consists of 7200 signed and numbered prints, 600 Special Series prints, and 500 Executive Series prints. A gold medallion accompanies each print in the latter two series.

1986

SIXTEENTH CALIFORNIA DUCK STAMP

Cackling Canada Goose
Sherrie Russell

The original art depicts a lone Cackling Canada Goose swimming in the water. The design was chosen from 98 entries.

The stamp is numbered on the front. It sold for $7.50. There were 200,000 stamps printed.

The print is 6½" x 9". The edition was time-limited, with a minimum number of 750 signed and numbered prints. Also available were pencil and color remarques and 200 Executive Edition prints.

1986

SEVENTH DELAWARE DUCK STAMP

Misty Morning Widgeon
Robert Leslie

The original art depicts Widgeon in the early morning. The design was chosen from 85 entries.

The stamp is not numbered. It sold for $5.00. There were 35,000 stamps printed.

The print is 6½" x 9". The edition consists of 1980 signed and numbered prints; pencil and color remarques were available with this edition.

1986
EIGHTH FLORIDA DUCK STAMP

Canvasbacks
Robert Steiner

The original art depicts Canvasbacks in flight. The design was selected by the Florida Game and Freshwater Fish Commission by a bid proposal.

The stamp is numbered on the front. It sold for $3.50. There were 42,000 stamps printed.

The print is 6½″ x 9″. The edition consists of 1000 signed and numbered prints; pencil and color remarques were available with this edition.

1986
SECOND GEORGIA DUCK STAMP

Mallards
Jim Killen

The original art depicts three Mallards coming in for a graceful landing in a marsh. Mr. Killen was commissioned to design the art for this year's stamp/print.

The stamp is not numbered. It sold for $5.50. There were 60,000 stamps printed.

The print is 6½″ x 9″. The edition consists of 2264 signed and numbered prints. An additional gold medallion edition of 242 were also available.

1986
TWELFTH ILLINOIS DUCK STAMP

Gadwalls
Art Sinden

The original art was chosen from 57 entries. This marks the second time that Mr. Sinden has won the Illinois contest.

The stamp is numbered on the front. It sold for $5.50. There were 177,450 stamps printed.

The print is 8″ x 10″. The edition consists of 600 signed and numbered prints; pencil remarques were available with this edition.

1986

ELEVENTH INDIANA DUCK STAMP

Wood Duck
Ron Louque

The original art depicts a single Wood Duck drake. The design was chosen from 241 entries.

The stamp is numbered on the front. It sold for $5.00. There were 51,000 stamps printed.

The print is 7½″ x 10″. The edition consists of 119 signed and numbered prints.

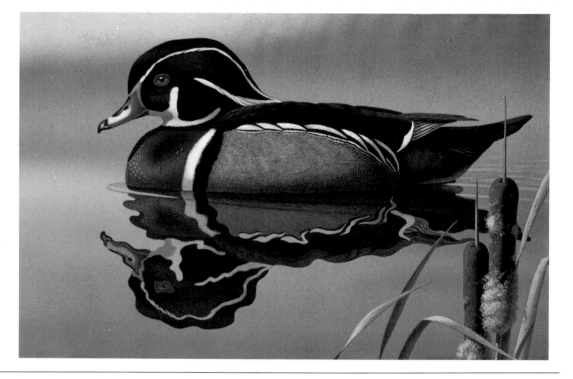

1986

FIFTEENTH IOWA DUCK STAMP

Blue-Winged Teal
Paul Bridgford

The original art depicts a pair of Blue-Winged Teal flying over cattails. The design was chosen from 51 entries. Mr. Bridgford became the first three-time winner of the Iowa Duck Stamp contest with this victory.

The stamp is not numbered. It sold for $5.00. There were 100,000 stamps printed.

The print is 6½″ x 11″. The edition consists of 500 signed and numbered prints; pencil remarques were available with this edition.

1986

SECOND KENTUCKY DUCK STAMP

Wood Ducks
Dave Chapple

The original art depicts a pair of Wood Duck drakes in flight. The design was commissioned from the artist.

The stamp is numbered on the front. It sold for $5.25. There were 45,000 stamps printed.

The print is 6½″ x 9″. The edition consists of 8189 signed and numbered prints. Added to this were 566 signed and numbered prints with gold medallion, 65 signed and numbered prints with companion color etching, and 273 signed and numbered prints with companion color etching and gold medallion.

1986
THIRD MAINE DUCK STAMP

Wood Ducks
David Maass

The original art was again commissioned from David Maass. This was the third year of a special collector's three-year David Maass waterfowl art program.

The stamp is numbered on the front. It sold for $2.50. There were 40,000 stamps printed.

The print is 6½″ x 9″. The edition consists of 1815 signed and numbered prints. Added to this was a Gold-Plated Medallion Edition of 310.

1986
THIRTEENTH MARYLAND DUCK STAMP

Hooded Mergansers
Louis Frisino

The original art depicts a pair of Hooded Mergansers swimming. The design was chosen from 164 entries.

The stamp is numbered on an attached tab. It sold for $6.00. There were 90,000 stamps printed.

The print is 6½″ x 9″. The edition consists of 2000 signed and numbered prints; pencil and color remarques were available with this edition.

1986
THIRTEENTH MASSACHUSETTS DUCK STAMP

Scaup Decoy
Robert Piscatori

The original art depicts a preening drake Bluebill, or Scaup, by an unknown Martha's Vineyard carver. The design was chosen from 52 entries.

The stamp is not numbered. It sold for $1.25. There were 50,400 stamps printed.

The print is 6½″ x 10¼″. The edition consists of 400 signed and numbered prints; pencil and color remarques were available with this edition.

1986
ELEVENTH MICHIGAN DUCK STAMP

Common Goldeneyes
Russell Cobane

The original art depicts a pair of Common Goldeneyes resting in the water near some rocks. The design was chosen from 84 entries.

The stamp is numbered on the front. It sold for $3.75. There were 110,000 stamps printed.

The print is 6½″ x 9″. The edition consists of 950 signed and numbered prints; pencil and color remarques were available with this edition.

1986

TENTH MINNESOTA DUCK STAMP

Lesser Scaup
Brian Jarvi

The original art depicts a pair of Lesser Scaup resting in the water. The design was chosen from 148 entries.

The stamp is numbered on the back. It sold for $5.75. There were 250,000 stamps printed.

The print is 6½" x 9". The edition consists of 3150 signed and numbered prints; pencil and color remarques were also available with this edition.

1986

ELEVENTH MISSISSIPPI DUCK STAMP

American Widgeon
Joe Latil

The original art depicts a pair of American Widgeon standing at the shore of a marsh. The design was chosen from 50 entries.

The stamp is numbered on the front. It sold for $2.00. There were 50,000 stamps printed.

The print is 6½" x 9". The edition consists of 500 signed and numbered prints and a gold-plated, stamp-shaped medallion to accompany each print; pencil and color remarques were also available with this edition.

1986

EIGHTH MISSOURI DUCK STAMP

Hooded Mergansers
Tom Crain

The original art depicts a scene with Hooded Mergansers. The design was chosen from 45 entries.

The stamp is numbered on the front. It sold for $3.00. There were 130,000 stamps printed.

The print is 6½" x 9". The edition consists of 1000 signed and numbered prints; pencil and color remarques were available with this edition.

1986
FIRST MONTANA WATERFOWL STAMP

Canada Geese
Joe Thornbrugh

The original art depicts a flock of Canada Geese flying over mountainous terrain. The design for this first-of-state waterfowl stamp was chosen from 60 entries.

The stamp is numbered on the front. It sold for $5.00. There were 70,000 stamps printed.

The print is 6½″ x 9″. The edition consists of 9212 signed and numbered prints. Also available were a Medallion Edition consisting of 1025 prints and gold-plated medallions, and an Executive Edition consisting of 300 matching prints, gold-plated medallions, and color remarques hand-painted by the artist.

1986
EIGHTH NEVADA DUCK STAMP

Redheads
Nolan Haan

The original art was chosen from 183 entries.

The stamp is numbered on the front. It sold for $2.00. There were 25,000 stamps printed.

The print is 6½″ x 9″. The edition consists of 2000 signed and numbered prints; pencil and color remarques were also available with this edition.

1986
FOURTH NEW HAMPSHIRE DUCK STAMP

Hooded Mergansers
Durant Ball

The original art design was chosen by bid proposal.

The stamp is numbered on the front. It sold for $4.00; 71,000 stamps were printed, in sheets of 30 and in books of 10.

The print is 6½″ x 9″. The edition consists of 5507 signed and numbered prints. Added to this were a Medallion Edition of 500, featuring a gold-plated medallion, and 100 color remarques.

1986
THIRD NEW JERSEY DUCK STAMP

Pintails
by Ronald J. Louque

The original art depicts a pair of Pintails swimming in calm water. The design was commissioned from the artist.

The stamp is numbered on the front. It sold for $2.50 ($5.00 nonresident). There were 102,000 resident stamps printed and 60,000 nonresident stamps.

The print is 6½" x 9" The edition consists of 10,011 signed and numbered prints; the Medallion Edition comprises 1210 prints and medallions. Also available were an Executive Edition of 650, consisting of print, medallion, and color remarque, and an Artist's Proof Edition of 150, consisting of artist's proof print, medallion, and color remarque.

1986
SECOND NEW YORK DUCK STAMP

Mallards
David Maass

The original art depicts a flock of Mallards flying over a marsh. The artist was commissioned to create the design.

The stamp is not numbered. It was sold for $5.50. There were 200,010 stamps printed.

The print is 6½" x 9". The edition consists of 14,040 signed and numbered prints; the Medallion Edition comprises 1035 prints and gold-plated medallions. An Executive Edition of 580 was also available, consisting of print, medallion, and color remarque.

1986
FOURTH NORTH CAROLINA
DUCK STAMP

Canada Geese
Tom Hirata

The original art depicts a pair of Canada Geese swimming in calm water. The artist was chosen for the second time in a row to do the North Carolina Duck Stamp design.

The stamp is not numbered. It sold for $5.50. There were 100,050 stamps printed.

The print is 6½" x 9". The edition was time-limited, with a minimum number of 5020 signed and numbered prints; color remarques were available with this edition. Also available was an Artist's Proof Edition of 150, consisting of artist's proof print and color remarque.

1986
FIFTH NORTH DAKOTA DUCK STAMP

Pintails
Mario Fernandez

The original art depicts a trio of Pintails in the water. The artist was commissioned to create the design.

The stamp is numbered on the front. It sold for $9.00. There were 159,970 stamps printed.

The print is 6½″ x 9″. The edition consists of 3438 signed and numbered prints. Also available were 340 artist's proof prints.

1986
FIFTH OHIO DUCK STAMP

Canvasback
Lynn Kaatz

The original art depicts a Canvasback drake at rest in quiet water. The design was chosen from 47 entries.

The stamp is not numbered. It sold for $5.75. There were 60,000 stamps printed.

The print is 6½″ x 9″. The edition consists of 2000 signed and numbered prints, including 100 color remarques.

1986

SEVENTH OKLAHOMA DUCK STAMP

Snow Geese
Hoyt Smith

The original art depicts a pair of Snow Geese in flight. The design was chosen from 33 entries.

The stamp is numbered on the back. It sold for $4.00. There were 35,500 stamps printed.

The print is 6½" x 9". The edition consists of 1980 signed and numbered prints; pencil or color remarques were also available with this edition.

1986

THIRD OREGON DUCK STAMP

Pacific Black Brant
Michael Sieve

The original art depicts a coastal Brant hunt in the early days of Oregon. The design was chosen from 45 entries.

The stamp is numbered on the front. It sold for $5.00. There were 90,000 stamps printed.

The print is 6½" x 9". The edition consists of 11,825 signed and numbered prints. Also available were a Medallion Edition of 2975 and an Executive Edition of 75.

1986
FOURTH PENNSYLVANIA DUCK STAMP

Blue-Winged Teal
Robert C. Knutson

The original art depicts a pair of Blue-Winged Teal swimming in calm water. The design was chosen from 109 entries. This marks the first time that the Pennsylvania design was chosen by a contest; the previous designs had been commissioned from the artists.

The stamp is not numbered. It sold for $5.50. There were 35,000 stamps printed.

The print is 6½″ x 9″. The edition consists of 7380 signed and numbered prints. Also available was a Medallion Edition of 625, featuring a silver medallion with gold-plated trim.

1986

SIXTH SOUTH CAROLINA DUCK STAMP

Canvasbacks
Daniel Smith

The original art depicts a pair of Canvasbacks riding the waves in rugged coastal waters. The design was chosen from 211 entries.

The stamp sold to hunters is numbered on the back; the stamp sold to collectors is not numbered. In any case, it sold for $5.50. There were 99,960 stamps printed.

The print is 6½″ x 9″. The edition consists of 4000 signed and numbered prints. Also available was a Governor's Medallion Edition of 500, featuring a gold-plated medallion.

1986

FIRST SOUTH DAKOTA WATERFOWL RESTORATION STAMP

Canada Geese
John Wilson

The original art was chosen from 42 entries. The South Dakota legislature passed a law requiring that waterfowl hunters have this Waterfowl Restoration Stamp.

The stamp is numbered on the front. It sold for $2.00. There were 135,000 stamps printed.

The print is 6½″ x 9″. The edition consists of 950 signed and numbered prints; pencil remarques were also available with this edition.

1986
EIGHTH TENNESSEE DUCK STAMP

Mallard
Ralph McDonald

The original art depicts a scene featuring a Mallard duck. In 1986 the state adopted a commission system for choosing artists to design its duck stamps.

The stamp is numbered on the front. It sold for $6.50. There were 50,000 stamps printed.

The print is 6½″ x 9″. The edition consists of 1000 signed and numbered prints. Also available was an Artist's Proof Edition of 250 prints with color remarques.

1986
SIXTH TEXAS DUCK STAMP

Green-Winged Teal
Herb Booth

The original art depicts a flock of Green-Winged Teal flying over duck hunters in a blind setting out decoys. The artist was commissioned to create the design.

The stamp is numbered on the front. It sold for $5.00. There were 210,000 stamps printed.

The print is 6½″ x 9″. The edition consists of 8600 signed and numbered prints. A special Conservation Edition of 350 prints was also available, as were 100 artist's proof prints.

1986
FIRST UTAH WATERFOWL STAMP

Tundra Swans
Leon Parson

The original art depicts a pair of Tundra Swans in flight. The design for this first-of-state waterfowl stamp was chosen from 61 entries.

The stamp is numbered on the front. It sold for $3.30. There were 120,000 stamps printed.

The print is 6½" x 9". The edition consists of 14,028 signed and numbered prints. Also available were a Silver Medallion Editon of 1600, a Gold Medallion Edition of 250, and Color Remarqued Edition of 150.

1986
FIRST VERMONT DUCK STAMP

Wood Ducks
Jim Killen

The original art depicts a trio of Wood Ducks in flight. The artist was commissioned to create the design.

The stamp is not numbered. It sold for $5.00. There were 50,000 stamps printed.

The print is 6½" x 9". The edition consists of 13,910 signed and numbered prints. Also available were a Gold Medallion Edition of 1590 and an Executive Edition of 195, consisting of print, medallion, and color remarque.

1986
FIRST WASHINGTON DUCK STAMP

Mallards
Keith Warrick

The original art depicts a pair of Mallards resting on a snow-covered shoreline. The design was chosen from 109 entries.

The stamp is numbered on the front. It sold for $5.00. There were 160,000 stamps printed.

The print is 6½″ x 9″. The edition consists of 12,180 signed and numbered prints. Also available were a Gold Medallion Edition of 1775 and an Executive Edition of 300, consisting of print, medallion, and color remarque.

1986
NINTH WISCONSIN DUCK STAMP

Canvasbacks
Don Moore

The original art depicts a pair of Canvasbacks. The design was chosen from 121 entries.

The stamp is numbered on an attached tab. It sold for $3.25. There were 160,000 stamps printed.

The print is 6½″ x 9″. The edition consists of 1250 signed and numbered prints. Also available were a separate pencil remarque edition of 100 and a watercolor remarque edition of 50.

1987–88

FIFTY–FOURTH FEDERAL DUCK STAMP

Redheads
Arthur G. Anderson

The original art depicts the flight of three Redheads sweeping across a backwater marsh. It was chosen from 798 entries.

The stamp, which is unnumbered, was printed in full color and sold for $10.00. Four million were printed. The first day of sale was July 1, 1987.

The print, 6½″ x 9″, is on 100% acid-free rag stock. The separation maker was Graphic Arts Systems and the printer was Overland Printer. The first edition consists of 20,000 prints. In addition to the regular edition, there was a Medallion Edition of 5000 gold-plated, stamp-shaped medallions accompanied by a print.

1987
NINTH ALABAMA DUCK STAMP

Pintail Ducks
Robert C. Knutson

The original art depicts a pair of Pintails. The design was chosen from 56 entries.

The stamp sold for $5.00. A total of 20,000 stamps were printed.

The print is 6½″ x 9″. The edition consists of 1000 signed and numbered prints and includes pencil and color remarques.

1987
THIRD ALASKA DUCK STAMP

Spectacled Eider
Carl Branson

The original art depicts a male and a female Spectacled Eider standing on the shoreline. The design was chosen from 39 entries.

The stamp is unnumbered and sold for $5.00. There were 61,000 printed.

The print is 6½″ x 9″. The edition consists of 4675 signed and numbered prints, 1075 medallions and prints, and an Executive Edition of 250 that comprises a print, a medallion, and a remarque.

1987
FIRST ARIZONA DUCK STAMP

Pintail
Daniel Smith

The original art depicts a pair of Pintails swimming in the water. The design was chosen from 21 entries.

The stamp (as well as the sheet) is numbered. It sold for $5.50. There were 70,500 printed, 30,000 in books and the rest in sheets.

The print is 6½″ x 9″. The edition consisted of 10,400 signed and numbered prints. Added to this were a Medallion Edition of 1390, consisting of stamp, print, and gold-plated medallion, and an Executive Edition of 198, consisting of stamp, medallion, and print with hand-painted color remarque.

1987
SEVENTH ARKANSAS DUCK STAMP

Hurricane Lake
Robert Bateman

The original art depicts four Wood Ducks swimming. The state of Arkansas commissioned the noted Canadian artist Robert Bateman to create this design. This marks the first time that a state stamp/print design was created by an artist residing outside the United States.

The stamp is numbered and sold for $7.00. A total of 100,000 were printed.

The print is 6½″ x 9″. The edition consists of 8855 signed and numbered prints, 600 Special Series prints, and 500 Executive Series prints. A gold-plated medallion accompanies each print in the latter two series.

1987
SEVENTEENTH CALIFORNIA DUCK STAMP

Redheads
Robert Steiner

The original art depicts a pair of Redheads in flight. The design was chosen from 90 entries.

The stamp is numbered and sold for $7.50. There were 5949 books of stamps printed, each containing 25 stamps, for a total of 148,725. The stamp was a salute to Ducks Unlimited.

The print is 6½″ x 9″. The edition consists of 750 signed and numbered prints and an Executive Edition of 200 prints. Medallions and pencil and color remarques were available for all editions.

1987
EIGHTH DELAWARE DUCK STAMP

A Touch of Red
Bruce Langton

The original art depicts a pair of Redheads, a drake and a hen, swimming in springtime. The design was chosen from 65 entries.

The stamp is unnumbered (though the sheets are) and sold for $5.00. There were 35,000 printed.

The print is 6½″ x 9″. The edition consists of 1980 signed and numbered prints; pencil and color remarques were also available.

1987
NINTH FLORIDA DUCK STAMP

Untitled
Ronald J. Louque

The original art depicts a pair of Mallards in flight. The design was selected from 48 entries.

The stamp was numbered on the front and sold for $3.00. There were 48,000 stamps printed.

The print is 12″ x 14″. The signed and numbered edition consists of 1,000 prints. Pencil remarques were available.

1987
THIRD GEORGIA DUCK STAMP

Untitled
James Partee, Jr.

The original art depicts a pair of Canada Geese. The design was chosen from 140 entries.

The stamp was sold for $5.50. Sheets of stamps are numbered. There were 40,000 stamps printed.

The print is 12″ x 14″. The edition consists of 5000 signed and numbered prints. Pencil and color remarques, as well as gold medallions, were available, as were 250 signed and numbered artist's proof prints.

FIRST IDAHO DUCK STAMP

Untitled
Robert Leslie

The original art depicts a pair of Cinnamon Teal in the water. The design for this first-of-state stamp/print was chosen from 40 entries.

The stamp sold for $6.00. There were 80,000 printed.

The print is 6½″ x 9″. The edition of signed and numbered prints is limited to orders received by April 1988. A companion print of 16½″ x 25″ was also available. Also issued were a Medallion Edition and an Executive Edition consisting of print, medallion, and hand-painted color remarque.

1987
THIRTEENTH ILLINOIS DUCK STAMP

Buffleheads
Bart Kassabaum

The original art depicts two drakes and a hen in low flight over bulrushes. The design was chosen from 90 entries. This marks the fourth time that Mr. Kassabaum has won the Illinois stamp/print contest.

The stamp sold for $5.50. There were 99,000 printed.

The print is 8″ x 10″. The edition consists of 600 signed and numbered prints; pencil and color remarques were available with this edition.

1987
TWELFTH INDIANA DUCK STAMP

Two Canvasbacks
Susan Bates

The original art depicts two Canvasbacks. The design was chosen in a state contest.

The stamp is numbered and sold for $5.00. There were 51,000 printed.

The print: no print of the 1987 design was marketed.

1987
SIXTEENTH IOWA DUCK STAMP

Canada Goose
John Heidersbach

The original art depicts a lone Canada Goose flying through the morning mist. The design was chosen from 25 entries.

The stamp, which is unnumbered, sold for $5.00. There were 80,000 printed.

The print is 11″ x 6½″. The edition consists of 750 signed and numbered prints. Pencil and color remarques were also available.

1987
FIRST KANSAS DUCK STAMP

Green-Winged Teal
Guy Coheleach

The original art depicts a pair of Green-Winged Teal taking off from marshy water. The design for this first-of-state stamp/print was commissioned.

The stamp is numbered and sold for $3.00. There were 100,000 printed.

The print is 6½″ x 9″. The edition of signed and numbered prints is limited to the orders received through February 1988. A Medallion Edition of 2500 was also available, consisting of a print using the same paper as that used for the signed and numbered edition and a gold-plated medallion facsimile of the stamp. Also available was an Executive Etching Edition of 950 hand-colored 6½″ x 9″ etchings by the artist. The Executive Etching Edition consists of etching, medallion, mint stamp, and portfolio.

1987
THIRD KENTUCKY DUCK STAMP

Black Ducks
R. J. McDonald

The original art depicts a pair of Black Ducks resting at the water's edge. The design was commissioned from the artist.

The stamp is numbered and sold for $5.25. There were 55,000 printed.

The print is 6½″ x 9″. The edition consists of 8189 signed and numbered prints. A bronze, gold-plated medallion about the size of the stamp was also available; a color remarque was available to medallion purchasers.

1987
FOURTH MAINE DUCK STAMP

Along the Coast—Buffleheads
Ron Van Gilder

The original art depicts a pair of Buffleheads in flight. The design was commissioned.

The stamp (as well as the sheet) is numbered. It sold for $2.50. There were 60,000 printed, in sheets of 10.

The print is 6½″ x 9″. The edition consists of 2450 signed and numbered prints. Also available were a Medallion Edition of 350 and a companion print set.

1987

FOURTEENTH MARYLAND DUCK STAMP

Americana
Francis E. Sweet

The original art depicts a pair of Redheads at rest in the open water. The design was chosen from 103 entries.

The stamp is numbered and sold for $6.00. There were 80,000 printed.

The print is 6½″ x 9″. The edition consists of 1500 signed and numbered prints; pencil or color remarques were available with this edition.

1987

FOURTEENTH MASSACHUSETTS DUCK STAMP

Widgeon Drake Decoy
Peter Baedita

The original art depicts a Widgeon drake decoy by the famous carver Joe Lincoln. The design was chosen from 41 entries.

The stamp, which is unnumbered, sold for $1.25. There were 50,400 printed.

The print is 4¾″ x 9″. The edition consists of 475 prints, including pencil and color remarques and signed and numbered prints.

1987

TWELFTH MICHIGAN DUCK STAMP

Untitled
Larry Hayden

The original art depicts a pair of Green-Winged Teal against an autumn sky. The design was chosen from 77 entries.

The stamp is numbered and sold for $3.85. There were 110,000 printed.

The print is 14″ x 12½″. The edition consists of 975 signed and numbered prints. In addition, 150 artist's proofs were available.

1987
ELEVENTH MINNESOTA
DUCK STAMP

North Shore Goldeneyes
Ron Van Gilder

The original art depicts several North Shore Goldeneyes. The design was chosen from 13 entries.

The stamp is numbered and sold for $5.00 each. There were 250,000 printed.

The print is 6½" x 9". The edition consists of 4200 signed and numbered prints. Also available was a larger companion print, 15" x 25" that incorporated the basic design in a larger composition.

1987
TWELFTH MISSISSIPPI DUCK STAMP

Ring-Necks
Robert Garner

The original art depicts a pair of Ring-Necks swimming. The design was chosen from 40 entries.

The stamp is numbered and sold for $2.00. There were 1200 printed.

The print is 6½" x 9". The edition consists of 500 signed and numbered prints; pencil and color remarques were also available with this edition.

1987
NINTH MISSOURI DUCK STAMP

Pintails
Ron Ferkol

The original art depicts a pair of Pintails swimming in the water. The design was chosen from 49 entries.

The stamp is numbered and sold for $3.00. There were 130,000 printed.

The print is 6½" x 9". The edition consists of 1000 signed and numbered prints, some of which have pencil remarques. A Special Collector's Set, consisting of matching number sets of the 1987 Missouri Duck Stamp print and the 1988 Missouri Trout Stamp print, was also available.

1987
SECOND MONTANA WATERFOWL STAMP

Redheads
Roger Cruwys

The original art depicts a pair of Redheads taking off over choppy marsh water. The design was chosen from 47 entries.

The stamp is numbered and sold for $5.00. There were 21,000 printed.

The print is 6½″ x 9″. The edition consists of 9212 signed and numbered prints. Available also were 1025 gold-plated medallions. An Executive Edition of 300 was available, too, consisting of print, gold-plated medallion, and color remarque.

1987
NINTH NEVADA DUCK STAMP

Buffleheads
Sherrie Russell

The original art depicts a pair of Buffleheads resting in the water. The design was chosen from 152 entries.

The stamp is numbered and sold for $2.00. There were 25,000 printed.

The print is 6½″ x 9″. The edition consists of 1990 signed and numbered prints. Also available were a Conservation Edition of 50 prints and an Artist's Proof Edition of 150 prints.

1987
FIFTH NEW HAMPSHIRE
DUCK STAMP

Untitled
Robert Steiner

The original art depicts two Canada Geese in flight. The design was selected as the result of a nationwide bidding process.

The stamp is numbered and sold for $4.00. There were 51,000 printed.

The print is 12″ x 14″. The number of signed and numbered prints in the edition was determined by the number of orders received by March 1, 1988. Also available were pencil and color remarques and a fifth anniversary gold-plated bronze medallion to accompany the regular edition.

1987
FOURTH NEW JERSEY DUCK STAMP

Canada Geese
Louis Frisino

The original art depicts a pair of Canada Geese in flight with a sitting Retriever watching them. The design was commissioned.

The stamp is of two types. There are 102,000 resident's stamps and 60,000 nonresident's stamps printed. Both stamps and sheets of stamps are numbered. The resident stamp sold for $2.50, the nonresident for $5.00.

The print is 6½″ x 9″. The edition consists of 10,011 signed and numbered prints; the Medallion Edition comprises 1210 prints and medallions. Also available were an Executive Edition of 650, consisting of print, medallion, and color remarque, and an Artist's Proof Edition of 150, consisting of artist's proof print, medallion, and color remarque.

1987
THIRD NEW YORK DUCK STAMP

Wood Ducks
Lee LeBlanc

The original art depicts Wood Ducks in flight over a pond. The design was commissioned.

The stamp sold for $5.50. Only the sheets were numbered. There were 99,000 stamps printed.

The print is 6½″ x 9″. The edition consists of 14,040 signed and numbered prints; the Medallion Edition comprises 1035 prints and medallions. Also available were an Executive Edition of 580, consisting of print, medallion, and remarque, and an Artist's Proof Edition of 250, consisting of artist's proof print, medallion, and remarque.

1987
FIFTH NORTH CAROLINA DUCK STAMP

Pintails
Larry Barton

The original art depicts a pair of Pintails rising above a pond. The design was commissioned.

The stamp sold for $5.50. Only the sheets were numbered. There were 105,000 stamps printed in sheets of 30.

The print is 6½" x 9". The edition consists of 5020 signed and numbered prints; color remarques were available with this edition. Also available was an Artist's Proof Edition of 150, consisting of artist's proof print and color remarque.

1987
SIXTH NORTH DAKOTA DUCK STAMP

Snow Geese
Ronald J. Louque

The original art depicts a flock of Snow Geese dropping into a field of wheat stubble. The artist was commissioned to create the design.

The stamp is numbered and sold for $9.00. There were 146,000 printed.

The print is 6½" x 9". The edition consists of 3438 signed and numbered prints; remarques were available with this edition. Also available were 340 artist's proof prints.

1987
SIXTH OHIO DUCK STAMP

Blue-Winged Teal
Harold Roe

The original art depicts a pair of Blue-Winged Teal at the shore of a pond. The design was chosen from 71 entries.

The stamp sold for $6.00. Only the sheets were numbered. There were 60,000 stamps printed in sheets of 16.

The print is 6½″ x 9″. The edition consists of 2000 signed and numbered prints; 100 pencil and 100 color remarques were separately available.

1987
EIGHTH OKLAHOMA DUCK STAMP

Canvasbacks
Rayburn T. Foster

The original art depicts a trio of Canvasbacks, two drakes and a hen, flying low over a shore-line. The design was chosen from 44 entries.

The stamp is numbered and sold for $4.00. There were 35,000 printed.

The print is 6½″ x 9″. The edition consists of 1980 signed and numbered prints, including pencil or color remarques that were also available.

1987
FOURTH OREGON WATERFOWL STAMP

White-Fronted Geese
D. M. Smith

The original art depicts three White-Fronted Geese. The design was chosen from more than 40 entries.

The stamp is numbered and sold for $5.00. There were 90,000 printed.

The print is 12″ x 14″. The number of signed and numbered prints in the edition was determined by the number of orders received. Also available were silver medallions, a poster, and pins featuring the design.

1987
FIFTH PENNSYLVANIA DUCK STAMP

Pintails
Robert Leslie

The original art depicts a pair of Pintails resting on a pond. The design was chosen from 73 entries.

The stamp sold for $5.50. Only the sheets were numbered. There were 40,000 stamps printed.

The print is 6½″ x 9″. The edition consists of 7380 signed and numbered prints. Also available was a Medallion Edition of 625.

1987
SEVENTH SOUTH CAROLINA DUCK STAMP

Black Ducks
Steve Dillard

The original art depicts a pair of Black Ducks in flight. The design was chosen from 145 entries.

The stamp sold for $5.50. Only the sheets were numbered. There were 99,960 stamps printed.

The print is 6½″ x 9″. The edition consists of 4000 signed and numbered prints; remarques were available with this edition. Also available was a Governor's Medallion Edition of 500.

1987
SECOND SOUTH DAKOTA WATERFOWL RESTORATION STAMP

Blue Geese
Rosemary Millette

The original art depicts a pair of Blue Geese resting in a cornfield. The design was chosen in a contest run by the South Dakota Ducks Unlimited Council in cooperation with the Game, Fish, and Parks Department. This is the second in a three-year program that features geese.

The stamp is numbered and sold for $2.00. There were 135,000 printed.

The print is 6½″ x 9″. The edition consists of 950 signed and numbered prints; pencil and color remarques were also available with this edition.

1987
NINTH TENNESSEE DUCK STAMP

Canada Geese
Tom Hirata

The original art depicts a pair of Canada Geese standing on a rocky shore. The artist was commissioned to create the design.

The stamp is numbered and sold for $6.50. There were 50,000 printed.

The print is 6½″ x 9″. The edition consists of 1000 signed and numbered prints. Also available were 250 artist's proof prints with color remarques.

1987
SEVENTH TEXAS DUCK STAMP

White-Fronted Geese
Gary Moss

The original art depicts a pair of White-Fronted Geese standing in a marsh. The artist was commissioned to create the design.

The stamp is numbered and sold for $5.00. There were 210,000 printed.

The print is 6½" x 9". The edition consists of 7000 signed and numbered prints. A Ducks Unlimited 50th Anniversary Medallion Edition of 200 prints was available through Texas Ducks Unlimited. Also available were a Conservation Edition of 200 prints and an edition of 100 artist's proof prints.

1987
SECOND UTAH WATERFOWL STAMP

Pintails
Arthur S. Anderson

The original art depicts a pair of Pintails in flight over water. The design was chosen from more than 60 entries.

The stamp sold for $3.30. There were 120,000 printed.

The print is 6½" x 9". The size of the signed and numbered edition was limited to orders received by March 1988. Also available were a Gold Medallion Edition of 1600 and a remarqued Executive Edition of 150, consisting of print, hand-painted remarque, and gold medallion.

1987
SECOND VERMONT DUCK STAMP

Winter Goldeneyes
Jim Killen

The original art depicts three common Goldeneyes flying over Lake Champlain in the winter. The design was commissioned from the artist.

The stamp is not numbered, but numbering was available on request with orders from the state. A total of 40,000 stamps were printed, each stamp selling for $5.00.

The print is 12" x 14". The size of the signed and numbered edition was determined by the number of orders received by March 31, 1988. A medallion edition was also available, as well as a special Executive Edition, which consisted of a mint stamp, print, medallion, and color remarque.

1987

SECOND WASHINGTON DUCK STAMP

Canvasbacks
Ray Nichol

The original art depicts a trio of Canvasbacks resting near a shoreline. The design was chosen from 46 entries.

The stamp is numbered and sold for $5.00. There were 130,000 printed.

The print is 6½" x 9". The edition consists of 12,180 signed and numbered prints. Also available were 1775 medallions and pencil and color remarques.

1987

FIRST WEST VIRGINIA DUCK STAMP

Canada Geese
Daniel Smith

The original art depicts a pair of Canada Geese in flight. The design was commissioned.

The stamp, which is unnumbered, sold for $5.00. There were 58,000 printed.

The print is 6½" x 9". The edition consists of 10,064 signed and numbered prints. Added to that were a Gold Medallion Edition of 1101 and an Executive Edition of 145, consisting of resident and nonresident stamps, color remarqued print, and medallion.

1987

TENTH WISCONSIN DUCK STAMP

A Pair of Kings
Al Kraayvanger

The original art depicts three Canada Geese in flight. The design was chosen from 114 entries.

The stamp is numbered and sold for $3.25. There were 160,000 printed.

The print is 12" x 14". The edition consists of 1500 signed and numbered prints. A separate edition of 150 prints with color and pencil remarques was also available.

ARTISTS' BIOGRAPHIES

JACKSON MILES ABBOTT
1957–58 Federal Duck Stamp

Jackson Miles Abbott was born in Philadelphia on January 25, 1920. He started at age six with the hobby of ornithology and still maintains a very active interest in the subject. During World War II, Mr. Abbott was in military engineering and pursued a career in both the Army and the civil service. But over the years, he has made birds the focus of his art. In 1957 he won both first and second place in the Federal Duck Stamp competition and since that year has conducted an annual nesting survey of the bald eagle population in the Chesapeake Bay region for the Audubon Society and the U.S. Fish and Wildlife Service. As well as writing and illustrating articles on birds for books and magazines, he has written and illustrated a Sunday magazine column on the birds in Washington, D.C. Some of his writing and illustration can be found in Austin's *New Encyclopedia of Useful Information* (1948) and Hausman's *Beginner's Guide to Attracting Birds* (1951).

GREG ALEXANDER
1985 Wisconsin Duck Stamp

Greg Alexander was born in Sault Ste. Marie, Michigan, on February 29, 1960. After high school, he continued his interest in art while attending the Minneapolis College of Art and Design. However, he found that the best way to enhance his talents was to spend more time in the field among the subjects he loved to paint. He moved into a wild part of Michigan, living in a log home near the Cranberry River close to Lake Superior's south shore. There he could monitor his wildlife subjects freely. In addition to the 1985 Wisconsin Duck Stamp contest, Mr. Alexander won the 1987 Minnesota Trout Stamp contest.

CHARLES ALLEN
1983 California Duck Stamp, 1983 Nevada Duck Stamp

Charles Allen was born in Fresno, California, on November 10, 1922. After graduation from Fresno State College and service as a pilot in World War II, he attended the Art Center in Los Angeles. That was followed by a successful career in illustration in San Francisco. He has always had an interest in wildlife and waterfowl painting. In 1983, at age sixty, Mr. Allen became the first artist ever to win two different state waterfowl contests in the same year. They were, moreover, the first two contests that he had ever entered.

ARTHUR G. ANDERSON
1987 Utah Duck Stamp, 1987–88 Federal Duck Stamp, 1987 Utah Duck Stamp

Arthur G. Anderson was born in Eau Claire, Wisconsin, on December 10, 1935. At the early age of twelve, he began painting with a set of oils his uncle gave to

him. Mr. Anderson studied art at the University of Wisconsin at Eau Claire and also at the Art Instruction School in St. Paul, Minnesota. He supported himself as a graphic artist while continuing to paint at home on evenings and weekends. In 1983, he began to devote his full time to wildlife art. An avid outdoorsman, Mr. Anderson admits he "hunts mostly with his camera." He lives with his family now in Onalaska, Wisconsin, a town near La Crosse that overlooks the Mississippi and is close to the marsh habitat frequented by ducks and other waterfowl in their annual migrations. In 1985, he gained international recognition when his painting "Riding the Wind" was selected as one of the companion pieces to the Ducks Unlimited Artist of the Year painting.

HARRY ANTIS
1933 Ohio Duck Stamp

Harry Antis was born in Dearborn, Michigan, on October 18, 1942. He was exposed to art from day one, for his father was a painter and his mother had a great love for and knowledge of fine painting. Mr. Antis was always provided with a large assortment of art materials to work with, and his creativity and experimentation were encouraged. After high school, he entered the Society of Arts and Crafts in Detroit. He soon needed to find gainful employment, though, and he joined an exclusive group that did full-color illustrations for General Motors Fisher Body Division. In 1970, Mr. Antis began painting full time, and he has since developed into one of the country's truly well-rounded artists. His subjects range from song birds to game birds, from big game to small mammals.

PETER BAEDITA
1987 Massachusetts Duck Stamp

Peter Baedita was born in Malden, Massachusetts, in 1961. He studied at the Massachusetts College of Art, and he currently works for a Boston advertising agency. He is a realistic painter who uses mostly acrylics to capture wildlife in its natural environment. He divides his work between his agency commitments and his private wildlife painting. In addition, he spends many hours observing, photographing, and researching the wildlife subjects he paints. This painstaking preparation comes out in the detailed, realistic style of his work. Mr. Baedita was the youngest winner of the Massachusetts Waterfowl Stamp contest to date. He resides in Massachusetts.

DURANT BALL
1986 New Hampshire Duck Stamp

Durant Ball was born in Hickory, North Carolina, on April 2, 1940. He studied art formally at Brigham Young University in Utah, receiving a Master of Arts

degree in painting and a Bachelor of Science degree in commercial art. In addition to his extensive commercial art background, Mr. Ball also taught for eleven years. He retired in 1982 to devote all his time to his painting career. His works have won many awards and have been exhibited in the Leigh Yawkey Woodson Art Museum in Wisconsin. He resides in Newport News, Virginia.

DEAN R. BARRICK
1980 Indiana Duck Stamp

Dean R. Barrick graduated from the University of Washington in Seattle with a degree in zoology. He turned his attention to wildlife art—a wise decision, as can be seen from the noted publications in which his work has appeared, including *National Wildlife, Ranger Rick, Defenders of Wildlife, Science,* and *Pacific Search.* He has also illustrated *Mule Deer and Black-Tailed Deer of North America* for the Wildlife Management Institute and *Waterfowl Ecology and Management* for the Wildlife Society. In addition, he has designed many of the National Wildlife Federation stamps and has displayed his work throughout the country. Mr. Barrick currently resides in Seattle, Washington.

LARRY BARTON
1985 New York Duck Stamp, 1987 North Carolina Duck Stamp

Larry Barton grew up on the shores of Lake Huron in the Michigan "thumb" region, where he early developed an interest in wildlife. He continued this interest by studying wildlife biology and management. He also pursued a journalism career, becoming a popular award-winning editorial cartoonist whose works have appeared in such publications as *Time,* the *Washington Post,* the *New York Times,* and the *Los Angeles Times* as well as newspapers in Ohio and North Carolina. He was able to return to wildlife painting full-time in 1979, and has steadily gained recognition. His artwork has appeared in many prestigious shows and galleries, and in the Leigh Yawkey Woodson Art Museum. He lives in North Carolina with his wife and family.

JUSTUS H. ("SONNY") BASHORE
1976 Indiana Duck Stamp, 1977 Indiana Duck Stamp

Justus H. ("Sonny") Bashore was born in Paulding, Ohio, on November 12, 1935. He served in the armed forces following high school, and on his return to civilian life, he began his career with the Ohio Department of Natural Resources. He worked as a wildlife artist and area manager at the Oxbow Lake Wildlife Area at Defiance, Ohio, and served with the Indiana Department of Natural Resources at Curtis Creek Trout and Salmon Station at Mongo, Indiana. He continues to paint and carve as a full-time wildlife artist. In 1977 he placed first in the Indiana Trout and Salmon Stamp competition. In 1987 he was the winner in the First Annual Michigan Duck Hunters' Tournament and Midwest Decoy Contest Poster competition.

ROBERT BATEMAN
1987 Arkansas Duck Stamp

Robert Bateman was born in Canada. In his early years as an artist, he experimented with a number of styles and techniques. Under the influence of the work of Andrew Wyeth, though, he returned in the 1960s to a realistic style of painting. He combined his artistic abilities with his knowledge and love of wildlife to create his own style of wildlife art—a style that is strong and dramatic. Honored with major one-man exhibitions at more than fifteen museums, he has also participated in numerous group shows. He has been the subject of three films, and three books have been written about his art. He painted the waterfowl design for Canada's first Wildlife Habitat Stamp Print—the most popular conservation stamp print ever issued.

SUSAN HASTINGS BATES
1987 Indiana Duck Stamp

Susan Hastings Bates grew up in New York City and eastern Long Island. Her interest in birds and nature began in the Maine woods where she spent her summers. Ms. Bates was awarded a B.A. in graphic design from Stanford University in 1978. She then worked as a jewelry designer for Shreve and Co. in San Francisco and won three national design awards in as many years. To pursue a career in fine art, spend more time outdoors, and help advance conservation, Ms. Bates spends a good part of each year in both the Atlantic and Pacific flyways working full-time as a wildlife artist. She placed second in the 1986 California Duck Stamp competition and was a finalist the same year in the Federal Duck Stamp contest. Ms. Bates now makes her home in San Francisco, California.

FRANK W. BENSON
1935–36 Federal Duck Stamp

Frank W. Benson, M.A., was born in Salem, Massachusetts, on March 24, 1862. When he was eighteen he began his art studies at the Boston Museum of Fine Arts. Three years later, in 1883, he went to Paris to study at the Academie Julien under Boulanger and Lefebvre. On his return in 1885, Mr. Benson taught painting and drawing and continued with his own work, painting portraits that featured his subjects out of doors in scenes of brilliant light and color. In 1912, he took up etching and afterwards made over three hundred plates, which gained wide acclaim for his work. As he developed, his style became more noted for simplicity and sparseness of detail. It is a style more appreciated by the expert than the layman, as it makes a statement so bare and brief that only the most technically competent artist could bring it off. Mr. Benson died in 1951 at the age of eighty-nine.

EDWARD J. BIERLY
1956–57 Federal Duck Stamp, 1963–64 Federal Duck Stamp, 1970–71 Federal Duck Stamp

Edward J. Bierly was born in 1920, in Buffalo, New York. His job as a designer of natural history exhibits for the National Park Service led to an appointment by UNESCO as a museum consultant to the government of Rhodesia. It was on this assignment that he first saw the wildlife of Africa. Moved by what he saw, he determined to use his art to attract attention to the plight of endangered fauna everywhere. In 1970 he left the Park Service to devote his full time to his art. His paintings have appeared on the covers of national magazines and have been exhibited at natural history museums throughout the country. Many of his print editions have been used to raise funds for wildlife conservation programs. He is a three-time winner of the Federal Duck Stamp competition and a member of the Society of Animal Artists.

BOB BINKS
1979 Florida Duck Stamp, 1982 South Carolina Duck Stamp, 1985 Florida Duck Stamp

Robert Binks was born in St. Louis, Missouri, on September 19, 1941. From his earliest memories he has always been vitally interested in wildlife. Mr. Binks began his working career as a technical illustrator and gradually went into advertising. While working at his then full-time job as art director, he never lost sight of his real love—wildlife art. A self-taught artist, he was commissioned to design the first duck stamp for the state of Florida in 1979. In 1982 he won the competition for the South Carolina Duck Stamp, and in 1985 he again designed the Florida Duck Stamp. He has given numerous one-man shows, and exhibited at Easton's Waterfowl Festival and at the National Waterfowl Art Show in Kansas City. He was also selected as Artist of the Year for Florida's Ducks Unlimited.

RICHARD E. BISHOP
1936–37 Federal Duck Stamp

Richard E. Bishop was born in Syracuse, New York, on May 30, 1887. Early in his career at a manufacturing plant, he found himself faced with a pile of inviting copper plates. With a phonograph needle, on a waxed plate, he inscribed the first of his many etchings. Mr. Bishop traveled widely in search of wildlife material, joining two African safaris organized by the American Museum of Natural History and also making trips to Great Britain, the Pacific Islands, and North and South America. His decorated glassware and china are highly regarded, but the books of his etchings are most widely cherished. Among these are *Bishop's Birds* (1936), *Bishop's Waterfowl* (1948), and *Prairie Wings* (1962) in collaboration with Edgar M. Queeny. Mr. Bishop rendered wildlife in many media: watercolors, oil painting, aquatints, dry points, etchings, jewelry, tiles, metal, glassware, and china. He died in 1975.

WALTER E. BOHL
1943–44 Federal Duck Stamp

Walter E. Bohl was born in Columbus, Wisconsin, on September 10, 1907. In 1931 and 1932, when he was recovering from a serious illness, he began making pen and ink drawings, just to pass the time. At the suggestion of the manager of the Marshall Field Art Galleries of Chicago he turned to making etchings. Because he loved the outdoors, it was natural that his subjects were birds, animals and outdoor scenes. In 1935, some of his work came to the attention of *Esquire*, which featured his etchings and paintings for nine years. With no formal art education, he has firmly established his reputation as an etcher and painter. Some of his etchings can be found in the permanent collection of the Smithsonian National Museum of American Art, Washington, D.C. His etchings are also in collections of Arizona State University, Tempe, Arizona, the University of Wisconsin at Madison, and the State House, Phoenix, Arizona. His paintings are in the collection of the Phoenix Art Museum, Phoenix, Arizona. In 1971 he was awarded a gold medal by the Arizona Chapter of the National Society of Arts and Letters.

HERB BOOTH
1986 Texas Duck Stamp

Herb Booth was born in La Junta, Colorado, on June 5, 1942. His introduction to serious painting came early in his life when, as an Explorer Scout, he formed a unique relationship with Buck Burshears, who led the Koshare Indian Dancers and was himself a collector of Southwestern and Indian art. Mr. Booth traveled with the Koshare Indians throughout the Southwest, learning many art techniques and becoming acquainted with many painters. He has had his work featured in *Ducks Unlimited*, *Texas Highways*, *Sports Afield*, and *Southern Outdoors*. He was selected in 1983 as the first Texas Ducks Unlimited Artist of the Year. In 1984 his design of speckled trout was selected for the 1984 Gulf Coast Conservation Stamp and Print. He has made his home in Texas since 1970.

CARL BRANSON
1987 Alaska Duck Stamp

Carl Branson was born in Redwood City, California, in 1937. His early outdoor life of hunting, fishing, and trapping undoubtedly influenced his later artistic interests. He came under Alaska's spell when he was stationed there with the Air Force during the Korean War. He moved to Peters Creek, near Anchorage, in 1982, following a stay of seven years in Alberta, Canada. Most of his art is in private collections throughout the state and Canada. He resides in Peters Creek with his family.

DON BREYFOGLE
1985 Delaware Duck Stamp

Don Breyfogle was born in Marshall, Minnesota, on November 25, 1947. He worked for seventeen years as an automobile painter, and in 1981 he began painting full-time. A self-taught artist, Mr. Breyfogle has consistently placed among the top ten finalists in the stamp competitions he has entered. His work has been shown at many national shows, including the Easton Waterfowl Festival and the Ducks Unlimited National Wildlife Show in Kansas City, Missouri. In the summer of 1986, he was selected for master class studies with Robert Bateman. Mr. Breyfogle still lives in Marshall, Minnesota.

PAUL BRIDGFORD
1980 Iowa Duck Stamp, 1983 Iowa Duck Stamp, 1986 Iowa Duck Stamp

Paul Bridgford was born in Davenport, Iowa, on March 15, 1952. In 1973, his lifelong interest in wildlife was intensified during his service at an Air Force base in a remote part of Idaho. Finding himself in the midst of a great raptor reserve, he delighted in observing falcons, hawks, eagles, and owls, carefully studying their habits and habitats. Fascinated by what he saw, he began trying to capture it in painting. From these early studies and paintings of birds of prey, Mr. Bridgford has developed into one of the most talented wildlife artists in the country. Currently, he is a commercial artist for an advertising agency in Des Moines, but his dream of becoming a full-time wildlife artist is fast approaching reality.

LYN BRIGGS
1984 Indiana Duck Stamp

Lyn Briggs was born in Payson, Utah, on August 25, 1946. As a youth, he lived in Provo, Utah, and graduated from Provo High School. He continued his education at Brigham Young University, from which he graduated in 1970 with a B.S. in zoology. He began work the following year with the Utah Division of Wildlife Resources as a conservation officer. Mr. Briggs is a self-taught artist, having received no formal art training. He lives now in Annabella, Utah, and hopes that winning the Indiana competition will help him pursue his career as a wildlife artist.

ROGER BUCKLIN
1982 Maryland Duck Stamp

Roger Bucklin was born in Portland, Maine, on October 8, 1927. He began his formal art training at the age of ten with his grandmother, Annie Pinkham Hall, an accomplished artist. He then studied with local artists, including Roger Deering and Nunzio Vayana. For almost twenty years Mr. Bucklin pursued art as a hobby while working as an electronics engineer, but in 1973 he began to devote full time to his art. His work is in the permanent collections of Maryland (Annapolis) and of Montgomery County, Maryland. In 1985, 1986, and 1987 several of his works were commissioned for use by the National Zoo in Washington, D.C.

LOIS M. BUTLER
1982 Delaware Duck Stamp

Lois M. Butler was born in Egypt, Pennsylvania, on June 19, 1950. She is a graduate of Kutztown State College, and she is now working as a graphic designer and biological illustrator at the College of Marine Studies,

University of Delaware. Ms. Butler lives in Newark, Delaware, and is an avid birdwatcher and a member of the Guild of Natural Science Illustrators. She has exhibited paintings at several local galleries, and examples of her work have been published in a variety of scientific and conservation publications. Ms. Butler's design for the 1982 Delaware Duck Stamp contest was selected from among sixty-four entries.

LEE CABLE
1982 Florida Duck Stamp

Lee Cable was born in Greenville, Ohio, in 1943. Even as a young child, he was enthusiastic about the outdoors, and he still retains happy memories of his early experiences with wildlife. He studied design, composition, and anatomy while in his teens, and he kept up his art studies throughout his service in the Air Force. After leaving the service, Mr. Cable took on the position of art director for a company in Greenville. He went on to become an editorial artist for the *Tampa Times* in 1968. Since 1975 he has pursued his lifelong ambition to work as a wildlife artist. He is a member of the Society of Animal Artists and has exhibited in the Leigh Yawkey Woodson Bird Art Exhibition.

KEN CARLSON
1982 Texas Duck Stamp, 1985 Arkansas Duck Stamp

Ken Carlson was born in Morton, Minnesota, on August 12, 1937. His interest in art began at an early age, and he began studying with a private teacher when he was sixteen. After his formal art training, he began a career as a commercial illustrator, while he continued to develop his interest in painting, drawing, and photographing animals. His works have appeared in many magazines and in numerous galleries throughout the country and he was the winner of the 1979 National Wild Turkey Federation Stamp contest. He was commissioned to do the 1982 Foundation for North American Wild Sheep Stamp. In that same year, he also did the Texas Duck Stamp, and his First of Issue Texas Turkey Stamp design was an instant hit. Mr. Carlson was also selected to design the 1985 First of Issue Texas Nongame Whooping Cranes Stamp.

GLENN D. CHAMBERS
1984 Missouri Duck Stamp

Glenn D. Chambers was born in Butler, Missouri, on June 14, 1936. He obtained his Master of Arts in wildlife management from the University of Missouri, then worked as a biologist and photographer for the Missouri Department of Conservation. He became a regional director for Ducks Unlimited in 1979 and still holds that post. Mr. Chambers currently resides in Columbia, Missouri.

DAVID CHAPPLE
1986 Kentucky Duck Stamp

David Chapple was born on March 30, 1947. His study of taxidermy has obviously helped him to master the anatomical details of his wildlife subjects. He has used his knowledge to create accurate, authentic, and artistic bird and animal scenes. Mr. Chapple was a three-time finalist in the California Duck Stamp contest, and he was invited to exhibit at the Leigh Yawkey Woodson Bird Art Show in Wausau, Wisconsin, and at the Easton Waterfowl Festival in Maryland. In addition to winning the 1986 Kentucky Duck Stamp contest, he also has won the 1985 First of State California Turkey Stamp, the 1985 North Dakota Trout and Salmon Stamp, the 1986 Quail Unlimited Grand Slam Quail Stamp, and the 1987 Quail Unlimited Stamp contests. Mr. Chapple resides in Irvine, California, with his wife and family.

JOSEPH CIBULA

1984 Massachusetts Duck Stamp

Joseph Cibula was born in Meriden, Connecticut. He obtained his formal art training at the Paire School in Connecticut, but he has also studied with such noted artists as Ken Davies and Paul Lipp. Mr. Cibula has worked in the commercial art field, but in 1982 he

decided to devote his full time to painting. He is not himself an avid hunter, but he does admire decoys as an art form and is happy to use them as subjects for his paintings. He currently lives and works in Marstons Mills, where he has his studio.

ROLAND H. CLARK
1938–39 Federal Duck Stamp

Roland H. Clark was born in New Rochelle, New York, on April 2, 1874. He attended private schools in New York City and received his formal art education under tutors at the Art Students League. Mr. Clark lived for 22 years in Gloucester, Virginia, on an offshoot of Chesapeake Bay. He went into oystering as a business, but he found too many opportunities there for wildlife painting to be diverted for long. He is principally noted for some five hundred etchings he did of game birds and wildfowl, but he has done oil paintings of sporting scenes and watercolors as well. In addition, he wrote four books—mostly recollections of his hunting trips —all illustrated by himself. He was a charter member of the American Sporting Artists and also a member of Ducks Unlimited, Inc. He died in Norwalk, Connecticut, on April 13, 1957.

RON CLAYTON
1985 Missouri Duck Stamp

Ron Clayton was born in St. Louis, Missouri, on September 5, 1957. He is a self-taught artist who works in a lively, realistic style. He participates regularly in national and local jury shows and he exhibits in galleries. He has received many awards. His two most satisfying accomplishments to date may be winning the 1985 Missouri Duck Stamp contest and the commission to design the cover artwork for Missouri Conservationist magazine. Mr. Clayton was in the Ducks Unlimited Wildlife Art Show in Kansas City and the Missouri Historical Society's "America in Paint and Bronze" show. He is a member of the Missouri Wildlife Artist Society.

RUSSELL COBANE
1986 Michigan Duck Stamp

Russell Cobane was born in Detroit, Michigan, on August 10, 1946. He is a nationally known commercial artist who specializes in technical paintings of mechanical products. His first wildlife painting dates from 1982, and in 1984 he entered stamp competitions for the first time. In 1985 he was chosen Michigan Ducks Unlimited Artist of the Year. In 1986 he was chosen Print of the Year Artist by the National Wildlife Federation, was the winner of the 1986 Michigan Duck Stamp contest, and has recently won the 1988 Michigan Trout Stamp contest. In addition, he was designated Indiana State Sponsor Print Artist for 1988. Mr. Cobane lives with his wife and family in rural Clarkston, Michigan.

GUY COHELEACH
1987 Kansas Duck Stamp

Guy Coheleach was born in New York. He has been in the forefront of contemporary wildlife art for the last thirty years. He is listed in *Who's Who in the World*, *Who's Who in America*, and *Who's Who in American Art*. His work has been exhibited in the National Collection of Fine Art, the White House, and the Royal Ontario Museum. Incidentally, he was the first American artist to exhibit in Beijing, China. Among his honors was his selection in 1983 as Master Artist of the Year by the Leigh Yawkey Woodson Museum. Visiting heads of state have received his eagle print.

ARTHUR M. COOK
1972–73 Federal Duck Stamp

Arthur M. Cook was born in Oak Park, Illinois, on September 15, 1931. At the age of ten, he moved with his family to the Minneapolis area. He began his formal art studies in high school and pursued them through Hamline University and the Minneapolis School of Art. He held a number of positions in commercial art with different studios and is now industrial art director at Honeywell. Always an active conservationist, he is a

member of both the National and International Wildlife Federations, Ducks Unlimited, the National Audubon Society, and Trout Unlimited. He has also found time to gain recognition as a lily hybridizer and do botanical drawings for the North American Lily Society Yearbook. He loves hunting and fishing and always brings a camera with him to do research for his wildlife paintings.

LARRY CORRY
1984 Michigan Duck Stamp

Larry Corry was born in Detroit, Michigan, on September 15, 1941. He took his formal art training at the Art School of the Society of Arts and Crafts in Detroit, an institution now known as the Center for Creative Studies. After that, Mr. Corry worked as an advertising illustrator for fourteen years. Since 1984, however, he has been a freelance illustrator, working in the commercial art field as well as pursuing his own vocation of wildlife art. His illustrations have appeared in such magazines as *Michigan Out-of-Doors*, *Michigan Natural Resources*, and *New Mexico Wildlife Magazine*. He won the 1980 and 1983 Michigan Trout Stamp contests as well as the 1984 Michigan Duck Stamp contest.

JOHN P. COWAN
1985 Texas Duck Stamp, 1986 Arkansas Duck Stamp

John P. Cowan was born in Bristol, Tennessee, on October 20, 1920. He graduated from the art school of Pratt Institute in Brooklyn, New York, in 1942, obtaining a degree in illustration. Mr. Cowan worked from 1949 to 1962 first as an agency art director and then as an award-winning freelance illustrator. In 1962, he left advertising and editorial illustration, devoting his time and talent to wildlife and sporting art. His works have appeared in many national outdoor magazines, and well-known galleries and museums throughout the country have displayed his watercolor paintings. Mr. Cowan was honored in 1977 as Ducks Unlimited Artist of the Year. Recently, he won the competition for the 1988 Texas Duck Stamp. He resides in Montgomery, Texas.

TOM CRAIN
1981 Missouri Duck Stamp, 1986 Missouri Duck Stamp

Tom Crain was born in La Junta, Colorado, on February 4, 1952. He has been painting wildlife ever since he was a small boy growing up in the countryside around Colorado Springs. He is a two-time winner of the Missouri Duck Stamp competition, and he is one of Missouri's most popular wildlife artists. He lives with his wife and family in Willard, Missouri.

RODNEY CROSSMAN
1981 Indiana Duck Stamp

Rodney Crossman took his undergraduate degree in art education at Marion College in Marion, Indiana, in 1976. He has received over one hundred awards at juried art shows, many of which include first-place ribbons and "Best of Show" awards. His work has also been seen in a number of national and regional exhibitions and has been featured in over twenty one-man exhibits. He has shown in colleges, galleries, and public places, and his work is now in the collections of many corporations, museums, and private homes throughout the country. As well as winning the 1981 Indiana Duck Stamp contest, he was also commissioned by the Indiana Department of Natural Resources to design the 1982 Indiana Habitat Stamp.

PHILLIP CROWE
1980 Tennessee Duck Stamp, 1983 Tennessee Duck Stamp, 1984 New Hampshire Duck Stamp

Phillip Crowe was born in McMinnvile, Tennessee, on September 8, 1947. After earning a B.A. from the Ringling School of Art in Sarasota, Florida, he went to work as an executive art director for an advertising agency in Nashville, Tennessee. In 1976, he opened The Art Office in Nashville, a commercial design studio, and shortly thereafter he was approached by Grey Stone Press, print publishers, to render some wildlife paintings for them. The results led Mr. Crowe to focus his main attention on wildlife art. Besides the Tennessee and New Hampshire Duck Stamps he also painted the 1985 Louisiana Turkey Stamp, the 1986 Waterfowl U.S.A. Stamp, the 1986 Quail Unlimited Stamp, and the 1986 International Woodduck Conservation Stamp. In 1982, he was selected as the first designer of the National Retriever Club Stamp; he also did their 1985 stamp.

ROGER CRUWYS
1987 Montana Duck Stamp

Roger Cruwys was born in Buffalo, New York, on November 8, 1938. He early developed an interest in nature and outdoor pursuits in rural Wellsville, where he haunted the trout streams and grouse coverts of the local countryside. He was a successful landscape architect–designer with undergraduate and graduate degrees from Syracuse University and the University of California. In 1978, he turned to wildlife art as a career. A self-taught artist, he has found ready acceptance for his work in major galleries, private collections, and many national sports magazines. His art concentrates on bird dogs, fly-fishing, and waterfowl. Mr. Cruwys lives in Bozeman, Montana.

JAY NORWOOD ("DING") DARLING
1934–35 Federal Duck Stamp

Jay Norwood ("Ding") Darling was born on October 21, 1876, in Norwood, Michigan, which gave him his middle name. He early acquired the nickname "Ding," and it stuck. His art career began during a stint as a reporter on the Sioux City Tribune, where he began cartooning. In 1906, he took a job with the Des Moines Register and Tribune, where he stayed until his retirement in 1949. Beginning in 1917, his cartoons were syndicated in 130 daily newspapers, and his drawings were compiled and published in a book every two years from 1908 to 1920. In 1934, he designed the first duck stamp himself. He received many honors over the years, including two Pulitzer Prizes for journalism, two honorary doctorates, and other medals and awards. Mr. Darling died in 1962.

JACK C. DELONEY
1981 Alabama Duck Stamp

Jack C. DeLoney was born in south Alabama in 1940. He majored in fine arts at Auburn University, graduating with a B.A. in 1964. A highly successful painter, Mr. DeLoney spends his studio time painting well-designed watercolors that display directness and purity of design. He has over eighty awards to his credit, and he has exhibited in many regional, national, and international juried shows. He is an associate member of the American Watercolor Society and a member of the Southern Watercolor Society.

JOHN H. DICK
1952–53 Federal Duck Stamp

John H. Dick was born in Islip, New York, on May 12, 1919. As a child he did not take up drawing but maintained a respectable collection of wildfowl. In 1947, Mr. Dick moved to a plantation in South Carolina that had belonged to his mother. There he began his first professional drawings of birds. At that time, he worked on commissions and as the illustrator for numerous magazines and books. Photography, another of his interests, has taken him throughout the world to take pictures of birds and animals. His works have appeared in *The Bird Watchers of America, Carolina Low Country Impressions, A Gathering of Shore Birds, Florida Bird Life,* and *South Carolina Bird Life,* as well as *A Pictorial Guide to the Birds of India* and *The Birds of China.* Throughout, Mr. Dick has maintained aviaries and closed pens of birds at Dixie Plantation.

STEVE DILLARD
1987 South Carolina Duck Stamp

Steve Dillard was born on May 13, 1956. He graduated in 1978 from Clemson University with high honors and a degree in zoology. He was soon to combine his natural artistic talent with his training in zoology to become a full-time professional wildlife artist. In recognition of

his talent, the South Carolina Wildlife Federation selected him to design its Print of the Year in both 1984 and 1986. He has also exhibited at several major art shows, including the Easton Waterfowl Festival and the Southeastern Wildlife Exposition. His entries have finished in the top ten in Federal Duck Stamp competitions. He was chosen to do the 1987 and 1988 South Carolina Ducks Unlimited Sponsor Print of the Year. Mr. Willard was also chosen to design the 1988 West Virginia Duck Stamp.

DANNY DORNING
1986 Alabama Duck Stamp

Danny Dorning was born in Blount County, Alabama, on January 7, 1950. Blount County is a rural area, and there he began to draw and paint wildlife subjects at an early age. His love of the outdoors is an advantage to him, since he has for thirteen years made a living working in the timber business while using every spare minute to paint. The knowledge of the outdoors that he has acquired is evident in the accuracy with which he depicts plants, animals, and their native habitats in his paintings.

AL DORNISCH
1984 South Carolina Duck Stamp

Al Dornisch was born in St. Marys, Pennsylvania, on October 27, 1931. Basically he is a self-taught artist. In spite of that, or perhaps because of it, he has developed a unique style in his works that has led him to become one of the country's most popular wildlife artists. His works have been exhibited in all of the major wildlife art shows throughout the nation, and his works are also found in private collections throughout the world. Mr. Dornisch is president of Northern Precision Materials, Inc., a manufacturer of metallurgical components. He lives in Minneapolis with his wife and family.

ARTHUR R. EAKIN
1981 Maryland Duck Stamp

Arthur R. Eakin was born in Elizabeth, New Jersey. He has a lifetime association with springer spaniels, field trials, rail birds, broad bills, widgeons, and black ducks. As a young man, he worked with Ted Mulliken, starting the now famous Wildlife Decoy Company. He has long been a colorful figure in the sporting game, winning the Springer National Field Trial, and he has judged, and gunned, the National Spaniel Trials, both here and in England. He owned a kennel farm in Bucks County, Pennsylvania, where he raised pheasants and mallards that were flown for released shoots. He studied art at the Grand Central Art School in New York and later received the advice—and friendship—of several of the great local artists of the Bucks County area. Mr. Eakin now lives in Chestertown on the eastern shore of Maryland.

JOHN F. EGGERT
1979 Illinois Duck Stamp, 1980 Massachusetts Duck Stamp, 1982 Massachusetts Duck Stamp

John F. Eggert was born in Chicago, on September 11, 1934. After finishing high school, he started work at an art studio where, as an apprentice, he received his formal training. Known for the striking detail of his work, he also designed the 1978, 1979, 1980, and 1981 Illinois Salmon Stamp and did the artwork for the 1982 Massachusetts Deer Stamp. Mr. Eggert's wildlife illustrations have appeared in the *World Book Encyclopedia, National Geographic, Reader's Digest,* and *Field & Stream.* He has done nine collectors' plates, which included the "Angler's Dream" series, "Cats," and "Swans." His original paintings and limited edition prints can be found in many private collections throughout the United States. At present, Mr. Eggert resides in Cape Cod, Massachusetts.

DICK ELLIOTT
1979 Tennessee Duck Stamp

Dick Elliott was born on November 30, 1931. A graduate of Austin Peay State College and the Harris School of Art, he is a professional illustrator and designer. Mr.

Elliott has had years of experience in the art field both as a teacher at the University of Tennessee and as a commercial art director for the Methodist Publishing House and Genesco in Nashville. Crisp, bright watercolors are the hallmark of his work, and he is adept at blending the designs of nature and of man into one unified piece. His landscapes and life portraits bring a vivid and refreshing style to contemporary subjects. Mr. Elliott is a member of the Tennessee Watercolor Society and has had numerous exhibitions and one-man shows. He now resides in Hendersonville, just outside Nashville.

ROBERT ESCHENFELDT
1975 Illinois Duck Stamp

Robert Eschenfeldt was born on October 14, 1930. He is a graduate of Chicago's American Academy of Art. For the past twenty years, Mr. Eschenfeldt has worked as an illustrator and an art director. He prides himself in capturing detail and accuracy in his paintings.

RON FERKOL
1987 Missouri Duck Stamp

Ron Ferkol was born in Cleveland, Ohio. He spent his youth in the Missouri Ozarks, where he developed a love of the outdoors that now leads him to study nature and to hunt and fish whenever time permits. He is a self-taught artist with a great deal of natural talent. Mr. Ferkol won the 1987 Missouri Duck Stamp contest and, in addition, he won the 1988 Missouri Trout Stamp contest. He also won Honorable Mentions in the Missouri competitions in 1983, 1984, and 1986. He resides in Gerald, Missouri, with his wife.

MARIO FERNANDEZ
1986 North Dakota Duck Stamp

Mario Fernandez was born in Havana, Cuba. He is now one of the country's most widely collected wildlife artists. He has won numerous Best of Show awards, beginning with his "Spirit of Freedom" painting at the 1981 National Wildlife Show in Kansas City. He was featured artist for the National Wildlife Show in 1983, and in 1984 he won both the Minnesota Trout and Pheasant Stamp contests. Mr. Fernandez was named Featured Artist for the 1985 Southeastern Wildlife Exposition in Charleston, South Carolina, and he was Wildlife Artist of the Year for the 1985 International Wildlife, Western and American Art Show in Chicago. He was also honored as the 1986 Wildlife Artist of the Year for the Wildlife and Western Art Collectors Society Show in Minneapolis, Minnesota.

JAMES P. FISHER
1975–76 Federal Duck Stamp

James P. Fisher was born in Wilmington, Delaware, on February 25, 1912. At the age of seventeen, while attending art school, he decided that if he was to succeed in his goal of becoming an artist, he would have to work harder. He took on the task of copying each of the plates from E.S. Thompson's *Art Anatomy of Animals.* Completing this project indelibly printed on his mind the importance of anatomical knowledge in drawing. He spent three years at the Wilmington Academy of Art, and after that he turned to commercial advertising art for his livelihood. He kept, however, his old interest in wildlife. A fascination with old derelict decoys prompted him to go to a decoy show in 1973, where he met a collector who allowed him to borrow from his collection for painting. Out of this came his first and only entry in the Federal Duck Stamp contest.

RAYBURN T. FOSTER
1987 Oklahoma Duck Stamp

Rayburn T. Foster was born on January 22, 1947, in El Reno, Oklahoma. He is a self-taught artist who began his career doing freelance artwork; now he is employed as a visual information specialist for the government. He is known for his acrylic and watercolor paintings of wildlife and for his humorous cartoons about the world of hunting and fishing that regularly appear in *Outdoor Oklahoma* magazine. He begins his wildlife art with research, sketches, and photographs. He is a meticulous craftsman who pays great attention to detail. He often goes to the field to study his subjects in their natural habitat and to observe their behavior, anatomy, and color firsthand. He even visits zoos and wildlife refuges to observe and sketch. His works are in several private and corporate collections throughout the country.

KEITH FREEMAN
1983 Indiana Duck Stamp

Keith Freeman was born in Auburn, Indiana, on March 7, 1921. After graduation from high school, he completed a two-year art course at Fort Wayne Art School. He continued his formal art training at the Corcoran Art School in Washington, D.C., the Meinzinger Art School in Detroit, and the Art Center School in Los Angeles. He worked as an art director in a Los Angeles advertising agency for three years and then became an illustrator in a Los Angeles art studio. In 1951, Mr. Freeman returned to Indiana, where he worked in an art studio for two years before opening up his own studio. He has done many wildlife calendars as well as illustrations for the *World Book Encyclopedia* and other educational books. Mr. Freeman has competed with distinction in several state duck stamp contests and won the 1988 Indian Game Bird Stamp design competition.

JEFFREY FREY
1982 Oklahoma Duck Stamp

Jeffrey Frey was born in Cleveland, Oklahoma, on August 5, 1929. After attending Oklahoma State University, where he studied art, he went to the Kansas City Art Institute for two semesters. For the next twenty years, he neglected to pursue his art career, and only ten years ago did he pick it up again. In 1980, he entered the Oklahoma Waterfowl Stamp contest and finished with Honorable Mention. He persisted and won the contest in 1982. He hopes this is the first of many wins for him in future contests.

LOUIS FRISINO
1976 Maryland Duck Stamp, 1986 Maryland Duck Stamp, 1987 New Jersey Duck Stamp

Louis Frisino was born in Baltimore, Maryland. He has been interested in art since childhood. Deaf since birth, he attended the Maryland State School for the Deaf in Frederick, and later he graduated with honors from the Maryland Institute College of Art, receiving at that time the Peabody Award. Since then, Mr. Frisino has appeared in art festivals all along the Atlantic seaboard, winning numerous awards for his work. He also won first place in the Maryland Trout Stamp contests of 1977 and 1979. In addition to his career as an artist, Mr. Frisino pursues his taxidermy and woodcarving hobbies.

LOTTI FULTON
1985 Mississippi Duck Stamp

Lotti Fulton was born in Angerburg, East Prussia, Germany, on September 17, 1935. She received her formal art training at Pratt Institute in Brooklyn, New York, where she studied commercial art and advertising. She combined her artistic talent and love of nature to become a professional wildlife artist. Ms. Fulton has made her home in Jackson, Mississippi, for over twenty years.

ROBERT GARNER
1987 Mississippi Duck Stamp

Robert Garner was born in Batesville, Mississippi, on May 8, 1945. He began drawing, painting, and creatively designing at an early age. He received his formal art training at Mississippi Valley State University. He has served as an art instructor in the public schools in and around his home town of Greenville, Mississippi, for the past eighteen years. He has exhibited in several local and statewide contests, gaining top honors in some of them. In November of 1983, he had a painting displayed in the auditorium of the Department of the Interior in Washington, D.C. In addition, some of his works are held in private collections.

ALBERT EARL ("GIL") GILBERT
1978–79 Federal Duck Stamp Winner

Albert Earl ("Gil") Gilbert was born in Chicago on August 22, 1939. His favorite place as a boy was the Brookfield Zoo, where he often skipped school to sketch animals and birds. After a brief stint as a park ranger, he began his career as a wildlife artist, doing illustrations for nature magazines and painting many of the National Wildlife Federation's stamps. Working with the American Museum of Natural History, he illustrated several books including *Eagles, Hawks and Falcons of the World*. Mr. Gilbert served as president of the Society of Animal Artists from 1977 through 1984. He was the first artist to paint full-color remarques for the Federal Duck Stamp prints. Originals of some of his works can be found in the Carnegie Museum, the Field Museum, and the Princeton University Art Museum. Mr. Gilbert was honored wth a chapter on his art in the recently published book *Twentieth-Century Wildlife Artists*. Possibly, his most widely published artwork is the wild turkey he painted many years ago for the Wild Turkey Bourbon label.

BOB GILLESPIE
1981 Tennessee Duck Stamp

Bob Gillespie was born in Birmingham, Alabama, on January 3, 1945. He developed a love of nature and the outdoors at an early age. When he was a teenager, his family moved to Tennessee, where he was introduced to the world of waterfowl. This experience plus his innate love of nature and fondness for birds led him to begin painting the waterfowl in a style all his own. Mr. Gillespie also attended the Art Institute of Pittsburgh, where he won school honors, and then moved back to middle Tennessee, where he now lives and operates his studio in Mt. Juliet.

JERRIE GLASPER
1983 Mississippi Duck Stamp

Jerrie Glasper was born in Chicago, on May 26, 1963. In 1971, his family moved to St. Louis, Missouri, where, during his early high school years, he developed into a very promising portrait painter. In 1980, he moved to Greenville, Mississippi, and attended Greenville High School, where he met Bobby Tompkins, a teacher and past winner of the Mississippi Duck Stamp contest. With the encouragement and guidance of Mr. Tompkins, he began working in oils on wildlife subjects. With his first entry into the Mississippi Duck Stamp competition, Mr. Glasper finished in the top ten finalists. Four months later, he won the Mississippi Duck Stamp contest for 1983 with a design of Lesser Scaup ducks. Currently, Mr. Glasper resides in Greenville.

TOMMY GOODMAN
1984 Mississippi Duck Stamp

Tommy Goodman was born in Meridian, Mississippi, on August 4, 1946. After receiving a degree in fine arts from Delta State University, he taught art in several high schools. He then entered the School of Architecture at Auburn University, and he now practices that profession full time. He continues with his painting as a hobby, using it mostly for pleasure and relaxation. Mr. Goodman now makes his home in Jackson, Mississippi.

JOHN C. GREEN
1983 Delaware Duck Stamp

John C. Green was born in Sioux Falls, South Dakota, on January 19, 1952. He has earned his living by painting wildlife since his high school days. His strong desire to learn new techniques and to strive for excellence in everything he paints are the twin driving forces behind his life's ambition to become one of this country's leading wildlife artists. He was helped in this endeavor by his father, Larry Green, also an artist, who is credited with teaching him the art of oil painting and how its ever-changing elements can be utilized by a wildlife artist. Mr. Green's works have been shown in major galleries throughout the country, and his illustrations have appeared frequently in major outdoor publications. His works have helped raise over $1,000,000 for Ducks Unlimited.

OWEN J. GROMME
1945–46 Federal Duck Stamp, 1978 Wisconsin Duck Stamp

Owen J. Gromme was born in Fond du Lac, Wisconsin, on July 5, 1968. Early on he was a hunter and outdoorsman, and his work reflects the great interest he always had in birds. During his years at the Milwaukee Public Museum, Mr. Gromme went on several expeditions, including several to Alaska and another to the Hudson Bay area. He also went in 1928 and 1929 to Africa, a trip that began his serious work in painting. Some of his paintings illustrated *Birds of Wisconsin* (1963); other publications featuring his work include *The Wild Turkey*, the book jacket and cover of *Birds Will Come to You*, *Circus World Museum, Baraboo, Wisconsin*, and several plates in *Birds of Colorado*. Mr. Gromme also provided a complete gallery of paintings for the Marshal & Ilsey Bank of Milwaukee, and a hall in the Milwaukee Public Museum was named in his honor.

THOMAS GROSS
1984 Minnesota Duck Stamp

Thomas Gross was born in St. Paul, Minnesota, on May 19, 1952. Except for art classes in grade school and high school, Mr. Gross is essentially a self-taught artist. In 1983, he entered the Minnesota Duck Stamp contest, his first wildlife competition, and placed sixth. The following year, he won. With that victory, he launched his career as a wildlife artist. He was a 1986 finalist in the Federal Duck Stamp competition. Mr. Gross resides in Woodbury, Minnesota, with his wife and family.

NOLAN HAAN
1984 Delaware Duck Stamp, 1986 Nevada Duck Stamp

Nolan Haan was born in Pennsylvania, on May 4, 1948. He was originally a portrait artist, and he entered the wildlife field when his first attempt at a duck painting placed second in the 1983 Federal Duck Stamp competition. In the following months, he placed second and fourth in the Maryland Duck Stamp competitions, third in the Nevada competition, and, finally, finished first in the 1984 Delaware contest. His works have already been exhibited in the Leigh Yawkey Woodson Art Museum Show, the Easton Waterfowl Festival, and the South Carolina Art Exposition. Mr. Haan now resides in Bethesda, Maryland, where he is actively pursuing his career in wildlife art.

JACK C. HAHN
1985 Iowa Duck Stamp

Jack C. Hahn was born in Middle Amana, one of the historical Amana villages in east central Iowa, on July 30, 1940. From an early age, he found that art and wildlife were an important part of his life. The two interests did not converge, however, until 1971, when he began carving realistic decoys. By the mid-1970s, he had received national recognition as a consistent winner of carving competitions across the country. From carving, his wildlife interest led to an involvement in painting outdoor scenes. Painting is now of equal importance with carving in his professional career. He still lives in Middle Amana with his wife, where they operate a century-old hearth oven bakery.

RAY HARM
1985 Kentucky Duck Stamp

Ray Harm was born in 1926, in Randolph County, West Virginia. His interest in wildlife began early in his life in West Virginia, where his father, who made a living digging and drying mountain herbs, taught him much. In his teen years, he traveled west, working as a ranch hand and as a rodeo rider. He then returned east to study at the Cooper School of Art and the Cleveland Institute of Art. Besides the recognition he has earned as a wildlife painter, he is also a lecturer and nature writer. Mr. Harm was also one of the two founders, in 1961, of what is known today as the limited edition print industy, and it was natural for him to be commissioned to do the design for the First of State Kentucky Duck Stamp. Mr. Harm currently operates a ranch southeast of Tucson, Arizona.

LARRY HAYDEN

1977 Michigan Duck Stamp, 1979 Nevada Duck Stamp, 1980 Michigan Duck Stamp, 1981 Texas Duck Stamp, 1984 Arkansas Duck Stamp, 1987 Michigan Duck Stamp

Larry Hayden was born in Detroit, Michigan, on March 21, 1934. An avid hunter and fisherman, he found it only natural to turn his artistic talents to his favorite pastime—waterfowl. Long recognized as one of the premier competitive decoy carvers, Mr. Hayden mixes both avocations; for instance, his hen Canvasback in the 1977 Michigan design is painted from the same reference material he used to carve the decoy that won Best of Show in the 1977 World Decoy Carving Championships. His works are very much in demand, with both his Duck Stamp prints and his annual ''Marsh Duck'' series being immediate sellouts. He was commissioned by bid selection to design the 1981 First of State Texas Stamp. Mr. Hayden is a full-time wildlife artist who lives with his wife and family in Framington Hills, Michigan.

JOHN HEIDERSBACH

1987 Iowa Duck Stamp

John Heidersbach was born in 1942, in Elmhurst, Illinois. His matching wins in the 1987 Iowa Waterfowl Stamp and 1987 Habitat Stamp design contests were only the latest in a long list of progressively higher-place finishes in state and national wildlife art competitions. Mr. Heidersbach tries to capture those rare moments when ''nature is quiet.'' At the same time, he tries to show as much detail as possible in every subject he paints. Thus he conveys in his paintings both mood and accuracy of detail.

TOM HENNESSEY

1975 Massachusetts Duck Stamp

Tom Hennessey was born in Bangor, Maine. The authentic realism of his paintings reflects his lifelong exposure to the sportsman's world and to the coastal fishing areas of Maine. He is a self-taught artist, and his works are represented by this country's leading art dealers. He has had many group shows and exhibits throughout the nation, and his works have also been used in numerous outdoor and wildlife publications. Among many of his awards, Mr. Hennessey is especially proud that several of his paintings were selected by the U.S. Department of the Interior to be displayed in the first showing of Western world sporting art in China and in eastern Europe. Mr. Hennessey currently resides in Bangor.

HEINER HERTLING

1983 Florida Duck Stamp

Heiner Hertling was born in Hamburg, Germany, on October 22, 1940. He came to the United States in 1965 with $700 in his pocket. Since that time he has established his own successful art studio in Detroit. A relative newcomer to wildlife art, he won his first major contest with the 1983 Florida Duck Stamp. His success in the Florida contest was followed by the 1984 Michigan Trout Stamp, the 1985 Kentucky Trout Stamp, and the 1985 First of State Colorado Trout Stamp. In 1984 and again in 1987, he was the Ducks Unlimited Artist of the Year for Michigan. Mr. Hertling lives with his wife and family in West Bloomfield, Michigan.

ROBERT W. HINES

1946–47 Federal Duck Stamp

Robert W. Hines was born in Columbus, Ohio, on February 6, 1912. Early in 1939, he was accepted as a staff artist for the Ohio Division of Conservation. Nine years later, he became an artist with the U.S. Fish and Wildlife Service in Washington. He illustrated *The Edge of the Sea* by Rachel Carson, his first supervisor at the Wildlife Service. Because he was working for a scientific organization, he had to make his art extremely accurate, and his drawings and paintings have been reproduced by conservation magazines in every state of the Union, in Canada, and even in the Soviet Union. He wrote and illustrated *Ducks at a Distance*. Moreover, Mr. Hines has done illustrations for more than eighty books and publications and has painted four wildlife murals for the Interior Building in Washington, D.C.

THOMAS HIRATA

1984 New Jersey Duck Stamp, 1985 New Hampshire Duck Stamp, 1985 North Carolina Duck Stamp, 1986 North Carolina Duck Stamp, 1987 Tennessee Duck Stamp

Thomas Hirata was born in Passaic, New Jersey, on January 11, 1955. His paintings, strong in design, reflect his tight, realistic approach to painting oil on board. Most of his works involve several textures and various lighting techniques. He received his formal art training from Colorado College in Colorado Springs, the Art Students League in New York City, and the Art Center College of Design in Pasadena, California. His work has been exhibited in shows at the Leigh Yawkey Woodson Art Museum, the Smithsonian, the Denver Museum of Natural History, and other shows throughout the United States. A member of the Society of Animal Artists and Ducks Unlimited, Mr. Hirata currently resides in Rutherford, New Jersey.

CARLA HUBER

1984 Maryland Duck Stamp

Carla Huber was born in San Francisco, on March 30, 1942. She holds a Bachelor of Fine Arts degree from Pratt Institute and has studied at the School of Visual Arts, both in New York City. A former fashion illustrator, in the past few years Ms. Huber has turned her attention to wildlife art. The success of this new emphasis is evidenced by her winning the 1982 Maryland Trout Stamp competition and the 1984 Maryland Duck Stamp competition. In addition, she finished in the finals of the Federal Duck Stamp contest, an impressive accomplishment for an artist new to the wildlife field. Ms. Huber's works are now gaining in popularity at a fast pace.

ALLEN HUGHES

1977 Mississippi Duck Stamp, 1984 Tennessee Duck Stamp

Allen Hughes, M.D., was born in Memphis, Tennessee, on July 20, 1939. While still a student at Southwestern College in Memphis, he began practicing taxidermy. Through this, he gained a better knowledge of the anatomy and detail of the subjects that he portrayed in his paintings and woodcarvings. Even so, he is a self-taught artist who has always loved the outdoors. His works have appeared in many national wildlife publications, and they are found in many private and public collections throughout the country. Mr. Hughes's paintings of waterfowl have consistently won Best of Show awards at the many juried shows he has entered, including thirteen at the National Wildlife Show in Kansas City. In 1972, he became the first person to win both the top painting and woodcarving awards at that show.

LYNN BOGUE HUNT

1939–40 Federal Duck Stamp

Lynn Bogue Hunt was born in 1878, in Honeoye Falls, New York. At the age of twelve, he went to Michigan to live and continued his strong interest in the study and drawing of wildlife. He also developed skills in taxidermy. After three years in college, Mr. Hunt became a staff artist at the *Detroit Free Press*. At the same time, he began sending wildlife artwork to various national magazines and soon moved to New York, where he continued to sell more and more of his work. He published in such magazines as *Saturday Evening Post, Field and Stream, Natural History*, and many others. In 1936, he published a book of bird paintings and drawings, *An Artist's Game Bag*. His illustrations also appeared in *A Book on Duck Shooting, American Big Game Fishing, Atlantic Big Game Fishing, American Neighbors of the Countryside, American Hunter*, and others. Mr. Hunt died in 1960.

FRANCIS LEE JACQUES

1940–41 Federal Duck Stamp

Francis Lee Jacques was born in Genesco, Illinois, on September 28, 1887. Although he began his career as an artist at age thirty-three, if all his works were put together they would total close to thirty thousand square feet, an outstanding amount. In 1924, he joined the American Museum of Natural History where he produced a multitude of background paintings that can

still be seen in many American museums. Mr. Jacques illustrated a number of books produced in collaboration with his wife, Florence Sarah Page, a writer. His illustrations appeared in other books, too, among them *Oceanic Birds of South America, American South Carolina Bird Life, Florida Bird Life*, and *Outdoor Life's Gallery of North American Game*. In addition, Mr. Jacques and his wife received the John Burroughs Medal, an award for the best nature study books. Mr. Jacques is deceased.

BRIAN JARVI

1986 Minnesota Duck Stamp

Brian Jarvi was born in Grand Rapids, Minnesota, on February 5, 1956. He began drawing early, influenced by his mother's artistic abilities. He also developed a fascination with wildlife and the outdoors. Gradually his interests in art and nature came together, and he took up painting and photographing wildlife around 1979. Basically a self-taught artist, he paints in oils, preferring the smooth texture and blending qualities of the medium. His entries placed high in the 1979 and 1983 Minnesota Duck Stamp contests, and he won the 1987 Minnesota Pheasant Stamp contest. An avid conservationist who has donated many of his paintings for fund-raising events, he was instrumental in starting the Floodwood, Minnesota, chapter of Ducks Unlimited.

RON JENKINS

1965–66 Federal Duck Stamp

Ron Jenkins was born in Pawtucket, Rhode Island, on August 18, 1932. After service in the Marines for three years, he attended the Philadelphia Museum of Art in 1955. He had to leave art study for a paying job, but he maintained his painting, and in 1964 he won the Federal Duck Stamp contest. Mr. Jenkins began freelancing in 1966. He has illustrations in *Pennsylvania Game News, Pennsylvania Angler, National Geographic*, and *Modern Game Breeding*. Mr. Jenkins works in any medium, but has said that the fast-drying media of opaque watercolor and polymer suit him best. He also teaches from time to time and gives lectures on art and conservation. Mr. Jenkins makes his home in Missoula, Montana.

JERRY JOHNSON

1982 Mississippi Duck Stamp

Jerry Johnson was born in Corinth, Mississippi, on July 13, 1947. He is a self-taught artist who works in both oils and watercolors, painting sporting scenes, wildlife, and the rapidly vanishing rural life of the South. Indeed, Mr. Johnson is as much at home in front of his canvas as he is roaming the hills of his native Mississippi. He has served six years as an art director for a local business and has done much freelance commercial art besides. He is especially proud of two of his works that are displayed in the White House.

PAUL B. JOHNSON

1971–77 California Duck Stamp

Paul Johnson was born in San Francisco on February 18, 1907. He attended the San Francisco School of Arts on a scholarship he won with his drawing and sculpture. He was the wildlife artist on contract for the California Department of Fish and Game from 1952 to 1985. His wildlife designs have been featured in many publications, including the *Outdoor California* magazine, which is the Fish and Game Department's bimonthly publication. He is the only artist to be commissioned to do more than one state duck stamp design: he was asked to do the art for the first seven California waterfowl stamps.

RANDY JULIUS

1979 Massachusetts Duck Stamp, 1981 Massachusetts Duck Stamp, 1983 Massachusetts Duck Stamp, 1985 Massachusetts Duck Stamp

Randy Julius was born in Roswell, New Mexico, on March 19, 1948. He has, however, lived in East Bridgewater, Massachusetts, for the past thirty-odd years. After high school, Randy studied commercial art in Boston for a short time, but found it too confining. Living in the Cape Cod area gave him ample opportunity to study waterfowl and learn the art of decoy carving, in which he also excels. In the winter of 1971, he spent a month by himself in the north woods, painting birds. It was then that he decided to pursue a career in wildlife art.

LYNN KAATZ
1986 Ohio Duck Stamp

Lynn Kaatz was born in Elyria, Ohio, on April 28, 1945. He has become internationally known for his wildlife paintings, landscapes, seascapes, and decoy carvings. He has traveled the world extensively for a thorough research into his subject matter. He has received numerous awards, including: winner of the national logo contest for Ducks Unlimited's Fiftieth Anniversary; 1988 Kentucky Duck Stamp; 1987 Watercolor Society Bronze Award; 1986 Ohio Wetlands Habitat Stamp; second place in the 1986 Federal Duck Stamp contest; selection as a Ducks Unlimited National Supplemental Artist every year since 1983. Mr. Kaatz's work has been published in many magazines as well as in *The Labrador Retriever*, by Richard Walters, and he is listed in *Who's Who in Waterfowl Art*.

EDWIN R. KALMBACH
1941–42 Federal Duck Stamp

Edwin R. Kalmbach, D. Sc., was born in Grand Rapids, Michigan, on April 29, 1884. His first job was as assistant director of the Kent Science Museum. He then worked as a biologist in the Biological Survey, a forerunner of the Fish and Wildlife Service. He did many field studies on the crow, blackbird, house sparrow, starling, magpie, and other wildlife. He was deeply involved in dealing with a baffling malady of Western waterfowl; his research led to the discovery of avian botulism, which formed the basis of a campaign against duck sickness. Dr. Kalmbach received the Leopold Medal of the Wildlife Society, and he was the recipient of the highest honor of the Department of the Interior —the Distinguished Service Award. Dr. Kalmbach is deceased.

BART KASSABAUM
1980 Illinois Duck Stamp, 1983 Illinois Duck Stamp, 1985 Illinois Duck Stamp, 1987 Illinois Duck Stamp

Bart Kassabaum was born in Granville, Illinois, on July 26, 1947. He developed an interest in painting and the outdoors at an early age, and he became a basically self-taught freelance commercial artist who now concentrates almost entirely on wildlife art. He currently does many commissions for private collectors as well as entering other state waterfowl competitions that are opened to nonresidents. He was the first artist in the country to win four duck stamp competitions in his home state.

BARBARA KEEL
1979 Alabama Duck Stamp

Barbara Keel was born in Opelika, Alabama. She has spent many hours around her home studying the abundant wildlife of the area. Her main interest is painting the big cats—tigers and lions—that are gradually vanishing from the earth due to poaching and loss of their native habitat. The detail and perfection of her work reflects her love for these animals. Her honors include many first place awards in the International Wildlife Art Show, and first place awards for three years in the Southeastern Wildlife Art Exhibit. In 1979, Ms. Keel was one of two artists who were the first women to do state duck stamps. And she is the first woman to have done a First of State duck stamp.

GEORGE KIEFFER
1984 Illinois Duck Stamp

George Kieffer was born in Rock Island, Illinois, on May 25, 1932. He grew up there, hunting and fishing on the Mississippi River. In 1974, he began carving decoys and is now one of the most popular carvers in the Midwest, having won awards for his decoys in all the major shows and exhibits. In 1982, Mr. Kieffer entered his first piece of flatwork in the Illinois Duck

Stamp contest and finished second. His high finish encouraged him to try again, and in 1984 he won the contest. Although he prefers to carve decoys, he will almost certainly enter more stamp and wildlife contests, with an excellent chance of success if past performance is any indication.

JIM KILLEN
1983 South Carolina Duck Stamp, 1984 North Carolina Duck Stamp, 1984 Pennsylvania Duck Stamp, 1986 Georgia Duck Stamp, 1986 Vermont Duck Stamp, 1987 Vermont Duck Stamp

Jim Killen was born in Montevideo, Minnesota, on January 22, 1934. He ranks among the country's foremost wildlife artists, his memorable watercolors earning him acclaim wherever they are shown. After winning many awards and honors at art shows, Mr. Killen was presented the President's Award as the Outstanding Wildlife Artist of the Ducks Unlimited National Wildlife Art Show in Kansas City in 1980 and again in 1981. He was also commissioned by the Marshlands Fund, Inc. to design that organization's first annual stamp. He has done six winning state duck stamp designs for five states, and he was selected Ducks Unlimited Artist of the Year in 1984. Mr. Killen lives in rural Minnesota, where he manages the acreage surrounding his house for the wildlife which abounds there.

NICK KLEPINGER
1976 Iowa Duck Stamp, 1978 Iowa Duck Stamp

Nick Klepinger was born in Charlton, Iowa, on November 30, 1945. He went to high school in Charlton and then attended the University of Oregon at Eugene, from which he graduated with a Bachelor of Arts degree in journalism. He got a sort of false start as a broadcaster with an Iowa radio network, but in 1976 he set out in his present direction and became a full-time freelance artist. Well known as a woodcarver and sculptor, Mr. Klepinger now owns and operates his own art gallery and custom frame shop in Newton, Iowa. He resides in Reasnor, Iowa, with his wife and family.

JOSEPH D. KNAP
1937–38 Federal Duck Stamp

Joseph D. Knap was born in Scottsdale, Pennsylvania, in 1875. His first business had always been real estate, with artwork a hobby, never a profession. At age forty-nine, at the insistence of one of his hunting companions, he first exhibited some of his watercolors at the Ackerman Galleries in New York. He met with almost immediate success. Mr. Knap preferred watercolor for most of his work, but he did make two sets of etchings, each set a limited edition of one hundred signed proofs for which the plates were destroyed after printing. In addition, Mr. Knap's paintings have been exhibited in many cities and were hung at the Grand Central Galleries and the American Museum of Natural History, both in New York. Mr. Knap died in 1962.

CARL ("SPIKE") KNUTH
1978 Indiana Duck Stamp

Carl ("Spike") Knuth was born in Milwaukee, Wisconsin, on August 18, 1937. After graduating from high school in 1955, he went to work for Mercury Outboards and was a commercial artist with the firm for more than eleven years. In 1974, he was hired by the Virginia Commission of Game and Inland Fisheries as audiovisual supervisor and staff artist and photographer for the *Virginia Wildlife* magazine. For the past five years, he has coproduced twenty-six programs entitled *Virginia Wildlife*, which are on seven PBS and five cable television stations. Mr. Knuth's works have not only appeared in that magazine but also on the covers of over seventy outdoors magazines and publications throughout the country, such as *Fur-Fish-Game*, *South Dakota Conservation Digest*, *Minnesota Sportsman*, *Midwest Outdoors*, and *Wisconsin Sportsman*.

ROCKNE ("ROCKY") KNUTH
1979 Wisconsin Duck Stamp, 1983 Wisconsin Duck Stamp

Rockne "Rocky" Knuth was born in Milwaukee, Wisconsin, in 1941. He moved with his family to Fond du

Lac at the age of nine. Rockne has been fascinatd by birds since the age of six when he first tagged along birdwatching with his older brother, Carl "Spike" Knuth, who is also a noted wildlife artist. Rockne's boyhood fascination grew into a serious lifelong interest. His works have appeared in many national publications. For seven years he has been selected to exhibit in the Leigh Yawkey Woodson Birds in Art Exhibition. Besides winning the 1979 and 1983 Wisconsin Duck Stamp, he also won the 1984 Wisconsin Great Lakes Trout and Salmon Stamp competition.

ROBERT C. KNUTSON
1986 Pennsylvania Duck Stamp, 1987 Alabama Duck Stamp

Robert C. Knutson was born in Minneapolis, Minnesota, on May 10, 1913. He was a commercial artist for over fifty years, until he retired and moved to Lillian, Alabama. There he began a new career as a wildlife artist. He has placed in the top five in the Federal Duck Stamp contest. In 1987, he won the Alabama Wildlife Federation Print contest and was named the Alabama Wildlife Federation Artist of the Year. Mr. Knutson feels that, even in his seventies, he has much to learn.

WILLIAM KOELPIN
1982 Wisconsin Duck Stamp

William Koelpin was born in Milwaukee, Wisconsin, on January 24, 1938. Besides his paintings, he has become famous for his wood carvings and bronze sculptures, and he has become one of the nation's most respected artists. His works have been exhibited at the Smithsonian Institute, Leigh Yawkey Woodson Art Museum, The Franklin Mint, and many galleries and art shows throughout the country. Mr. Koelpin currently resides in Hartland, Wisconsin, with his wife and family.

LESLIE C. KOUBA
1958–59 Federal Duck Stamp, 1967–68 Federal Duck Stamp, 1978 Minnesota Duck Stamp, 1985 North Dakota Duck Stamp

Leslie C. Kouba was born in Hutchinson, Minnesota, on February 3, 1917. He had an early interest in drawing and, at age fourteen, began taking art courses by correspondence from Art Instruction, Inc. These constituted the only formal art training he ever had, but they proved to be all he needed. In addition to being a respected wildlife artist, Mr. Kouba is also the founder and proprietor of one of the most respected art galleries of the country—the American Wildlife Art Galleries. This gallery represents some of the best work of the top artists of the nation in this field. Mr. Kouba has also met with success outside of his gallery, with his work in the form of prints achieving a wide distribution. Mr. Kouba has also spent much time photographing wildlife and traveling with Mrs. Kouba in search of Indian artifacts.

AL KRAAYVANGER
1987 Wisconsin Duck Stamp

Al Kraayvanger was born in Milwaukee, Wisconsin, on January 8, 1927. A lover of the outdoors since childhood, Mr. Kraayvanger developed as a wildlife artist even as he juggled the demands of numerous corporate clients in his career as a commercial illustrator. He has placed among the top ten in most of the contests in which he has participated. He was first runner-up in the 1982 Wisconsin Duck Stamp competition.

DIETMAR KRUMREY
1981 Michigan Duck Stamp

Dietmar Krumrey was born in Germany on March 11, 1948. He emigrated to the United States with his family at the age of three. After living in the Chicago area for several years, the family discovered the upper peninsula of Michigan and made their home there. Mr. Krumrey spent the greater part of his youth fishing, hunting, and gaining respect for the wildlife he now enjoys painting. He attended the American Academy in Chicago, then accepted employmnent with Hallmark Cards in Kansas City as an artist. His works have been exhibited in many prestigious shows including the Bird Art Show at the Leigh Yawkey Woodson Art Museum. Mr. Krumrey won the Michigan Ducks Unlimited Artist of the Year Award in 1980 and in 1984, the only artist to win it twice. Among his other honors, he was designated 1987 National Ducks Unlimited Sponsor Artist as well as 1987 Michigan Ducks Unlimited Sponsor Artist.

ANDREW KURZMANN
1979 Michigan Duck Stamp

Andrew Kurzmann was born in Troisdorf, Germany. Educated in the United States, he received his formal art training at the Meinzinger Art School and the Detroit Institute of Arts. He has worked as an illustrator, graphic designer, art director, and as an art instructor at Kellogg Community Colllege. His studio is located in Battle Creek, Michigan. Among his most noted paintings are "Bear Lake Mallards," the design he used when he was chosen Michigan Ducks Unlimited Artist of the Year in 1977, and "Island Lake Mallards," which was used as a Ducks Unlimited nationally distributed auction print. His works have also appeared in many national and foreign publications.

ROBERT KUSSEROW
1976 South Dakota Duck Stamp
1985 Wyoming Duck Stamp

Robert Kusserow was born in Pennsylvania on September 2, 1929. He is a 1954 graduate of West Liberty State College, where he attained a Bachelor of Arts in fine arts. Until 1974, Mr. Kusserow was a commercial artist in Denver and also a biological illustrator for the University of Colorado. His works have appeared on several covers of the South Dakota *Conservation Digest* magazine. His paintings are noted for their characteristic attention to detail, and his exhibits across South Dakota have gained him recognition as one of the state's foremost wildlife artists. He now makes his home in Rapid City, South Dakota, where he has an art studio.

JAMES F. LANDENBERGER
1974 Iowa Duck Stamp

James F. Landenberger was born on February 6, 1938. Unlike most painters, he did not begin his career with a brush but rather with books—books on zoology and ornithology, texts that would teach him the precise details of form, fin, and feather that have come to mark his work. Combining this approach, which is perhaps a vestige from his college days at the University of Iowa, with his meticulous documentation in field research has allowed Mr. Landenberger to develop a distinctive portrait-type wildlife art in which each subject is individualized. He has also designed the Iowa Trout Stamps for 1975 and 1979. His works have appeared in numerous juried and invitational shows, including the elite Mzuri Safari Foundation Convention, which annually exhibits the work of only a dozen or so of the country's top wildlife artists.

BRUCE LANGTON
1987 Delaware Duck Stamp

Bruce Langton was born in Fairmont, Minnesota, in 1951. He was raised in Delavan, Wisconsin, where he spent his boyhood hunting, fishing, and observing nature with his father and brother. He is now a freelance illustrator, who devotes his evenings and weekends to wildlife art. He has studied taxidermy and made good use of photography and sketches to develop a style that is now bringing him acclaim as a wildlife artist. He is an active member of Ducks Unlimited and the Audubon Society. In 1987, he won the 1988 Indiana Duck Stamp contest, and he has been selected Indiana Ducks Unlimited Sponsor Print Artist for 1989.

ROBERT G. LARSON
1976 Illinois Duck Stamp

Robert G. Larson was born in southern Minnesota, in 1921. He studied art at the Layton School of Art in Milwaukee, Wisconsin, and at Sul Ross State University in Alpine, Texas. His interests in natural science, conservation, and North American history prompted him to pursue a museum career. He is presently Artist-Curator of Exhibits at the Illinois State Museum in

Springfield, Illinois. The painting of wood ducks that Mr. Larson entered in the 1976 Illinois Duck Stamp contest was chosen from one hundred entries in the first open competition in Illinois; open, that is, to Illinois residents only. This print is unique because of its size, being the largest of state prints issued thus far. Mr. Larson's works, including watercolors, oils, and sculptures, are in both private and public collections.

JOE LATIL
1986 Mississippi Duck Stamp

Joe Latil was born in Biloxi, Mississippi, on May 7, 1952. He is a self-taught artist and has been a professional since the age of sixteen. His work is very popular in his home state and throughout the South. He was selected as the Mississippi Ducks Unlimited Artist of the Year for 1985. He was also chosen for the Mississippi Ducks Unlimited Supplemental Print program of 1985 and the First Sequel Mississippi Ducks Unlimited Print for 1986. He lives in Ocean Springs, Mississippi, with his wife and family.

ROD LAWRENCE
1983 Michigan Duck Stamp

Rod Lawrence was born in Flint, Michigan, on February 20, 1951. He studied art at Flint Junior College and in 1973 graduated magna cum laude from the University of Michigan at Ann Arbor. He was named Michigan Wildlife Artist of the Year in 1981 and Waterfowl Artist of the Year by Michigan Ducks Unlimited in 1979. Mr. Lawrence's paintings are in various collections, galleries, and museums in the United States and Canada. His work has also appeared on the covers of such magazines as *Michigan Out-of-Doors*, *Michigan Sportsman*, and *Michigan Angling Report*, and has been used for illustrating many books. A snug cabin in the woods overlooking the North Branch of the Manistee River in Kalkaska County in Michigan is home now for Mr. Lawrence and his wife and family.

LEE LeBLANC
1973–74 Federal Duck Stamp, 1981 Arkansas Duck Stamp, 1981 South Carolina Duck Stamp, 1987 New York Duck Stamp

Lee LeBlanc was born in Powers, Michigan, on October 5, 1913. He received his formal training at the Frank Wiggins Trade School in Los Angeles, the LaFrance Art Institute in Philadelphia, the Art Students' League in New York, the Chouinard School of Art and Jespen Art School in Los Angeles, plus private tutoring with Will Foster and Nicolai Fechin. Mr. LeBlanc worked for Western Lithographic as a commercial artist and as an artist and animator for Walt Disney Studios, 20th-Century Fox Studios, and MGM Studios. In 1962, he left film work to pursue a career as a freelance artist and returned to the only place he really could call home —Iron River, Michigan. Mr. LeBlanc is a member of Ducks Unlimited, the National Wildlife Federation, The Audubon Society, the National Geographic Society, the Ornithologists Union, and the Cornell Laboratory of Ornithology. He was the 1981 Deer Unlimited Artist of the Year.

JOHN P. LEE
1983 Alabama Duck Stamp

John P. Lee was born in LaFayette, Alabama, on February 13, 1941. He attended Troy State University in Troy, Alabama, where he majored in art and received a Master of Science degree in criminal justice administration. He became Chief of Police in Troy, a job he held until retiring just two days before he won the 1983 Alabama Duck Stamp contest. After a short retirement he returned to law enforcement as Chief of Police at the University of Montevallo in Alabama. He currently resides with his wife in Brierfield, Alabama.

ROGER E. LENT
1983 Maryland Duck Stamp

Roger E. Lent was born in Brooklyn, New York, on December 29, 1939. His love for the outdoors started while he was growing up in the small town of Plainfield,

New Jersey, where he spent countless hours hunting and fishing. He majored in art at the University of Miami in Florida, and while there he served as the art director and assistant director of alumni relations. Following school, Mr. Lent returned to Maryland and worked as a salesman and then as a sign painter. Having always liked the eastern shore of Maryland for its wide-open spaces and abundant wildlife, he moved there in 1977 and began painting full-time. He works in his studio at home, a mile from Chincoteague Bay.

ROBERT LESLIE
1986 Delaware Duck Stamp, 1987 Idaho Duck Stamp, 1987 Pennsylvania Duck Stamp

Robert Leslie was born in Oconomowoc, Wisconsin, on August 8, 1947. He credits his love of the outdoors to his father and his artistic interests to his mother. His earliest exposure to wildlife was in the forests and marshes of Wisconsin, where he acquired the knowledge of natural habitats that can be seen in his paintings today. He was also a professional musician for twelve years and a recording artist for Motown Studios. He even entertained troops in Vietnam while on tour. It was only in 1985 that he launched his career as a wildlife artist. He decided to make art a full-time profession after competing in two shows and capturing first prize in each.

RONALD J. LOUQUE
1985 Ohio Duck Stamp, 1986 Indiana Duck Stamp, 1986 New Jersey Duck Stamp, 1987 Florida Duck Stamp, 1987 North Dakota Duck Stamp

Ronald J. Louque was born in New Orleans, Louisiana, on March 3, 1952. He developed his interest in nature and wildlife through his school years, which led him to embark on a career in ornithology at Louisiana State University in 1970. It was there that he also discovered his talent for painting, and, although he received no formal instruction, in two years he was painting as a full-time professional artist. His works have appeared in several national publications, and he has won eight state stamp competitions. Mr. Louque also won the first annual World Painting Competition held in 1984 by the Ward Foundation in Maryland. He placed third in the 1986 Federal Duck Stamp competition. In addition, his works have been shown at many of the popular wildlife exhibits throughout the country.

GARY LUCY
1982 Missouri Duck Stamp

Gary Lucy was born in Caruthersville, Missouri, on February 5, 1949. He attended the Southeast Missouri State University where he received a B.S. degree in art education in 1971. After teaching art for one year, he realized that he really wanted to devote his full time to art as a profession, and so, in 1972, he began a career that proved to be most rewarding. He has been receiving national recognition for his work, which he creates in his secluded studio located near Gerald, Missouri. Many of his works have been featured in publications, exhibited in art shows, and hung in public and private collections throughout the country.

RICHARD LYNCH
1977 Illinois Duck Stamp

Richard Lynch was born on January 16, 1929. A graduate of Washington University of Fine Arts in St. Louis, Missouri, Mr. Lynch began painting seriously only a few years before winning the 1977 Illinois Duck Stamp contest. He had for twenty-five years been in the advertising business as a graphic designer. His paintings have won awards at the prestigious National Wildlife Art Show in Kansas City, and he was also commissioned by the Hallmark Company of Kansas City to design a series of twelve songbirds in watercolor.

DAVID A. MAASS
1974–75 Federal Duck Stamp, 1977 Minnesota Duck Stamp, 1979 Minnesota Duck Stamp, 1982–83 Federal Duck Stamp, 1983 Arkansas Duck Stamp, 1984 Maine Duck Stamp, 1984 North Dakota Duck Stamp, 1984 Texas Duck Stamp,

1985 Maine Duck Stamp, 1985 New Jersey Duck Stamp, 1986 Maine Duck Stamp, 1986 New York Duck Stamp

David A. Maass was born in Rochester, New York, on November 27, 1929. He early developed a love of wildlife and began his career without any formal art education but with extraordinary native talent. He took a job as an illustrator with a manufacturer of high school and college jewelry, where he finally rose to the position of art director. In 1961, he became a full-time artist. By 1966, Mr. Maass's originals were selling so well that he began to produce limited-edition prints. He won the 1974 Ducks Unlimited Artist of the Year award. He holds this to be his proudest achievement because it comes from the votes of more than seven hundred Ducks Unlimited officers, conservationists, and hunters, all of whom know well the birds and habitats. His oil paintings and pencil sketches appear in Gene Long's book, *A Gallery of Waterfowl and Upland Birds.*

ALDERSON MAGEE
1976–77 Federal Duck Stamp

Alderson Magee was born in Hartford, Connecticut, on October 5, 1929. He began in industrial management with Pratt and Whitney Aircraft, but he always maintained an interest in painting and drawing. Finally, by 1971, he felt he could make it in the art world and retired from Pratt and Whitney. To improve his native talent, he enrolled in several courses at the Hartford Art League. There he studied with Estelle Coniff. In 1972, he decided to try the medium of scratchboard, which he had read about in an old artbook. He was fascinated by this technique and has used no other medium since.

LARRY MARTIN
1985 Alabama Duck Stamp

Larry Martin was born near Anniston, Alabama, on June 7, 1939. His background and training seem unlikely for a wildlife artist. For most of the fifteen years he was in medical research, he was also in the Army. After leaving the service, he returned to Anniston and worked for three years as the curator of a natural history museum. But finally, developing an interest in wildlife art, he turned to a full-time artistic career. Since then he has gained national acclaim as a wildlife artist. Perhaps because of his background, his approach to design is distinctively personal, as evidenced in the bi-level design of wood ducks with which he won the Alabama Duck Stamp contest for 1985. This was the first time that such a design had ever appeared on a stamp and print.

NED MAYNE
1980 Delaware Duck Stamp

Ned Mayne grew up amidst the numerous creeks, rivers, and marshes of the Del-Mar-Va Peninsula near the Chesapeake Bay—one of the richest waterfowl wintering areas in the world. As a youngster he was interested in taxidermy and waterfowl hunting. From this, he gained his basic knowledge of waterfowl anatomy. Mr. Mayne received a Bachelor of Arts in art from the University of Delaware. He has won many awards at such events as the U.S. National Decoy Show at Babylon, New York, the Greater Goose Decoy Contest at Chincoteague, Virginia, and the Ward Foundation World Championships.

RALPH J. McDONALD
1986 Tennessee Duck Stamp, 1987 Kentucky Duck Stamp

Ralph J. McDonald was born in Nashville, Tennessee, on November 27, 1934. His works have a strong appeal to collectors. Over 90 percent of the prints he has published in the last ten years have sold out. Mr. McDonald was named Ducks Unlimited Artist of the Year for 1981, and he is the Southeastern Wildlife Exposition Artist of the Year for 1988. He now lives with his wife and daughter in Gallatin, Tennessee.

DICK McRILL
1980 Nevada Duck Stamp

Dick McRill was born on January 13, 1941. Raised in Los Angeles, California, he early developed an interest in painting outdoor scenes. Basically a self-taught artist,

Mr. McRill now restricts his subjects to those he loves best—waterfowl and waterbirds. The winning of the Nevada contest was his finest achievement in art to date. Currently, he lives in Eugene, Oregon.

JAMES MEGER
1980 Minnesota Duck Stamp, 1986 Alaska Duck Stamp

James Meger was born in Minneota, Minnesota, on April 19, 1942. He developed a love for waterfowl at an early age, and during his high school years he began painting and drawing wildlife, although his school had no formal art course. After entering a fine arts college with hopes of becoming a professional wildlife artist, he found that, unfortunately, the art faculty there held wildlife art in low esteem. This disappointment resulted in a fifteen-year period in which Mr. Meger neither drew nor painted wildlife. In 1977, though, he returned to his first love and began painting waterfowl. In the 1979 Minnesota Duck Stamp contest, he finished tenth. This encouraged him to give up his teaching career entirely to devote his full time to painting.

GEORGE METZ
1982 Indiana Duck Stamp

George Metz was born on January 22, 1931. Fishing and hunting as a young boy were instrumental in creating in Mr. Metz a strong interest in the outdoors and in painting. After graduating from high school, where he majored in art, he joined a Chicago art studio as an apprentice. He has worked as a commercial artist for the past thirty years. His works have appeared in catalogues of Sears, Montgomery Ward, J.C. Penney, and Marshall Field and have been seen on the covers of such magazines as *Fur-Fish-Game, Sports Liquidator,* and *Freshwater Fisherman.* Mr. Metz now resides in Chicago, and, having won in the 1983 Illinois Salmon Stamp contest, he hopes someday to win his state's waterfowl stamp contest.

LAWRENCE K. ("KEN") MICHAELSEN
1978 California Duck Stamp, 1979–80 Federal Duck Stamp

Lawrence K. ("Ken") Michaelsen was born in San Francisco on October 1, 1936. He has been painting ever since his childhood, when his father, an artist, was his mentor. After a hitch in the Air Force, he held a number of jobs in the commercial art world. It wasn't until the 1970s, though, that he started doing the wildlife paintings he is famous for today. It was in 1972 that a friend commissioned him to paint a Dall sheep, his first wildlife subject. After several other commissions to paint wildlife subjects, he knew he had found his niche and dropped out of commercial art for good. Mr. Michaelsen, in addition, is an accomplished photographer. He has taught classes at the Mendocino Art Center in the community where he and his wife Judy, also an artist, reside.

JOE MICHELET
1982 Alabama Duck Stamp

Joe Michelet was born in New Orleans, Louisiana, on August 11, 1930. A self-taught artist, he has created intricately detailed paintings that can be found in numerous public and private collections throughout the United States and Great Britain. Prior to making art his full-time profession in 1968, Mr. Michelet was a crop duster; since then, he has won over one hundred awards in regional and national competitions, the most prestigious being the 1982 Alabama Duck Stamp.

ROSEMARY MILLETTE
1985 South Carolina Duck Stamp, 1987 South Dakota Duck Stamp

Rosemary Millette was born in Owatonna, Minnesota, on January 28, 1954. She later moved to South Dakota, where she drew on the wealth of animal life there for inspiration in her work. After spending seven years as a commercial artist, Ms. Millette now dedicates herself full-time to wildlife art. She has participated in national juried shows and has won many Best of Show awards. She is a member of the Society of Animal Artists and currently resides in Sioux Falls, South Dakota. She also won the contest for the 1983 New Hampshire Pheasant Stamp.

GERALD MOBLEY
1983 Oklahoma Duck Stamp, 1985–86 Federal Duck Stamp, 1985 Oklahoma Duck Stamp

Gerald Mobley was born in Rector, Arkansas, on February 6, 1938. He has been an avid outdoorsman since his early years. While in the service, he worked on technical training aids for aircraft systems, and afterwards went into commercial art, where he eventually founded his own now-successful commercial art studio in Tulsa. Since 1981, when he became seriously interested in wildlife art, he has spent most of his spare time at game preserves and zoos, photographing ducks and geese for reference material. Mr. Mobley separates his wildlife painting from his commercial work by painting wildlife subjects only in the studio in his home.

JOHN G. MOISAN
1978 South Dakota Duck Stamp

John G. Moisan was born in Watertown, South Dakota, on November 7, 1946. He spent his childhood in the northeastern South Dakota prairie, an area of the United States widely known for its abundance of waterfowl. In 1968 he graduated from the University of South Dakota with a major in advertising art. In 1972, after serving with the U.S. Army in Germany, Mr. Moisan returned to the University of South Dakota to do graduate work in the fine arts. It was then that he bagan developing his considerable skills as a wildlife artist. In 1974, he won first place in the Kansas City Ducks Unlimited Art Show. In 1976, he placed third in the state's duck stamp competition. Since his duck stamp win in 1978, he won first place in the 1980 and 1988 South Dakota Pheasant Stamp competitions. Mr. Moison continues his work from his studio in Fort Pierre, South Dakota, where he lives with his wife and children.

ROBERT MONTANUCCI
1984 California Duck Stamp

Robert Montanucci was born in California in 1953 and raised in the San Joaquin Valley. A descendant of artistic families from Italy and Poland, Robert graduated from college as an art major and was so successful with his first one-man show in 1974 that he has made a career of his art. Besides winning the 1984 California Duck Stamp competition, he has received other state and national awards. He has also gained recognition from articles in several prominent publications and is listed in the seventeenth edition of *Who's Who in California.* The artist is represented by galleries in the United States, and his works are included in public and private collections in North America, Australia, and Europe. Mr. Montanucci surrounds himself with the beauty of the high Sierras as he works in his studio at Lake Tahoe.

BURTON E. MOORE, JR.
1986–87 Federal Duck Stamp

Burton E. Moore, Jr. was born in Columbia, South Carolina, in 1945. A former Marine Corps captain, he is a self-taught artist and has made his living with his work since 1977. He is known nationally for outdoor scenes featuring sporting dogs, decoys, and waterfowl. His other honors include being selected as South Carolina Wildlife Federation Artist of the Year. Mr. Moore's works have been shown in galleries and at major exhibits throughout the nation. These include the Smithsonian Institution, Cleveland Museum of Natural History, the Southeastern Wildlife Exposition, the Easton Waterfowl Festival, and the well-known Leigh Yawkey Woodson Bird in Art Exhibition. A life sponsor of Ducks Unlimited, Mr. Moore resides in Charleston, South Carolina.

DON MOORE
1986 Wisconsin Duck Stamp

Don Moore was born in Lincoln, Nebraska, on October 16, 1947. Though he has been painting continuously since his high school days, he has concentrated only recently on wildlife subjects. His days are spent with binoculars and camera in hand studying and painting his subjects in their natural habitats. Mr. Moore is a self-taught artist whose works have been exhibited in many shows and are displayed in galleries throughout the country. He lives with his wife and family in Monona, Wisconsin.

EDWARD A. MORRIS
1962–63 Federal Duck Stamp

Edward A. Morris was born in Philadelphia, on July 28, 1917. After eight years with the Marines, he studied at the Philadelphia College of Art, where two of his instructors were Henry C. Pitz and W. Emerton Heitland. Mr. Morris is a painter as well as an illustrator, and his work appears in many private collections. He shares with good wildlife artists a keen appreciation for the outdoors. His work has appeared in *Gopher Historian, Naturalist, Linn's Weekly Stamp News,* and other magazines. He was also a contributor to *The Northwestern Banks Hunting Guide* (1962). Over the years, his work has appeared in a wide variety of media: oil, watercolor, pen and ink, bronze, stone, lithography, and dry-point etching, and ivory carving. He finds most interesting whatever he is working on at the moment.

WILLIAM C. MORRIS
1984 Alabama Duck Stamp, 1984–85 Federal Duck Stamp

William C. Morris was born in Mobile, Alabama, on June 8, 1945. He began sketching and enjoying the natural world around him ever since his early field trips as a young boy. Despite his interest in art, he studied engineering in college and joined Chevron Oil on graduation. On his own, he tried some watercolors, and one, a painting of football coach "Bear" Bryant, stirred up so much interest that he published a limited edition of a thousand prints. They sold out in four weeks and opened up a second career for him. Many of his original works are now in private collections. His two successes in 1984—the Federal and the Alabama Duck Stamp contests—will make his works even more highly prized by collectors.

GARY MOSS
1983 Minnesota Duck Stamp, 1987 Texas Duck Stamp

Gary Moss was born in Minneapolis, Minnesota, on December 15, 1946. After studying art throughout high school, he attended the Minneapolis College of Art and Design for four years, including one year of study in Holland. Mr. Moss also served as a Marine Corps combat artist in Vietnam, where he earned the title of Combat Artist of the Year in 1970. As one of the country's promising young wildlife artists, he has had his works shown at numerous exhibits, including the Bird Art Exhibition at Yawkey Woodson Art Museum, Wausau, Wisconsin, and the Smithsonian Institution in Washington, D.C.

MARTIN R. MURK
1977–78 Federal Duck Stamp, 1980 Wisconsin Duck Stamp

A native of Wisconsin, Martin R. Murk's wildlife art has earned him many awards, including the 1982 Wisconsin Wetlands for Wildlife Artist of the Year, 1984 Wisconsin Ducks Unlimited Artist of the Year, 1986 Wisconsin Waterfowler's Artist of the Year, and the 1987 Great Lakes Wildlife Artist of the Year. Winner of the 1977 Federal Duck Stamp competition, the 1979 Wisconsin Trout Stamp, and the 1980 Wisconsin Duck Stamp contest. Mr. Murk also designed Wisconsin's first Great Lakes Salmon and Trout Stamp and the first North American Endangered Species Conservation Stamp in 1982. Among the many places his work has been exhibited are the Great Lakes Wildlife Art Festival, National Wildlife Federation, Southeastern Wildlife Exposition, Waterfowl Festival and the Leigh Yawkey Woodson Art Museum Birds in Art Exhibition. He is listed in *American Artists of Renown* and *Who's Who in Waterfowl Art* (1982).

THOMAS MURPHY
1973 Iowa Duck Stamp

Thomas Murphy was born in Ottawa, Iowa, on June 27, 1926. He entered, and won, the 1973 Iowa Duck Stamp competition with his painting, "Poetry in Motion." In addition, he also had the distinction of finishing second and even third in the same contest. In the first contest opened to all Iowa artists by the Conservation Commission, artists were allowed to enter three paintings each in the competition, and Mr. Murphy had only himself as competitor for the top three spots. He is

basically a hobby painter, but he does do some commission work from time to time. His other hobbies are fishing, hunting, photography, and amateur radio. Mr. Murphy is now retired and lives with his wife at a private lake near Brooklyn, Iowa.

JACK MURRAY
1947–48 Federal Duck Stamp

Jack Murray was born in Pittsburgh on August 12, 1889. He showed an early interest in sketching and taxidermy, and after graduation from Massachusetts State College in 1914, he completed his training at the Massachusetts School of Art. He went into the commercial art world and gradually got more and more assignments to do drawings and paintings for advertising agencies. He kept up with painting wildlife scenes as a hobby until the turning point in his career, when one of his wildlife paintings was published on the cover of the *Saturday Evening Post.* After that he was kept busy with magazine work, appearing in *Country Home, Better Homes and Gardens, Woman's Home Companion, Successful Farming, Good Housekeeping, Farmer's Wife, Boy's Life,* and others. Mr. Murray is deceased.

RAY NICHOL
1987 Washington Duck Stamp

Ray Nichol was born in 1945. He has been painting in oils since 1980. In 1987 he began entering various state wildlife contests, submitting winning entries in the Illinois and Washington competitions. With a painting of a Rainbow Trout, he won the Illinois Salmon Stamp competition, prevailing over 226 other entries. His winning entry in the Washington contest was one of 47 entries from around the nation. His portrayal of three Canvasbacks took six weeks to paint, plus two weeks of in-depth research. Although a commercial photographer by profession, Ray Nichol enjoys painting wildlife scenes along with still lifes, landscapes, and portraits. He lives with his wife in Seattle.

JAMES PARTEE, JR.
1987 Georgia Duck Stamp

James Partee, Jr., is a native of Georgia and the first state resident to win the Georgia Duck Stamp competition. Part of his success in his career as a wildlife artist has been the great popularity of his work with the National Wild Turkey Federation, 3500 Ducks Unlimited, Quail Unlimited, and Waterfowl U.S.A. He has contributed original paintings and limited edition prints to a number of conservationist causes, thus helping to raise thousands of dollars to protect wildlife and their habitat.

LEON PARSON
1986 Utah Duck Stamp

Leon Parson was born in Provo, Utah, on May 13, 1951. He spent most of his life near Jackson Hole, Wyoming, close to Yellowstone Park—an ideal place for a wildlife artist. He was raised in a family that now counts five professional artists among its members, including his father. It is no surprise, then, that he began painting animals very early in life and is, today, primarily a big-game painter. His formal education includes a Bachelor of Fine Arts from the Art Center College of Design in Pasadena, California, and graduate study for his Master of Fine Arts in illustration from Syracuse University in New York. His works have appeared on the covers of such magazines as *Outdoor Life, Petersen's Hunting, North American Hunter,* and others. Mr. Parson lives in Rexburg, Idaho, with his wife and family.

RICK PAS
1985 Indiana Duck Stamp

Rick Pas was born in Flint, Michigan, on March 27, 1958. He works now in graphic design and technical illustration in the Flint area, while pursuing an up-and-coming career as a wildlife artist. With the one exception of 1986, his works have shown each year since 1983 in the Leigh Yawkey Woodson Art Museum's national tour of Birds in Art. His 1985 win of the Indiana Duck Stamp contest was his first win on the national level of art competition. In 1982 and again in 1987 Mr. Pas was named Artist of the Year by the Michigan United Conservation Clubs.

CARROL J. AND GWEN K. PERKINS
1976 Mississippi Duck Stamp

Carroll J. and Gwen K. Perkins, husband and wife naturalists, submitted their winning photograph for the 1976 Mississippi Duck Stamp competition jointly. Dr. Perkins was born in Leesville, Louisiana, on May 21, 1915. Dr. Gwen Kirtley Perkins was born in Marlow, Oklahoma, on March 23, 1918. Mr. Perkins has retired from a professorship in Wildlife Management at the School of Forest Resources, Mississippi State University. Their photographs have appeared in numerous national publications under the credit Kirtley-Perkins.

ANDREW D. PETERS
1979 Iowa Duck Stamp

Andrew D. Peters was born near Council Bluffs, Iowa, on November 8, 1954. He took an early interest in birds and hunting, and in the early 1970s he began working with ink, acrylics, and watercolors. In 1977, he placed second in the Iowa Duck Stamp contest. He graduated from Iowa State University with a degree in wildlife biology. After winning the 1979 Iowa Duck Stamp competition and the 1980 Iowa Habitat Stamp contest, he opened his own wildlife gallery in Omaha, Nebraska. When not traveling, he can be found working in his studio above his gallery.

DIANE PIERCE
1979 Indiana Duck Stamp

Diane Pierce was born in Ohio in 1939. Fascination with collecting feathers in childhood led to sketching in the field and, eventually, to enjoying her own aviary of over a hundred species of birds. Throughout her twenties, working on her aviary helped lay the foundation for an extensive understanding of bird behavior and habitats. Ms. Pierce works well in transparent watercolor, scratchboard, and oils. She participated in illustrating the National Geographic Society's *Field Guide to North American Birds.* Twenty-nine of her oils and watercolors are part of the Florida Hidden Heritage Collection in Ocala, Florida. Ms. Pierce's works can be found in other collections as well. Diane Pierce was the first woman to win a conservation stamp competitition—in Long Island in 1979—and is one of the first two women to win a state duck stamp competition—in Indiana in 1979.

CAROLE HARDY PIGOTT
1979 Mississippi Duck Stamp

Carole Hardy Pigott was born in Houston, Texas. She graduated from Mississippi State University for Women in 1970 with a Bachelor of Fine Arts degree, and then worked with an advertising agency for six years. Ms. Pigott has been painting professionally for the past twelve years, doing mostly landscapes and wildlife. In 1979, she was named Mississippi Ducks Unlimited Artist of the Year, and, in the past few years, she has been accepted in many competitions and shows, such as the New York Arts Club Watercolor Competition and the Watercolor Southeast Competition. Ms. Pigott has also been listed in the 1981–82 *American Artists of Renown,* and she is now recognized as one of the nation's leading female wildlife artists.

BOB PISCATORI
1986 Massachusetts Duck Stamp

Bob Piscatori was born in Bridgewater, Massachusetts, on October 17, 1946. He grew up near the Hockmock Swamp wetlands, which doubtless fostered his interest in nature and led to his Bachelor's degree in wildlife management from the University of Maine in 1968. Since then, he has been a biology teacher at Taunton High School in Massachusetts. He also has a Master's degree in instruction media from Bridgewater State College. His paintings have been featured in *Massachusetts Wildlife,* and he has exhibited in several outdoors art shows and in antique decoy shows, and his paintings are in private collections throughout the country. Mr. Piscatori also won the Massachusetts Duck Stamp contest for 1988. He now resides in Taunton, Massachusetts, with his wife and family.

DAVID PLANK
1980 Missouri Duck Stamp

David Plank was born near Salem, Missouri, in 1934. It was a year that fell right in the middle of a drought and a depression. Nevertheless, Mr. Plank began at an early age to observe and sketch birds. After high school and a three-year tour of duty in the Army as a photographer, he went to work at *The Salem News* as a photo-offset lithographer and pressman. He continued to paint birds in his spare time. In 1973, he realized his dream of becoming a full-time painter, and since then his works have been shown throughout the country at many museums and exhibitions. *Arkansas Birds, Their Distribution and Abundance*, a recently published book, contains a number of drawings and paintings by Mr. Plank.

RICHARD W. PLASSCHAERT
1980–81 Federal Duck Stamp, 1982 North Dakota Duck Stamp, 1983 New Hampshire Duck Stamp, 1983 North Carolina Duck Stamp

Richard W. Plasschaert was born in New Ulm, Minnesota, on April 25, 1941. Very soon he realized that he possessed a special ability to capture the beauty of nature in painting. His art, however, does not always reflect his lifelong interest in wildlife, much of it comprising landscapes and portraits. Mr. Plasschaert has spent over twenty-five years in the fields of commercial art, layout and design, portrait, landscape, and wildlife painting. He is skilled in the use of oils, acrylics, and watercolors. Most of his paintings have sold well in the New York market; additionally, he received a great honor when he was accepted into the National Academy. His work, both originals and prints, can be found in many of the nation's galleries.

ROGER E. PREUSS
1949–50 Federal Duck Stamp

Roger E. Preuss was born in Waterville, Minnesota, on January 22, 1922. After service in the Naval Reserve he attended the Minneapolis College of Art. When he was only twenty-six, he won the Federal Duck Stamp contest; he is the youngest artist to date ever to have won the competition. He has also won twenty-one national and international juried art honors. His paintings have been exhibited in twenty leading art museums, including the Joslyn Art Museum and the Institute of Contemporary Arts. He was elected a Fellow by the International Institute of Arts and Letters and Vice President by the Wildlife Artists of the World. Mr. Preuss is also a member of the Society of Animal Artists. He is the author of *Outdoor Horizons*, and his work has appeared in sixty-five national magazines. Named United States Bicentennial Wildlife Artist in 1976, Mr. Preuss is listed in thirty of the world's standard references, including Marquis's *Who's Who in the World*.

CLAREMONT G. ("BUD") PRITCHARD
1968–69 Federal Duck Stamp

Claremont G. ("Bud") Pritchard was born in Kenesaw, Nebraska, on June 18, 1910. His formal art training took the form of correspondence courses, and he received certificates from the Washington School of Art and later from the Federal School of Art, now Art Instruction Schools, of Minneapolis. He served in World War II and, back in civilian life, he gained increasing artistic recognition. At the Nebraska Game and Parks Commission, his chief responsibility was illustrating that agency's *Outdoor Nebraska*. At the same time, he did illustrations for *The Pronghorn Antelope, Animal Behavior*, and *Mammals of North America*. Moreover, he exhibited throughout the country. He was a charter member of the Audubon Naturalists' Club in Lincoln, Nebraska. Mr. Pritchard is deceased.

TERRY REDLIN
1981 Minnesota Duck Stamp, 1983 North Dakota Duck Stamp, 1985 Minnesota Duck Stamp

Terry Redlin was born in Watertown, South Dakota, on July 11, 1937. Following his graduation from high school there, he enrolled in the commercial art program at the School of Associate Arts in St. Paul, Minnesota.

After working as a layout artist, illustrator, and magazine art director, Mr. Redlin made the decision in 1979 to devote his time and talent to wildlife art. It is a decision that has come to please many avid art collectors, for he developed into one of the country's most popular wildlife artists in perhaps the shortest time of any previous painter. Mr. Redlin was also selected as the 1983 Ducks Unlimited Artist of the Year.

BRAD REECE
1981 Iowa Duck Stamp

Brad Reece was born in Des Moines, Iowa, on December 21, 1955. He attended the Iowa State Univeristy in Ames, receiving an education degree in teaching. The son of renowned wildlife artist Maynard Reece, Mr. Reece is a self-taught artist who works mostly with acrylics. He also does some stone sculpture, metal sculpture, and woodcarving. He had a job with Mercury Marine and has worked under Paul Frederick at the Picture Framing Academy in San Francisco. Mr. Reece is now the owner and operator of Maynard Reece Gallery in Des Moines.

MARK REECE
1975 Iowa Duck Stamp

Mark Reece was born in Des Moines, Iowa, on June 10, 1953. He has spent his life associated with nature in one form or another, learning much from his father, Maynard Reece, the widely appreciated wildlife artist. The many trips Mark Reece has taken with his family to marshes, lakes, and various wildlife habitats have helped him develop a keen sense of detail, color, and composition that has served him well as a wildlife artist. He has also been active in academic fields and has become a medical doctor. His formal education includes a Bachelor of Science degree from Iowa State University, a Master of Arts degree in biology from Drake University, and an M.D. from the Creighton University Medical School.

MAYNARD REECE
1948–49 Federal Duck Stamp, 1951–52 Federal Duck Stamp, 1959–60 Federal Duck Stamp, 1969–70 Federal Duck Stamp, 1971–72 Federal Duck Stamp, 1972 Iowa Duck Stamp, 1977 Iowa Duck Stamp, 1982 Arkansas Duck Stamp, 1983 Texas Duck Stamp

Maynard Reece was born in Arnolds Park, Iowa, in 1920. His love of nature combined with undeniable artistic talent have made him one of America's foremost wildlife painters. He began drawing at an early age and won his first award in 1932 when he was twelve years old. After finishing school, he went into commercial art and then joined the Iowa Museum in Des Moines, where he stayed for ten years interrupted by World War II. In 1951, he turned to freelancing and has been a full-time artist ever since. He has won the Federal Duck Stamp contest an unprecedented *five* times, and in all he has a total of twenty-two stamp designs to his credit. Mr. Reece's works have appeared in many museums, books and publications, and they are now in such demand that most of his paintings are sold even before they are completed.

JOHN C.A. REIMERS
1978 Mississippi Duck Stamp, 1981 Mississippi Duck Stamp

John C.A. Reimers was born in Jackson, Mississippi, on December 25, 1948. He displayed an early talent for drawing and coloring; in addition he also developed a passionate interest in hunting and fishing. It was not until later, though, that he combined these loves. While studying art at Mississippi College in Clinton, Mr. Reimers experimented with all types of media. This was during the Pop Art era of large, brilliantly colored canvases often depicting familiar household objects. Mr. Reimers painted in this style with abandon. After a decade of this, he had occasion to do a portrait of a small dog, and its reception helped him to decide that this style suited him better. He then began and has continued to paint the birds he loves so much. He spends long hours in duck blinds pursuing these "favorite subjects" with brush and gun.

ROBERT RICHERT
1982 California Duck Stamp

Robert Richert was born in Oak Park, Illinois, on March 6, 1947. Shortly after his birth, he moved with his family to Long Beach, Califoria, and he has been a California resident ever since. He did a tour of duty in Vietnam and in 1973 he attended the California State University, Long Beach, where he studied illustration and biomedical art until 1977. In his painting style, he changed media from watercolors and gouache to acrylic, which he credited for his 1982 California Duck Stamp win. He has exhibited at many national shows including those at the Easton Maryland Waterfowl Festival, the Mzuri Safari Foundation, and the Leigh Yawkey Woodson Art Museum.

MICHAEL J. RIDDET
1984 Wisconsin Duck Stamp

Michael J. Riddet was born near Barrow-in-Furness on the northwest coast of England on June 26, 1947. In 1956, his family moved to the United States and settled in the suburban area around the city of Chicago. After earning a Bachelor of Arts from Roosevelt University in Chicago, Mr. Riddet embarked on a career as a wildlife artist. His works have been exhibited at the Leigh Yawkey Woodson Art Museum in Wausau, Wisconsin. They can also be found in private collections throughout the United States, Canada, and England. Mr. Riddet now lives amidst fifty acres of unglaciated hill country in southwestern Wisconsin.

ALDEN LASSELL RIPLEY
1942–43 Federal Duck Stamp

Alden Lassell Ripley was born in Wakefield, Massachusetts, on December 31, 1896. After serving abroad in World War I, he returned to a scholarship at the Museum of Fine Arts in Boston. He completed his studies there and was granted a fellowship for two years of study in Europe. Shortly after his return, he held an exhibition of his watercolors and was made a member of the Guild of Boston Artists. His murals and etchings are well known and widely respected. Two famous murals of his are "Purchase of the Land from the Indians" and "Paul Revere's Ride." His paintings are found in many noted galleries and in private collections as well. Mr. Ripley was a member of a number of artistic societies, and was elected to the National Academy of Design, a distinction generally considered to be the highest an artist in the United States can attain. Mr. Ripley died in 1969.

HAROLD ROE
1984 Ohio Duck Stamp, 1987 Ohio Duck Stamp

Harold Roe was born in Toledo, Ohio, on September 22, 1930. He graduated cum laude from the Ohio State University School of Architecture in 1953 and, after serving five years in the Navy, he returned to Toledo to be an architect. He began his career in wildlife art in 1973, and his works have been selected for exhibition at the prestigious Leigh Yawkey Woodson Art Museum International Bird Art Show. In 1985 he was named National Ducks Unlimited Artist of the Year. Basically, Mr. Roe combines a lifelong love of nature with his skills developed over the years as an architect to design his meticulously detailed waterfowl paintings.

DOUG ROSS
1983 Missouri Duck Stamp

Doug Ross was born in Galena, Missouri, on January 9, 1943. He studied at The School of the Ozarks for a year before working with various printing companies. Since 1968, he has been a graphic artist for the University of Missouri—Columbia Agriculture Extension Division, where he teaches, illustrates, and designs for displays and other teaching materials. His wildlife art is done primarily at night and on weekends, and he hopes one day to be able to devote full time to his art. Mr. Ross is a member of Ducks Unlimited and the National Wildlife Federation. Mr. Ross lives in Columbia, Missouri.

CHARLES ROWE
1981 Delaware Duck Stamp

Charles Rowe was born in Great Falls, Montana. He obtained a Bachelor of Fine Arts degree from the School of the Art Institute in Chicago, and a Master's degree from the Tyler School of Art, Temple University, Philadelphia. He is a professor of art at the University of Delaware, and many of his wildlife paintings have been published in limited edition prints. In addition, his works have been exhibited at many major museums and shows throughout the country. Mr. Rowe is listed in *Who's Who in American Art*, *Who's Who in the East*, *American Artists of Renown*, and the Victoria and Albert Museum Archives in London. He is currently living in Newark, Delaware.

SHERRIE RUSSELL
1986 California Duck Stamp, 1987 Nevada Duck Stamp

Sherrie Russell was born in Madison, Wisconsin, on July 1, 1950. Her move to her present home in Mt. Shasta, California, deepened her love of ducks. She has gained steadily in popularity among waterfowl art collectors since 1982, when she began painting waterfowl. Her style combines an attention to detail with a "softness" and almost Oriental simplicity that makes for striking compositions. Her acrylic paintings and limited edition prints are displayed in private collections and galleries across the nation.

JOHN A. RUTHVEN
1960–61 Federal Duck Stamp, 1982 Ohio Duck Stamp

John A. Ruthven was born in Cincinnati, Ohio, on November 12, 1924. After serving in the Navy during World War II, he attended the Art Academy in Cincinnati. In 1946, he started his own commercial art studio which he turned over to his employees in 1959. In 1961, he won the Federal Duck Stamp competition. By the time he was forty, Mr. Ruthven had achieved a national reputation as a naturalist and as an animal and bird artist. Among his many achievements, Mr. Ruthven painted the American Bald Eagle unveiled at a reception held in his honor in the East Room of the White House in 1976. He was the first Ducks Unlimited Artist of the Year, is a member of the Society of Animal Artists of New York City, and he is a trustee of the Cincinnati Museum of Natural History.

HARVEY SANDSTROM
1954–55 Federal Duck Stamp

Harvey Sandstrom was born in St. Paul, Minnesota, in 1925. In 1946, after serving in the Navy in World War II, he began four years of study at the Minneapolis School of Art. He then did freelance commercial artwork in Duluth, Minnesota, and began an art studio with three partners. It was also at this time that Mr. Sandstrom began painting wildlife in earnest. He held several one-man shows and displayed and sold original paintings in sporting goods stores and galleries in New York, Chicago, and other locations in the East, South, and Midwest. Inspiration from a hunting trip near Grand Rapids, Minnesota, led to the ring-necked duck design that later appeared as his winning entry in the Federal Duck Stamp competition.

PATRICK SAWYER
1980 Oklahoma Duck Stamp

Patrick Sawyer was born on August 5, 1948. Part of his experience with and understanding of wildlife comes from his nine years in Alaska working as a wildlife artist. Mr. Sawyer's works have been exhibited at the National Wildlife Art Show in Kansas City, the Safari Club, the Anchorage Audubon Show, and the Oklahoma Wildlife Art Show in Tulsa. He has works in collections of Remington Arms, Winchester Press, and *Outdoor Oklahoma* magazine. Mr. Sawyer was selected to do the 1986 Oklahoma Ducks Unlimited Sponsor print.

PHIL SCHOLER
1981 Nevada Duck Stamp, 1982 Minnesota Duck Stamp, 1983–84 Federal Duck Stamp

Phil Scholer was born in Rochester, Minnesota, on July 7, 1951. He developed an early love of nature from childhood camping trips with his family, and after high school, he enrolled in the Mankato State University College of Fine Arts. He supported himself with various jobs while trying freelance work, and he was on the verge of going freelance full-time when he won the Federal Duck Stamp contest. He was not always a wildlife painter; he worked on portraits and landscapes in college and for a time thereafter. One day he saw a painting by another local artist, David Maass, and was very impressed by the way Maass incorporated birds into his landscape. New horizons opened to him and his career in wildlife painting was born. He has continued to develop as one of the country's most talented waterfowl artists.

JACK SCHROEDER
1977 Maryland Duck Stamp, 1980 Maryland Duck Stamp

Jack Schroeder was born on September 13, 1927. He was originally attracted to Maryland's eastern shore by Chestertown's Washington College, which he attended, and he soon discovered the subtle charms of Chesapeake Bay and came to appreciate its unique way of life. In 1965, he was appointed field illustrator for a general ecological study conducted in Costa Rica. As he worked with curators of the Museum of Natural History, Smithsonian Institute, his exceptional talents were soon discovered. His long association with the Smithsonian as a contract natural history illustrator was begun. By 1975, Mr. Schroeder was sought after on the Eastern Shore for his exquisitely detailed artwork of local subjects. He started Schroeder Prints, Inc., a company that sells his work in prints and notecards.

KEN SCHULZ
1982 Tennessee Duck Stamp

Ken Schulz was born on January 19, 1920, in Racine, Wisconsin. In 1966, he moved to east Tennessee where he built his gallery, studio, and residence in the Great Smoky Mountains just east of Gatlinburg, Tennessee. Over the years, he has become one of America's foremost painters in watercolor and egg tempera. He is listed in *Who's Who in American Art*, and his works have appeared on the Artists of America Calendars, American Artists Group, and many others. Mr. Schulz's major exhibitions have been with the American Watercolor Society, of which he is a member, National Academy of Design in New York, National Arts Club, Allied Artists of America, Audubon Artists, and numerous others. He has received an impressive number of honors and awards.

TIMOTHY C. SCHULTZ
1981 Wisconsin Duck Stamp

Timothy C. Schultz was born in Fond du Lac, Wisconsin, in 1955. Through frequent childhood contacts with the lakes, marshes, and woodlands of east central Wisconsin, he developed an early interest in and respect for the natural world around him. He also discovered and began to develop his artistic talents. While attending high school and the University of Wisconsin Center in Fond du Lac, Mr. Schultz continued to intensify his studies in the art area. Upon completion of his formal education, he began to paint full-time. In addition to painting, Mr. Schultz enjoys hunting, fishing, camping, photography, and all forms of athletics.

CHARLES W. SCHWARTZ
1979 Missouri Duck Stamp

Charles W. Schwartz was born on June 2, 1914, in St. Louis, Missouri. He was commissioned by the Missouri Department of Conservation to design Missouri's initial state duck stamp. Mr. Schwartz has worked for nearly forty years in the Department as an artist, photographer, and writer. He is a biologist by academic training, receiving Bachelor of Arts, Master of Arts, and Doctor of Science degrees from the University of Missouri. He has written several award-winning scientific books and has produced some twenty-five motion pictures on wildlife, all of which have received national or international awards.

CLAYTON B. SEAGEARS
1953–54 Federal Duck Stamp

Clayton B. Seagears was born in 1897. At the University of Michigan, he majored in zoology and journalism. After a stint of teaching at the University, he spent the next thirteen years, 1924 to 1937, in newspaper work including cartooning. Mr. Seagears was a self-taught artist. He did general commercial work and later specialized in outdoor and wildlife subjects. He founded *The Conservationist*, the official publication of New York State's Conservation Department; most of his work was done for that journal until his retirement from the Department in 1962. His illustrations and writings have appeared in many books and publications. He worked mostly in tempera, specializing in birds with an emphasis on waterfowl and upland game. Mr. Seagears died in 1983.

MICHAEL SIEVE
1984 Oregon Duck Stamp, 1985 Oregon Duck Stamp, 1986 Oregon Duck Stamp

Michael Sieve was born in Wilmont, Minnesota, on September 2, 1951. He was raised in what was once known as the pheasant hunting capital of Minnesota. He spent much time as a youth hunting and fishing in southwestern Minnesota, Iowa, and northwestern Colorado, and he began drawing wildlife long before starting school. He studied art at Southern Minnesota State College in Marshall. Relying heavily on first-hand experience as the inspiration and basis for his painting, Mr. Sieve travels extensively and frequently to all parts of Canada, Alaska, the northern and western United States, and Central America. Although accomplished in many media, he prefers oils and specializes in big game subjects. He has exhibited in the Minnesota Wildlife Heritage Show and the Leigh Yawkey Woodson Bird Art Exhibit.

ERNEST SIMMONS
1980 Florida Duck Stamp

Ernest Simmons was born in Arlington Heights, Illinois, in 1957. He has been interested in birds as far back as he can remember. At the age of seven, while growing up in the suburbs of Chicago, he developed a gift for portraying his ideas on paper. As he developed his techniques, he experimented with many media, including acrylics, pastels, and oils; he finally settled on his watercolors. Mr. Simmons currently is a resident of Clearwater, Florida, but he travels extensively throughout the state to study the many native species of birds and their habitats.

ART SINDEN
1982 Illinois Duck Stamp, 1986 Illinois Duck Stamp

Art Sinden was born in Berwyn, Illinois, in 1935. Following high school, he attended Knox College in Galesburg, Illinois for two years. His only formal art training was a brief attendance at the Art Institute of Chicago. Basically a self-taught artist, he has found his favorite media to be acrylics and watercolors. Mr. Sinden has worked as a design engineer for the Ingersoll Milling Machine Company for the past twenty-seven years. Always at work on designs for future duck stamp competitions in hopes of furthering his art career, he recently won the Illinois Duck Stamp competition for 1988.

DANIEL SMITH
1985 Alaska Duck Stamp, 1985 Georgia Duck Stamp, 1986 South Carolina Duck Stamp, 1987 Arizona Duck Stamp, 1987 West Virginia Duck Stamp

Daniel Smith was born in Mankato, Minnesota, on August 1, 1954. Before devoting his life full-time to wildlife art, he spent eight years in the commercial art field as an illustrator. This experience broadened and deepened his technique and contributed greatly to his unique style—a style that has brought him widespread recognition. He won first-of-state selections for stamp designs in Alaska and Georgia in 1985. He won the 1986 South Carolina waterfowl contest, and he was also selected to design the First of State New Mexico Turkey Stamp and the First of State Arizona Waterfowl Stamp. His works have been selected for the Leigh Yawkey Woodson Art Museum Bird Art Exhibition, and he continues to participate each year in the Minnesota Wildlife Heritage Show. He resides with his family near Eden Prairie, Minnesota.

DOROTHY M. SMITH
1987 Oregon Duck Stamp

Dorothy M. Smith was born in West Linn, Oregon. Beginning with a lifelong interest in painting, she earned a degree in painting and a degree in biology and, after a career as an educator for many years, developed as an outstanding wildlife painter. Ms. Smith has devoted all of her time to her artistic career since 1982.

HOYT SMITH
1981 Oklahoma Duck Stamp, 1984 Oklahoma Duck Stamp, 1986 Oklahoma Duck Stamp

Hoyt Smith was born in Elkins, Arkansas, on March 14, 1938. He has a Master's degree in painting from the University of Tulsa and a Master's degree in medical and biological illustration from Johns Hopkins University School of Medicine. Mr. Smith is currently Director of Medical Graphics at the University of Oklahoma Medical School in Tulsa. His works have appeared in various medical publications throughout the country. He has traveled extensively, spending three years as a Peace Corps volunteer in Ethiopia. This gave him the opportunity to explore Kenya, Tanzania, and Uganda, where he photographed people and wildlife. Mr. Smith is a member of the Guild of Natural Science Illustrators and the Association of Medical Illustrators.

NED SMITH
1983 Pennsylvania Duck Stamp, 1985 Pennsylvania Duck Stamp

Ned Smith was born on October 9, 1919, in Millerburg, Pennsylvania, where he was introduced to the natural world of the Susquehanna Valley and its surrounding fields and mountains by his father, an avid botanist and outdoorsman. Mr. Smith, besides his talent with a brush, was also a naturalist, illustrator, and talented writer. He designed stamps for the Raptor Fund, the Pennsylvania Federation of Sportsman Clubs, the Pennsylvania Turkey Federation, and the National Wild Turkey Federation.

WAYNE SPRADLEY
1980 Alabama Duck Stamp

Wayne Spradley was born in Pell City, Alabama, on November 11, 1937. He began painting seriously when he was in high school, and, after a tour of duty with the Navy, he began his career doing commission work only. He then took a three-year course in art to complement his self-taught style. Mr. Spradley is a full-time artist whose works have won over 190 major art awards. He is a member of the Southern Watercolor Society and the Alabama Watercolor Society. In 1987, he was named Alabama Ducks Unlimited Artist of the Year. Mr. Spradley continues to live in Pell City with his wife and family.

EVERETT STAFFELDT
1978 Illinois Duck Stamp

Everett Staffeldt was born in Naperville, Illinois, in 1932. After a stint in the Marine Corps, he studied biology at North Central College and then went to work in the Biology Department of Argonne National Laboratory. Since 1975, he has painted and carved decorative birds almost exclusively. He does five or six paintings a year, making his works highly valued by collectors throughout the country. He placed third in the 1985 Illinois Duck Stamp competition. Mr. Staffeldt still makes his home in Naperville, Illinois.

STANLEY STEARNS
1955–56 Federal Duck Stamp, 1964–65 Federal Duck Stamp, 1966–67 Federal Duck Stamp, 1975 Maryland Duck Stamp, 1978 Maryland Duck Stamp

Stanley Stearns was born in Washington, D.C., on January 15, 1926. He spent much of his childhood in Hawaii, where his father was a geologist. He attended high school in Hawaii and Seattle, college in Seattle, and served in the Marine Corps in World War II. After the war, he attended the Vesper George School of Art and the Massachusetts School of Art in Boston, receiving training in both commercial and fine art. For some years, he worked full-time at commercial technical art, confining his painting and sculpture to the weekends. He did landscapes, city scenes, figures, and portraits, using various media. As time went by, though, he turned more and more to wildlife subjects. His first sale of wildlife art was a group of "spots" for *American Rifleman*. Mr. Stearns's work is in numerous public and private collections throughout the country.

DON STEINBECK
1977 South Dakota Duck Stamp

Don Steinbeck was born in Hartley, Iowa, on February 27, 1930. He developed an early interest in the outdoors and in wildlife, and he began painting in his early teens. Mr. Steinbeck attended the University of South Dakota, graduating with a Bachelor of Fine Arts in advertising art. Following four years as a jet pilot with the South Dakota Air National Guard, he was employed by an advertising firm and has been in advertising for over twenty years. Mr. Steinbeck's art media include acrylics, watercolors, and oils, and his favorite subjects to paint were birds. Mr. Steinbeck is deceased.

ROBERT STEINER
1981 California Duck Stamp, 1984 Nevada Duck Stamp, 1985 Michigan Duck Stamp, 1986 Florida Duck Stamp, 1987 California Duck Stamp, 1987 New Hampshire Duck Stamp

Robert Steiner was born in Philadelphia on October 10, 1949. As a youth, he lived in Miami, where his main interests were seascapes and modern art. It wasn't until 1971, upon his moving to the San Francisco area, that he developed his interest in wildlife. His training includes a Bachelor in Fine Arts from the Rhode Island School of Fine Arts in Providence and a Master's degree from San Francisco State. The abundant wildlife in the Bay area, especially birds, prompted him to begin painting wildlife with a style all his own. His works are extremely popular because of their attention to detail, dramatic composition, and ability to elicit a mood from the viewer. Mr. Steiner's works have been displayed at all major art shows and exhibitions throughout the country. Currently there is a two-year waiting list for his originals.

JIMMY STEWART
1985 Tennessee Duck Stamp

Jimmy Stewart was born in Montgomery, Alabama, in 1946, and raised on Alabama's Gulf Coast in Foley and Mobile. He has enjoyed the wildlife of his surroundings since his boyhood in Alabama, and he continues to enjoy them from his current home in Hixon, Tennessee. As part of that enjoyment, and with no formal art training, Mr. Stewart has been drawing and painting wildlife since he was a boy. A supporter of Ducks Unlimited and other wildlife conservation groups, Mr. Stewart has used originals and prints of his works to help raise thousands of dollars to aid these organizations in their efforts. In addition to winning the 1985 Tennessee Duck stamp contest, Mr. Stewart was a finalist in the 1986 Federal Duck Stamp competition, placed second in the 1987 Ohio contest, and ninth for the 1988 Indiana Duck Stamp competition.

CLARK SULLIVAN
1981 Florida Duck Stamp

Clark Sullivan was born on January 20, 1945. He was raised in Michigan's upper peninsula and early on developed an interest in and appreciation of the wildlife available to him in that area. In 1968, he graduated from Northern Michigan University with a Bachelor of Science in art and history. He began painting waterfowl as a hobby in 1977 and took up decorative decoy carving in 1980. Since then, he has been honored as a finalist in the Michigan Duck Stamp competition, and he has won many first-place ribbons for his decoy carvings. He has been a high school teacher and art director since 1968. He is also co-host of the P.B.S. television series, "Wildlife Woodcarvers." Mr. Sullivan lives with his wife and family in Swartz Creek, Michigan.

FRANCIS E. SWEET
1987 Maryland Duck Stamp

Francis E. Sweet was born in northern New York in 1938. Although he has been a lifelong wildlife enthusiast and self-taught artist, Mr. Sweet only began painting full-time in the autumn of 1986. Even so, he has already begun to make an impact in this highly competitive field. His goal is to produce wildlife paintings that set new standards in realism, and his paintings so far have shown a meticulous attention to detail. Currently his work is displayed in several galleries along the east coast and has been seen in numerous juried shows, including the Gold Room at the Waterfowl Festival in Easton, Maryland, and the Annapolis Wildfowl Art Exhibition. Mr. Sweet resides in Bowie, Maryland, with his wife and family.

JOHN W. TAYLOR
1974 Maryland Duck Stamp, 1979 Maryland Duck Stamp, 1984 Florida Duck Stamp

John W. Taylor was born in Washington, D.C., on April 19, 1931. He began an avid interest in birds when his fourth-grade teacher formed a Junior Audubon Club. The idea of bird painting as a profession did not develop until he started work for the Division of Birds at the U.S. National Museum in Washington where a close association with artists and ornithologists formed the basis and inspiration for his life's work. After service in the military, he returned to the Museum and studied art and design at the Corcoran Gallery School in Washington, D.C. After that he had a position as an artist and editor with the Maryland Department of Game and Fisheries. Mr. Taylor has been freelancing since 1965. In 1985, 1986, and 1987 he designed conservation non-game stamps for Maryland.

JOE THORNBRUGH
1986 Montana Duck Stamp

Joe Thornbrugh was born in Blackwell, Oklahoma, on June 24, 1948. His lifelong interest in wildlife and the outdoors was developed during his childhood in western Montana, where he has spent many years painting and sketching the local flora and fauna. Birds, however, are his most frequent subject. He works in acrylics, taking great pains to capture the brilliant colors and intricate designs of the birds' plumage. Mr. Thornbrugh's works have appeared in many national shows and in the Leigh Yawkey Woodson Art Museum. He lives in Victor, Montana, with his wife and family.

RICHARD TIMM
1978 Michigan Duck Stamp, 1982 Nevada Duck Stamp

Richard Timm was born in Lincoln Park, Michigan, on May 15, 1925. His formal art training began at the Meinzinger Art School in Detroit and proceeded to the Art Center in Los Angeles. There followed a twenty-year career as a commercial artist until 1971, when Mr. Timm was commissioned to paint his "Mammals of North America" series. This initiated his dream of becoming a full-time wildlife artist. He has gone on to complete his six-work series, "Geese of North America." He is also at work on publishing several limited edition prints commissioned by GMC Trucks & Bus Group for Ducks Unlimited. Mr. Timm's originals and prints are now sought by collectors throughout the country.

BOB TOMPKINS
1980 Mississippi Duck Stamp

Bob Tompkins was born in Greenville, Mississippi, in 1943. After graduating from Delta State University in 1965 with a B.S.Ed. degree, he went to Jacksonville, Florida, to teach art. In 1968, he moved back to the Delta area, where he taught art at Greenville High School. In 1973, he received his Master's degree in art education. Among Mr. Tompkins' many achievements are the Grand Award in the Southeastern Art Show in Panama City, Florida, in 1975 and first place in the 1980 Mississippi Duck Stamp competition. Mr. Tompkins resides in Greenville with his wife and family.

JIM TRANDEL
1981 Illinois Duck Stamp

Jim Trandel was born in Chicago on March 4, 1947. He began drawing at an early age and took up oil painting at seventeen. His love of duck hunting brought an interest in painting birds, and it is a goal of his someday to make painting his full-time occupation. Mr. Trandel is a self-taught artist with no training other than his direct, from-the-field knowledge of the birds he loves to hunt and paint. Currently he spends much of his time in northern Minnesota hunting, fishing, and painting.

DAVID TURNBAUGH
1985 Maryland Duck Stamp

David Turnbaugh was born in Baltimore, Maryland, on September 20, 1937. He graduated from the Maryland Institute of Fine Arts in 1959, having studied under the late Jacques Maroger. After graduation, he taught art in the Baltimore County school system for twelve years. In 1971, he gave up teaching in order to devote his full-time efforts to painting. As a painter, Mr. Turnbaugh is best known for his rendering of scenes from Maryland's eastern shore and the rural areas of the mid-Atlantic states. He has won numerous prizes in juried shows and is a member of the American Society of Marine Artists. Mr. Turnbaugh lives in Baltimore with his wife and family.

WILLIAM P. TYNER
1976–78 Massachusetts Duck Stamp

William P. Tyner was born in New Haven, Connecticut, in 1935. From his childhood—when he used to rescue ducks frozen in the Quinnipiac River's ice—to the present, Mr. Tyner's world has revolved around the outdoors of the New England area. His earliest contacts with nature came on field trips with his father, a commercial artist who encouraged his son's interest in nature. Mr. Tyner's development as a conservationist was triggered by his uncle, Ray E. Benson, who was a founder of Ducks Unlimited, Inc. The conservation aims of this organization have been constantly promoted by Mr. Tyner through many activities, appearances, and donations of his art works. Today, Mr. Tyner spends much time on expeditions to the fields, marshes, and woods of this country and Canada, where he photographs wildlife and collects mounted birds and decoys for studio use.

GIJSBERT VAN FRANKENHUYZEN
1982 Michigan Duck Stamp

Gijsbert van Frankenhuyzen was born in 1951 in the Netherlands. His interest in nature and wildlife go back to his boyhood. In 1968, he enrolled in the Royal Academy of Arts in Arnhem, Holland, and, after graduation, he worked as a commercial artist and photographer. In 1976 his work came to the attention of the *Michigan Natural Resources Magazine*. Shortly thereafter, he moved to the United States and is now the magazine's art director. His work has been shown in several invitational art exhibits and has won him noteworthy commissions. For his work on the *Michigan Natural Resources Magazine*, Mr. van Frankenhuyzen has received the Award of Excellence from *Communication Arts Magazine*. He is a member of the Society of Animal Artists and is currently working on an African wildlife series based on two trips he recently took to Kenya.

RON VAN GILDER
1987 Maine Duck Stamp, 1987 Minnesota Duck Stamp

Ron Van Gilder was born on May 17, 1946. He got a Bachelor of Fine Arts degree in graphic design from the Minnesota School of Art and Design. During his formal art training, he concentrated on drawing, especially life drawing. He translates this same care into his wildlife art, devoting three months every fall to field study, photographing wildlife in its natural habitat. He found 1987 an especially eventful year in that he won both the Maine Duck Stamp contest and the Minnesota Duck

Stamp competition. All in all, in fifteen years of painting he has published over forty-seven wildlife paintings as limited edition prints, of which forty so far are sold out.

TOM WALKER
1982 Iowa Duck Stamp

Tom Walker was born on June 18, 1947 in Jacksonville, Iowa. His boyhood days were spent in that rural community where a nearby wooded creek gave him his early appreciation of nature and wildlife. Always interested in art, he credits his high school art teacher with much of his success, since it was this teacher who encouraged him to pursue an art career. Mr. Walker has an Associate of Arts degree in fish and wildlife and a Bachelor's degree in business. Currently, he is working full-time as an artist and framer near Council Bluffs, Iowa, where he lives with his wife and family.

OSCAR WARBACH
1976 Michigan Duck Stamp

Oscar Warbach was born in Elizabeth, New Jersey, in 1913. After receiving a Bachelor of Science from Rutgers University and a Bachelor of Science in zoology from Michigan State University, he joined the Michigan Department of Conservation in 1941. After the war years, Mr. Warbach returned to the Michigan Department of Conservation and stayed there until 1948, when he became a research biologist for the U.S. Fish and Wildlife Service at the Patuxent Research Center in Laurel, Maryland. In 1954, he returned to the Michigan Department of Conservation, now the Department of Natural Resources, and remained there as an illustrator and biologist until retiring in 1977.

KEITH WARRICK
1986 Washington Waterfowl Stamp

Keith Warrick was born in Preston, Idaho, on February 7, 1938. He is a self-taught artist who received his only formal art training at the University of Washington, as a commercial artist. He is recognized as one of the West's most talented wildlife artists, and his works have appeared in numerous national publications and have been shown in galleries throughout the country. He has also designed the 1980 Washington Upland Game Bird Stamp, the 1981 and 1983 Washington Salmon Stamps, the 1986 First of State Washington Migratory Duck Stamp, and the 1985 through 1987 Ducks Unlimited Artist of the Year Print for Washington State. Mr. Warrick resides in Lake Stevens, Washington.

WALTER A. WEBER
1944–45 Federal Duck Stamp, 1950–51 Federal Duck Stamp

Walter A. Weber was born in Chicago on May 23, 1906. He received all his formal education there and worked there for several years after college. He attended the Chicago Art Institute, the American Academy of Art, and the Church School of Art. Trained as a scientific illustrator, he joined the Chicago Field Museum, now the Chicago Museum of Natural History, in 1928. He traveled extensively for the museum on field trips throughout the world. In the mid-1930s, Mr. Weber turned to freelance artwork, which he continued until 1949, when he went on staff as artist and naturalist for the National Geographic Society. In 1967, he was awarded the highest civilian honor the U.S. Department of the Interior can bestow—the Conservation Service Award. Mr. Weber died on January 10, 1979.

MILTON C. WEILER
1974 Massachusetts Duck Stamp

Milton C. Weiler graduated from the Syracuse College of Fine Arts and took up the painting of portraits. After a year he entered the teaching profession. From 1935 until his death, he was associated with the Garden City Public School system as head of the Fine and Industrial Arts Department. His watercolors of wildlife have the

authenticity of an artist who has lived the life he has painted. An outdoorsman and conservationist, he was devoted to trout and salmon fishing, waterfowl, and upland gunning. While he worked as a teacher, his work graced some of the Derrydale titles on gunning and fishing, and some other publishers' books as well, including Scribner's, Coward-McCann, Stackpole, and Winchester Press. Mr. Weiler died in 1974.

JOHN S. WILSON
1981–82 Federal Duck Stamp, 1986 South Dakota Duck Stamp

John S. Wilson was born in Sisseton, South Dakota, on June 6, 1929. Many of his boyhood days were spent hunting and fishing, activities he still enjoys and which help him gain first-hand knowledge for his wildlife paintings. He attended school in Sisseton and then enlisted in the Air Force in 1946. Returning to civilian life in 1954, he studied architectural drafting for a year and then worked as a designer and artist for a sign company for twenty-five years. For Mr. Wilson, painting was a hobby to be practiced on his own time. He did not paint any wildlife subjects until 1976, when he entered the state's duck stamp contest, taking second place. Fired with enthusiasm, he went on to win the 1981 South Dakota Pheasant and the 1981 Federal Duck Stamp contests.

RICHARD L. WILSON
1985 California Duck Stamp, 1985 Nevada Duck Stamp

Richard L. Wilson was born in Capetown, South Africa, on April 23, 1944. He moved to Bryan, Texas, in 1952 and later to southern California in 1961. During his undergraduate work, he took a pre-dental course and found that he enjoyed the "artistic" aspects of dentistry. A graduate of the Pacific Dental School in San Francisco in 1971, he practices general dentistry in San Leandro, near his Castro Valley, California, home. A self-taught artist, Dr. Wilson confines his painting to weekends and vacations. He does his outdoor research with cameras, telephoto lenses, and binoculars. A keen outdoorsman, he has taken vacation trips to the wilds of Alaska, Canada, Oregon, and to the Okefenokee Swamp in Georgia.

WALTER WOLFE
1979 California Duck Stamp, 1980 California Duck Stamp

A native Californian, Walter Wolfe was raised in the great southwest desert country, where he found a soul-deep kinship with nature and the wildlife she nurtures. He studied art with Art Instruction, Inc. and the California College of Arts and Crafts. His early adult years were spent successfully in visual advertising, but in 1976 he abandoned this security to paint full-time. In addition to his successful duck stamp designs, he won the 1980 National Wild Turkey Stamp competition. Today, he works from his home and studio just outside the boundaries of the Sacramento National Wildlife Refuge near Willows, California, painting in oil and gouache and filling orders for patrons and galleries throughout the country.

LARRY ZACH
1984 Iowa Duck Stamp

Larry Zach was born in Cedar Rapids, Iowa, on October 2, 1946. His love of nature developed as a child as he roamed the streams and forests of the Iowa River bottom near his father's farm. Long interested in nature study, wildlife photography, and taxidermy, he now expresses his deep appreciation for the natural world through his paintings. His very first entry in the Iowa Duck Stamp competition resulted in a first-place finish. He was also named 1987 Artist of the Year for the Iowa Turkey Federation, Iowa Ducks Unlimited, and Iowa Pheasants Forever.